Also by David Chanoff

A Vietcong Memoir (with Truong Nhu Tang)
The Vietnamese Gulag (with Doan Van Toai)
Portrait of the Enemy (with Doan Van Toai)
In the Jaws of History (with Bui Diem)
Warrior (with Ariel Sharon)

ORRIN DeFOREST
and
DAVID CHANOFF

SIMON and SCHUSTER

NEW YORK   LONDON   TORONTO   SYDNEY

TOKYO   SINGAPORE

SLOW

The Rise and Bitter Fall of American Intelligence in Vietnam

BURN

Simon and Schuster
Simon & Schuster Building
Rockefeller Center
1230 Avenue of the Americas
New York, New York 10020

Designed by Levavi & Levavi
Manufactured in the United States of America

1   3   5   7   9   10   8   6   4   2

Library of Congress Cataloging in Publication Data
DeForest, Orrin.
Slow burn: the rise and bitter fall of American intelligence in Vietnam/
Orrin DeForest and David Chanoff.
p.   cm.
1. Vietnamese Conflict, 1961–1975—Underground movements.
2. Vietnamese Conflict, 1961–1975—Personal narratives, American.
3. United States.   Central Intelligence Agency.
4. Counterinsurgency—Vietnam.   5. DeForest, Orrin.
I. Chanoff, David.   II. Title.
DS558.92.D44   1990
959.704'38—dc20   90-9496
CIP
ISBN 0-671-69258-5

For my wife, Lan, and my children:
Cecile, Julie, Coleen, and Michael,
and to all those we left behind—
the living and the dead.

CONTENTS

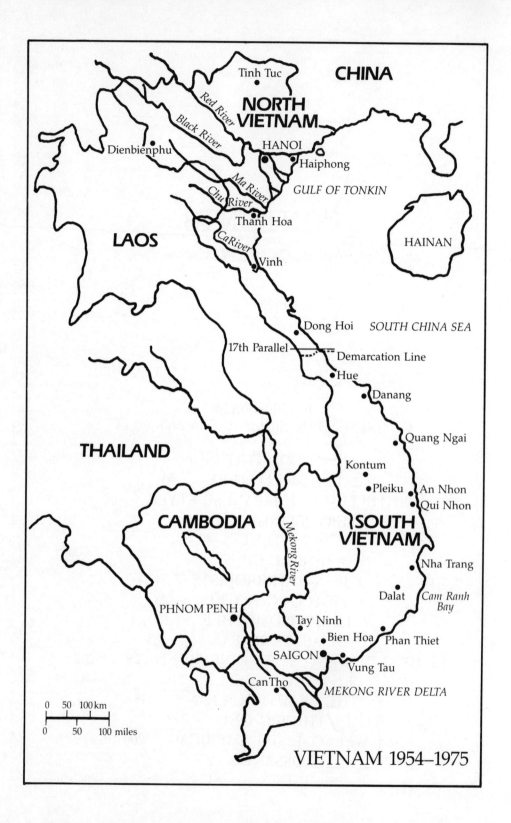

VIETNAM 1954–1975

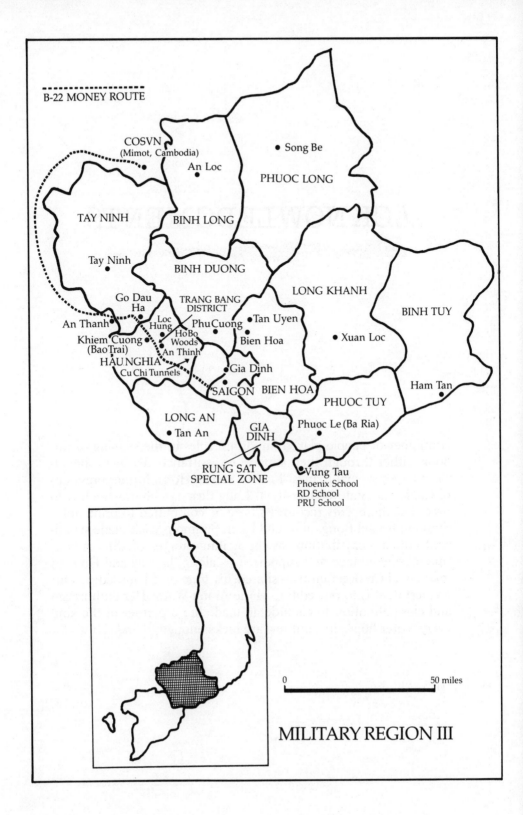

B-22 MONEY ROUTE

COSVN
(Mimot, Cambodia)

● Song Be

An Loc

PHUOC LONG

TAY NINH

BINH LONG

Tay Ninh

BINH DUONG

LONG KHANH

Go Dau
Ha

TRANG BANG
DISTRICT

BINH TUY

Loc
Hung

PhuCuong

● Tan Uyen

An Thanh

HoBo
Woods

Bien Hoa

● Xuan Loc

Khiem Cuong
(BaoTrai)

An Thinh

HAU NGHIA

Cu Chi Tunnels

Gia Dinh

Ham Tan ●

SAIGON

BIEN HOA

PHUOC TUY

LONG AN

● Tan An

GIA
DINH

Phuoc Le (Ba Ria)
●

RUNG SAT
SPECIAL ZONE

● Vung Tau
Phoenix School
RD School
PRU School

0   50 miles

MILITARY REGION III

ACKNOWLEDGMENTS

A number of people played important roles in the shaping of this book, either through their support or assistance. To them the authors owe a special thanks. First to Steven Horn, former president of California State University at Long Beach, who was the first to urge that the events recounted here be committed to print. John Sterling, Rafael Bouganim, and Ellen Simmons each made significant critical contributions as the writing progressed. Stuart Herrington encouraged and supported us along the way and Douglas Pike (as always) generously shared his time and knowledge. Our greatest debt is to our editor, Marie Arana-Ward. Her enthusiasm and close attention to each detail made her a partner of the kind every writer hopes for, but few are lucky enough to find.

INTRODUCTION

When I learned that Orrin DeForest was finally commit-
ting his Vietnam experiences to print, I silently ap-
plauded the good news. For while there has been a veritable
explosion of publications in the past few years purporting to "tell it
like it was" in Vietnam, few, if any, of these works have zeroed in
on the real crux of the problem we faced for more than a decade. I
mean, of course, the real strength of the insurgency—the Vietcong's countrywide organization, an organization that extended
into the central nervous system of South Vietnam—the villages
and the hamlets. No one can fathom what happened to us and our
South Vietnamese ally without understanding the nature of this
organization. Those who suggest that the United States erred by
focusing its power on the Vietcong when we should have known
all along that Hanoi was the enemy and "gone for Hanoi's jugular"
simply do not understand the nature of revolutionary warfare and
the key role played by Hanoi's Southern organization.

Orrin DeForest was one of the few Americans I met in my four
years in Vietnam who not only understood the Vietcong's organization and its tactics, but who also was in a position to *do* something about them. As a military intelligence officer in Vietnam
charged to ferret out the VC "shadow government" in Hau Nghia

province, I had a unique opportunity to observe Orrin and his CIA colleagues in action. Certainly there is no question that, while the Phoenix program administered by CORDS and manned by MACV advisers like myself varied from province to province in its effectiveness, the intelligence operation run by Orrin DeForest and the CIA's Military Region Three base in Bien Hoa was consistently the most effective in the war. The damage that I personally observed and occasionally participated in that Orrin and his operators inflicted on the Vietcong's political and military structure was massive.

Shortly after encountering Orrin for the first time in Bien Hoa, I realized that here (at last!) was an operator who understood the Asian mind-set, was determined to penetrate the Vietcong's organizational security, and, most importantly, had the time and resources to do the job and do it right. Unlike my military colleagues, who were almost invariably homeward bound in one year, Orrin could and did stick it out (he didn't give up until the country fell—which never would have happened had all our people been as dedicated and competent as he). Time and again I marveled as Orrin and his crew scored repeated successes against the Vietcong. On one occasion, when the South Vietnamese army, the ARVN, was planning an extremely ambitious cross-border operation into Cambodia, Orrin and his impressive stable of sources developed an intelligence estimate that showed clearly how fruitless the operation would be if launched as planned. Unveiling a map marked with detailed Vietcong rear-area order of battle, Orrin was able to convince the ARVN generals to reorient their attack. The results? A major victory for the ARVN, which marched directly into a hitherto undetected base area literally brimming with the enemy. Here was an individual whose targets were normally political in nature, but who outdid military intelligence at its own game.

I am particularly pleased about Orrin's book because his story and the story of the CIA in Military Region Three needs to be told. In my first book, *Silence Was a Weapon*, I tried to do so, but could not do justice to it because of security restraints still in force at the time, and because the only one who can tell the story the way it needs to be told is Orrin himself. Students of our Vietnam experience, professional intelligence officers, indeed the American people, should have the chance to finally learn of the exploits of the silent war fought by Orrin and his colleagues. In my view, we've had enough of the books by amateurs and disaffected CIA folks whose version of reality and their personal roles are self-serving and misleading. Orrin DeForest was one of a small number of true

professionals who were in the thick of the fray and he can speak
with unchallenged credibility. His contribution will undoubtedly
take its place as a classic in the literature on revolutionary warfare.

Colonel Stuart Herrington
United States Army Military Intelligence

A NOTE TO THE READER

In what follows, certain names, dates, places, and other particulars have been altered to avoid exposing any individuals who may still be at risk.

1

IN COUNTRY

As we walked through customs in the filthy civilian lobby of Saigon's Tan Son Nhut airport we saw the old man holding a sign. A tiny, dark-skinned, wrinkled man, unmistakably a peasant—one of the lucky ones who had managed to land a job in the city. The sign, drawn in heavy pencil with each letter traced three or four times, read "DeForest, Pinossa, Williams." When we smiled at him we were treated to a wide grin that was missing three top front teeth. Ushering us through the door and into a white air-conditioned Maverick, the old man got in the driver's seat and moved tentatively out into traffic, stretching to see over the wheel. "Duc full," he said, "Embassy not full."

The Duc Hotel belonged to the Agency, but I knew it was often crowded. The overflow went to the Embassy Hotel on South Tu Do Street, half a mile up from the famous commercial strip. "Everything looks the same," I said to John Pinossa and Cal Williams, the two agents I had flown out with straight from the Vietnam training course at CIA headquarters in Langley, Virginia. "But the car's a lot better. Last time I was here they picked me up in a jeep. At least no one's going to lob a grenade into this one."

It was late in the afternoon of November 11, 1968. Back in the States the elections were just over and Richard Nixon would be the

new president. He had, or so he said, a secret plan to end the war
in Vietnam. But everyone I knew thought it was a load of crap.
What the man wanted was to get elected; what he wanted for Vietnam was anyone's guess. But whatever Nixon wanted it would have
to be a change. Nine months before, the Vietcong's Tet Offensive
had knocked LBJ out of the box, had led him to stop bombing the
North, to agree to negotiations, and to opt out of a try for a second
presidential term. Exactly how Nixon was going to follow that lead
no one could predict. New man, new ball game. Not that I spent
much time wondering about what Nixon had in mind. I had a new
job, too, and I was excited about it.

I had already done one tour in Vietnam, not with the CIA, but
with the CID, the U.S. Army's Criminal Investigations Division.
Now I had joined what I still couldn't help thinking of as the first
team of the intelligence world. I had worked with CIA operatives
before, in Japan during the fifties and early sixties, and I had developed a fairly high opinion of them. Even the superficial and du-
bious training we had just completed hadn't dispelled my
enthusiasm for the Agency, or for the idea that now I might be
able to make a difference.

The windows that pierced the neat brick front of the Embassy
Hotel were covered by grenade screens. But inside there were no
signs of war. The delicate Vietnamese landscape paintings on the
walls and the lion statues with their toothy grimaces gave the Embassy lobby a look of slightly faded elegance. Guerrilla patrols
might be slipping through the Nha Be swamp a mile or two south
of the city and the Vietcong sappers might be walking along Saigon's streets, but in the lobby, French colonial times had not
passed. At the long mahogany reception counter where we
checked in an unsigned note was waiting for us. "Report by phone
tomorrow morning. A car will be sent for you."

Next to the restaurant door off to the left, a sign announced
"Garden Bar on Rooftop." The night was ahead, but all three of us
were exhausted from the flight. Seven hours from Hawaii to Guam,
then a layover, then another six hours into Saigon. When John
suggested we get settled into our rooms first, then meet on the
rooftop in a couple of hours for a drink, it sounded like just the
thing. I was looking forward to a bath and a nap. After that we'd
still have plenty of time to think about dinner and a stroll down Tu
Do.

Two hours later I walked slowly from the Embassy's ancient
grilled-in elevator out onto the rooftop garden, feeling languid
from my long soak in the claw-foot tub and an hour and a half of

unconscious sleep. John and Cal had already arrived and were standing near the Tu Do Street side looking out across the city. Joining them, I watched the street scene below us for a minute, feeling the slight evening breeze that was already cooling the sultry air. From six stories up the jumble arranged itself in a crazy pattern. Parked cars were jammed bumper to bumper on both sides of the street, leaving two narrow lanes in the middle where cars, motorbikes, and bicycles fought one another for open space. An army "deuce and a half" truck rumbled by, black exhaust curling out of its stack to mix with the smoky haze that always seemed to engulf Saigon, especially at dusk when all over the city women started cooking family dinners on their outdoor charcoal grills.

From the backyard kitchens the smell of sizzling fish rose to the rooftop garden, along with the sharp aroma of *nuoc mam* and *mam ruc*, the two most popular of Vietnam's fermented fish sauces. Hot steamy mint added its odor to the mix, reminding me instantly of *pho*, the bowls of noodle soup I used to enjoy so much in Vung Tau during my last tour. *Pho* was something I hadn't thought about since I had left. I had forgotten too that Saigon was always a city of smells, strong smells that blended together but seemed to demand that you decipher them individually. Now it all came back in a rush —the charcoal fish, the *nuoc mam*, the noodle soup—and the burning trash, always and forever the smell of burning trash.

Sitting down at a table in the rooftop bar, each of us ordered a dry martini from a pretty waitress with a vivacious smile. Leave it to Agency bureaucrats to hire good-looking ones, I thought; it's as if they think it's part of the perks. To the west the sun was setting into the ocean, a tremendous Chinese-red ball against a sky turning red and orange in the reflected glow. Then from a distance came the explosive pops of jet afterburners kicking in, and, a moment later, six black silhouettes streaked across the sun's face—F-104 Phantoms on a mission.

Pinossa, Williams, and I sipped our martinis and watched the Phantoms veer southward and bear down on the Nha Be peninsula just beyond Saigon's Cholon Chinatown. Nha Be had the U.S. Navy's big POL (petroleum, oil, lubricants) tank farm as well as the South Vietnamese army's central POL farm, almost all the petrol supply for South Vietnam. The peninsula was also a giant swamp with hundreds of little ocean inlets, ideal terrain for the Vietcong. In the distance the Phantoms swooped and dived, releasing their loads. Light flashed briefly against the sky, followed after a second or two by the dull roar of high explosives. "Well, friends," I said, "welcome to Vietnam."

. . .

The next morning at 7:45 another driver in a Maverick picked us up and drove us to the United States Embassy compound. Inside the wall next to the embassy itself was a two-story wooden building, the Norodom Complex, where much of the operational side of the CIA's Saigon Station activities was housed. Outside the building a white-clad Vietnamese guard watched us from his sandbagged circular concrete position. Along the wall that enclosed the compound were several other squat concrete cylinders, each with an M-60 machine gun protruding over the sandbags. A year earlier none of them had been there. They owed their existence to the Tet Offensive, when a Vietcong commando platoon had blown a hole in the wall and killed several marine guards before dying in a firefight inside the compound. That had been one of the war's more dramatic incidents. Early news reports even had it that the surprise assault had taken the embassy itself. It wasn't true, of course. The VC platoon had been annihilated on the grounds. But the results of their suicide mission were evident enough—a new approach at home, new machine-gun positions here.

Inside the complex we found the personnel office where a secretary greeted us and led us up to the top-floor office of Jack Lambert, the soon-to-be-departing head of the CIA's Saigon Station. Lambert's replacement had already been named—Ted Shackley, former chief of the Laos operation. But the tall, gray-haired Lambert still seemed to take a personal interest in his three new arrivals as he led us into the "glass house," the specially constructed room within a room that was reputedly a hundred percent bugproof.

Sitting at a large conference table that filled almost the whole of the glass-walled enclosure, Lambert welcomed us, then launched into a quick, upbeat overview of the Agency's Vietnam effort. The four pillars of that effort, as we knew, were the Provincial Reconnaissance Units, the Census Grievance program, the Rural Development program, and the Special Branch Police advisory program. As Lambert described them, it seemed clear that each was having an impact on the war. Our schedule for the rest of the day, he said, would include detailed briefings on these programs directly from their chiefs. Then tomorrow morning we should be prepared to leave for our assignments in the field.

Lambert's optimistic review was good to hear, especially after the ten-week training session we had gone through at CIA headquarters. Our instructors there had all been Agency veterans with experience in country. But I had come away from their lectures full of doubts. "You are going over there," we had been told the first day, "to work with and advise Vietnamese counterparts in carrying out one of our programs." But I could just imagine the enthusiasm with which the Vietnamese counterparts took to their American advisers. I had had plenty of experience working with the Japanese intelligence police during eleven years with CID and OSI (Air Force Office of Special Investigations). I couldn't quite conceive of what they would have thought had I or any other American presumed to advise them. I couldn't believe that at heart the Vietnamese were any different.

South Vietnam's police were not in the same ballpark as the Japanese. But like the Japanese, the Vietnamese had a long and heroic history, two thousand years of it. And like the Japanese, they had a tremendous sense of national pride. I was sure they did not take kindly to American ways and procedures being forced down their throats. They might need our help desperately; as I had seen during my previous tour, they *did* need help desperately, but that hardly meant they were going to respond well, or change anything they were doing in more than the most superficial ways.

More to the point, perhaps, my tour in 1966 and 1967 as an army CID investigator in Vung Tau, then as CID chief in Qui Nhon, had put me in daily contact with the Vietnamese National Police. That had been a frustrating experience. So many of the police were holding down outside jobs that often you could not find them in their offices. They tended to show up at the police station in the morning, then take off, with the full knowledge of their commanders. They were all trained in American procedures and American techniques of investigation and interrogation. But it seemed to go in one ear and out the other. It wasn't that they didn't understand; they understood perfectly. It was rather that they would not change ways they had been accustomed to for ages. You just could not get them to do it. But that was the National Police, Vietnam's criminal police. Now, as a CIA operative I would be working with the Special Branch, the intelligence police. But I doubted I'd find much of a difference.

So, even as we trained at CIA headquarters, I was starting off with a healthy skepticism about how effective we might be as advisers. But as the training at Langley progressed, I grew far more concerned about another subject: the Agency's approach to interrogation in Vietnam. Maybe it was my years as a detective, or my experience working with the highly effective Japanese security apparatus. But whatever the reason, the CIA concept of interrogation, at least as the trainers presented it, had left me with very uneasy feelings.

The one afternoon of our lectures on the subject had been hot and muggy, and looking around me as the instructor droned away it seemed that half the class had dropped off to sleep. For some reason, the Hungarian Joseph Cardinal Mindszenty was much on the lecturer's mind that day, particularly the psychological techniques the Communist interrogators had used to break him in the late forties. It was a parallel whose relevance to Vietnam wasn't altogether clear, neither to me nor (I guessed) to others who were still struggling to stay awake. There was some mention too about the Mutt and Jeff technique—the nice guy–bad guy routine—and about the order of subjects that had been developed for questioning Vietcong suspects. But that was it, and despite my own experience I had expected more. This was, after all, the Agency, playing in the big leagues along with the KGB, MI5 and 6, Mossad, and Japan's CIO. I expected some coherent approach—an inventory of methods, a psychological profile of the enemy, an analysis of proved tactics. There was none.

Nor had the instructor said anything about the context of interrogation, the single most essential tool of the inquisitor's trade. I had sat there in growing wonder as I realized that we were not going to be told anything about the structure of the Vietcong organization, or how we might get an accurate understanding of who our suspect was, or what role he played in his organization, or whom he interacted with. Without such essential background data, how would an interrogator know what to ask? How would he be able to verify anything he was told? Did this data exist somewhere and we were just not being told about it for some reason? Or was an interrogator in Vietnam really expected to question his suspect cold, without any knowledge of the man or his background?

For the most part I kept my mouth shut. But when the lecturer at one point told us that many Special Branch policemen were at "work night and day to penetrate the Vietcong infrastructure," I couldn't hold back. "Well, sir," I asked, "what exactly is the infrastructure they are penetrating? Which committees or subcommittees? What are the most important provinces in that structure, the most important districts?" "Oh," came the answer, "Tay Ninh is very important, Long An is very important, and, uh, Binh Dinh is very important. We're making lots of great strides in Binh Dinh." End of discussion.

That afternoon had left me stunned. If I was reading it right, intelligence interrogation in Vietnam was strictly an ad hoc affair, carried on against an enemy whose organization was mostly unknown and invisible. It reminded me of a GI in Vung Tau who once described what it was like to go out on patrol against the VC. "We never see them," he'd said. "Bingo, one or two guys go down, then the whole squad is down and firing into the bush. But we never see them." By the time our ten-week training course was over I was wondering if maybe the CIA was never seeing them, just as the GIs never did.

Still, even with my misgivings, the Agency's programs made a certain amount of sense on the whole, at least on a conceptual level. Whether the programs worked in the field, though, was another story. I had left Langley eager to find out, and eager to put my own experience to work with an organization that had real power. As a CIA case officer I would have funding at my disposal, logistical support, topflight communications, all the resources of the legendary first team. I would have substantial freedom of action, the likes of which I'd never known in the military, and I'd be in a position to help achieve the overall goals the Agency had set. Despite the warning signs at Langley that all was not right with the CIA's Vietnam programs, I continued to feel that I might be able to accomplish something important, something that would help the American cause, and that of the South Vietnamese. It was a feeling that Jack Lambert had now helped to stimulate anew.

Leaving the glass house, we were escorted to a downstairs briefing room where we would meet Colonel Sam Liddel, director of the Provincial Reconnaissance Units program, one of the Agency's four pillars. The briefing room was arranged as a small theater, with built-in theater-type seats and enough room for fifteen or twenty people. Already waiting for the colonel were several new State Department people whose work required them to know about the PRU. One introduced himself and his colleagues and looked slightly puzzled when none of us reciprocated the introduction. Officially there were no CIA personnel in the country. When pressed, all Agency employees automatically referred to themselves as OSA officers—Office of Special Assistance to the ambassador. It was a well-known cover; I never met a single soldier who didn't know what OSA was. But at least we could reasonably get around without announcing ourselves to the world.

After a couple of minutes Colonel Liddel strode energetically into the room, a tripod under one arm and a batch of charts under the other. He was a man in his forties, obviously an army career officer attached to the CIA to handle this program. In his green-and-black tiger suit and short haircut he looked as if he'd be hopping a chopper for some provincial hot spot as soon as he finished the briefing.

The first words out of Liddel's mouth were that until a few
months ago the Provincial Reconnaissance Units had been called
CTs—counterterrorists. But the name had drawn bad publicity.
"Counterterrorism" sounded a little too much like "terrorism," and
reporters were always asking to have the difference explained.
"Provincial Reconnaissance Units," on the other hand, sounded
nice and bland. It didn't provoke any questions.

Liddel then explained that the units were organized into teams
of between twenty and forty, a team in each province capital. Ordinarily these teams were assigned to the Agency's Province Officer
in Charge, its POIC (pronounced "poick"). They were housed in
or near his compound and were led operationally by a U.S. Army
officer or a U.S. Army noncom. In effect, then, the Provincial
Reconnaissance Units were a kind of private army, directly under
CIA command. The Agency ran a training facility for PRU personnel near Vung Tau where the instruction was quite similar to
American Special Forces training. The PRU has been responsible,
Liddel said in conclusion, for approximately seven thousand Vietcong killed per year for the past four or five years.

I did a quick multiplication, then looked up just in time to catch
looks from Cal and John, who had obviously done the same. I
couldn't imagine that the figure was accurate. If the PRU alone
had killed thirty-five thousand or so Vietcong, and the U.S. forces
added another fairly substantial figure, and South Vietnam's army
—ARVN—added its own, then in the last five years every single
Vietcong had probably been killed off at least once and maybe
twice. I didn't say that to Liddel of course, nor did Cal or John. But
later, when the three of us talked it over, we echoed one another's
skepticism. "I'm really curious," I said. "We should check the figures when we get out to the provinces. I'd like to find out what the
facts really are on this."

After Liddel's talk we went over to the Census Grievance office
to be briefed by its program director. Ostensibly, the Census Grievance program had been established to obtain information from
peasants who had grievances against the Saigon government. But
in reality, it was a way of cultivating peasants to provide information on the location, activities, and order of battle of the Vietcong,
a kind of mass, low-level spying program.

Just as each province had an Agency POIC with his own Provincial Reconnaissance Unit strike team, so each province had a CIA
Census Grievance adviser and a Vietnamese Census Grievance
chief. And each Census Grievance chief had hundreds of peasants
on his payroll, the money furnished to him monthly by Agency

liaison people who carried it to the provinces in black satchels. Since we did not have any actual Vietcong agents, the director said, this program and the Rural Development program were the Agency's main sources of information.

Though I was sitting there listening to this, I found it difficult to believe my ears. Could the Census Grievance director actually be saying that we had no agents of our own in Vietnam? No spies? This was a subject that had not been covered at Langley. How the hell, I thought, could we possibly win a war with no spies? And was he telling us that the Census Grievance program simply accepted (and paid for) information from peasants it had signed up? It seemed the perfect target for any double agent: any of these peasants could be Vietcong; no doubt many of them were. Many more were undoubtedly Vietcong sympathizers. And the Agency was paying them for their services and accepting what they said as intelligence?

The logistics alone seemed improbable. "If these people are out in the boonies," I asked the director, "or deep in the rubber plantations where they might acquire some knowledge about VC units, how does the Census Grievance chief in the province contact them?" The answer was that usually the chief could travel during the daytime in an Agency vehicle to the districts and villages to meet the people. "Individually or in groups?" I asked half facetiously. "Oh, individually of course, Mr. DeForest. Their information is highly confidential and they would not want to be seen or heard discussing these sorts of things in public."

I didn't continue the discussion, but it sounded very strange that an Agency official might drive a jeep, say, from Song Be, the capital of Phuoc Long province, down to some village to meet peasants near a Vietcong area, get information from them and pay them off. He just wouldn't be able to do that, nor would some backwoods peasant in one of these areas ever think of meeting a CIA official in that way. And if the Census Grievance adviser didn't handle the information collection and payments personally, then how was he to know the money was getting to real people who were actually submitting real reports of some sort? The program the director described immediately aroused all my old cop skepticism.

After breaking for a two-hour lunch—standard in government circles there, as we soon learned—we reconvened in the office of the Rural Development program (RD) for our next briefing. The model for this program was developed in Binh Dinh province by a Vietnamese colonel named Nguyen Be. Colonel Be, we were told, had been quite successful in recruiting villagers to teach the peasants in his area how to improve sanitation and animal husbandry, how to build irrigation projects and so on. Be's recruits also helped hamlets and villages organize self-defense forces.

The idea had worked so well that Colonel Be had been brought to Saigon by the CIA to set up a national program. Rural Development cadres went through training at their own school in Vung Tau, then were fed into sixty-man teams operating in each province. They lived in the hamlets permanently and were the leading edge of the Saigon government's rural pacification effort. Their objective was to neutralize the local Vietcong and "win the hearts and minds of the people."

During our Langley training, Rural Development had seemed a reasonable concept. It did here too, at least as the director explained it. But when he used the expression "winning the hearts and minds" it set me on edge, as that expression always did. How South Vietnam's peasants might be won over in the absence of a full-scale land-reform program was something I had never understood and still didn't. Without land reform, this "hearts and minds" business was a joke, the kind of bad joke you could find inscribed on the Zippo lighters the Vietnamese stole from the PXs; the Vietnamese would engrave them, then sell them back to the GIs. "Give me your hearts and minds," they read, "or I'll blow your fucking hut down."

Listening to the director talk, I decided that I had to get a good look at these training facilities for Rural Development and for the Provincial Reconnaissance units. If these programs along with Census Grievance were the Agency's main sources of information, I wanted to know how they really operated from the ground up, not just how they were supposed to operate. I made a mental note to ask that visits to these places be included as part of my orientation.

Our last meeting of the day was with Ted Coleburne, director of Special Branch Police Operations and Training. Coleburne and the other three directors were the CIA's operational chiefs in Vietnam, and since Coleburne would be meeting with us last, it was a good bet that all three of us would be working in his program.

When Pinossa, Williams, and I were shown into Ted Coleburne's office we found him sitting behind a desk that was piled with more paperwork than I had ever seen. The stack in front of him rose almost two feet off the desktop, leaving only his head and shoulders visible as he talked. This man must be either horribly overworked, I thought, or else he's the world's lousiest paper pusher. I never did find out whether either or both of these guesses was true. But whatever else he might have been, Coleburne seemed like a friendly guy with a sense of humor. "You do have some choice in your assignments," he said. "But of course we've already picked them out for you." Cal Williams was going to Chau Doc province in Military Region Four (Four Corps) as special police adviser; John Pinossa would have the same assignment in Tay Ninh, a hot province in Military Region Three next to the Cambodian border. I had been selected as chief interrogator for the same Military Region Three.

I must have looked momentarily crestfallen when I heard this, because Coleburne said, "Orrin, you've got a distressed expression on your face. Is something wrong?" "No," I told him. "Not really. Though I must admit I was thinking about Qui Nhon in Binh Dinh province. I was with CID there for a while and I know that area pretty well." The fact was that I was going to suggest that I be assigned to Qui Nhon. As CID chief in that bustling port city I had been friends with the Vietnamese chief of police, which meant I would have had an easy time getting close to the chief of the special police. "Well," said Coleburne, "I'm afraid that's out of the question. The chief interrogator's job in Region Three is a new position and it requires a lot of interrogation experience. We took a good look at your file, and you're the only one who has it. Tomorrow, John and Cal will be leaving," he continued, "but I want you to stay for the staff meeting. After that you'll meet Captain Zale. He's in charge of our nationwide Provincial Interrogation Center program. That's a program you'll have to know well, Orrin. We must get those interrogation centers to work."

That evening Cal, John, and I relaxed over martinis in the hotel's rooftop bar. I was a little disappointed, I told them; I had kind of been looking forward to Qui Nhon. "You're disappointed!" Cal exclaimed. "What about me? I'm going to Chau Doc. That's the real boonies." John seemed more contemplative. His destination, Tay Ninh, was a rough place. Right next to the Cambodian border, the province was home to many of the Vietcong and North Vietnamese base areas as well as significant numbers of enemy main-force troops. "Well," he said, taking a sip, "at least I don't suppose it will be boring."

After the martinis we had dinner in the hotel restaurant, then took a walk down Tu Do Street, Saigon's infamous shopping strip where everything in the world was available—electronics, cameras, military uniforms, holsters, hats, insignias, paintings, souvenirs, an immense array of liquors. Also drugs and girls, especially girls. The street was teeming with GIs, thousands of them, and with Vietnamese. The noise of wrangling and haggling enveloped us. Laughter and raucous music overflowed from the bars and massage parlors.

As the street traffic thickened, a little boy detached himself from a gang of barefoot boys gathered in front of a bar and walked up to us. Although he could not have been more than nine or ten, a cigarette dangled from his lips. I soon noticed that all of them were smoking, the whole ragged little bunch. Taking hold of my hand, the boy looked up and asked, "You GI?" With my free hand I felt for my watch. "You want short time, mister? You go *di di* me?" He had one of the dirtiest faces I had ever seen, but big eyes and, as he clenched the cigarette in his teeth, a big smile. "You like girl, mister? You like boy? You want blow job?" A nine-year-old pimp. The streets were full of them, little-boy pimps and harder-looking teenage pimps. As I shook him off, a taxi pulled up next to us. "Hey," said the driver, "you want number-one bang bang?" We started to laugh. The place was unbelievable, a true madhouse.

A half block farther down we saw the girls lounging against the walls or picking their way through the crowd, all of them in high heels and tight miniskirts, their breasts straining against low-cut blouses. Most of them were whores, others just bar girls who wanted to get us inside the bars that lined the street. It started immediately. "You buy me Saigon tea, GI, you buy me Saigon tea?" That meant "Come in with me, sit down with me, talk, feel, do anything, just buy the tea. Five hundred *p* a glass, just buy the tea, GI." These were pretty tough girls. When I waved them off, they spat out, "Booshit, GI, you number ten! You number ten thousand! You fucking number ten thousand!" "My God, Orrin" —Cal couldn't believe I was chasing them away—"some of these girls are really cute." This was Cal's first tour. "Cal," I said, "you really don't want to try one of these short timers. You'll get the biggest dose of clap you've ever seen."

The next morning John, Cal, and I had breakfast together, then said our good-byes, promising to keep in touch if possible. In fact, John and I knew we would be seeing each other since his assignment in Tay Ninh put him in Military Region Three, where I would shortly be taking over as chief of interrogation. Cal we might see in Saigon if we all happened to take a little R and R at the same time. But other than that, he was right, Chau Doc was the boonies.

Once they left I reported to the Norodom Complex to meet with Ted Coleburne and his staff for a detailed briefing on their work with the Special Branch. Their responsibility, as they described it, was to train Vietnamese special police agents for work on the village and district levels. The agents' task was to penetrate the Vietcong infrastructure and work within the Phoenix program. Phoenix, as I knew from training, was a CIA-initiated attempt to bring together the various Vietnamese security agencies with an American adviser in order to pool intelligence and coordinate efforts to crack the Vietcong organization. That was all I had heard about Phoenix at that time, though later I would get to know the program well.

When we were finished talking, Coleburne took me to see Robert Zale, national adviser for the Provincial Interrogation Centers the CIA had built throughout South Vietnam—PICs, or as everyone pronounced them, "picks." Captain Robert Zale had the butch haircut of a marine lifer, as well as a lifer's gung ho energy and imperious manner. Pleasant introductions were not his style. "Sit down, Orrin," he said, in a voice right off the drill field. "I'll explain your duties." Right to the point, anyway, I thought, deciding to ignore the rudeness. Over the years I had met quite a few jarhead marines who turned out to be decent guys after all.

The Provincial Interrogation Centers, Zale told me, had been constructed by the Agency in almost every province capital at a cost of $55,000 each. They consisted of a standard twenty-eight cells together with interrogation rooms and offices. The cells were small, five feet by four feet, designed to give a Vietcong suspect no room to do anything but sit or lie down curled up. Ventilation was minimal. My responsibilities as interrogation officer of Military Region Three would be: number one, to inspect the PICs; number two, to train Vietnamese field officers in interrogation techniques; and number three, to monitor the production of intelligence. I was to pay special attention to spotting operational leads and to the possibility of turning prisoners into agents, feeding them back into their old Vietcong units. Our program over the next two weeks would be to visit as many of the centers as we could, at least two a day, to meet the local people and see how they were doing.

The way Zale explained it, the business of gathering intelligence sounded pretty cut and dried. But during his efficient descriptions he used a telltale phrase I had heard Coleburne use the previous day. "We must make the PICs work, Orrin," Zale said at one point. "We must make them work." Apparently, then, the PICs were not working, at least not as they were supposed to. And despite his gung ho optimism, Zale was obviously nervous about it. "It's one of our most important programs," he said. "The chief's watching this one closely."

First thing next morning Zale and I were on a plane to Qui

Nhon, the most active interrogation center in Military Region
Two. I was happy about the choice, since it would allow me to see
Police Chief Nguyen Lang there and to talk to some of my old
friends who I knew were familiar with the Rural Development and
Provincial Reconnaissance Unit programs. I wanted to do whatever
I could to get the straight story on these programs myself.

The Qui Nhon PIC turned out to be quite different from the
standardized CIA centers. This one was housed in an old French
fort that seemed much better suited to interrogation than the
Agency-designed centers Zale had described. Here the prisoners
weren't cramped into tiny cells; they had cots to sleep on, they
could walk around, they had plenty of air. Just being in the cells
wouldn't make them feel angry and recalcitrant. It didn't look too
bad. But the interrogation we sat in on was terrible by any standards. The Vietnamese special police interrogator who was questioning the prisoner was painfully inept, while his American adviser
obviously had no idea of what to do. There was no context to the
questioning, no rationale to their line of thinking, no probing at all
into the suspect's background. When I asked if they had the ability
to check his story against information on file in the province special
police office, the answer was no. Was there anything on file about
the local district Vietcong structure? Again, no. "Do you have any
kind of wiring diagram of the VC organization?" I asked. The interrogator shook his head, confused. The special police adviser answered that he didn't think so. What, if he could ask, was a wiring
diagram?

At this Zale blew his stack and started shouting at the police
interrogator in Vietnamese. I kept my mouth shut, listening to Zale
chew him out right in front of the prisoner and in front of me. It
was a terrible thing to do, and embarrassing to watch. What is
wrong with this guy? I thought to myself. You don't do things like
this to the Vietnamese. But in objective terms, Zale was right; the
interrogation was appalling.

From Qui Nhon we flew south to the coastal city of Nha Trang.
The PIC there was an Agency project, a rectangular-shaped, tile-
roofed, whitewashed structure with a sandbagged guard position in
front of the door. Behind the offices of the PIC chief and his staff
were four or five interrogation rooms, and, behind these, the cells.
Each cell was meant for one man, and was vented by a single three-
by-five-inch hole at the top of the back wall. The door had a six-
by-six-inch peekaboo grated window in the front and a food slot
near the bottom. In the hundred-degree temperature the place
stank of urine, feces, and the odor of unwashed bodies.

When I looked into the first occupied cell through the six-by-six grate I saw a little man squatting motionlessly on his haunches. Seeing my face at the door, he gave me an angry stare and grunted something that I didn't ask to have translated. "Another one of those fuckin' foreigners," no doubt. Well, I thought, I'm seeing my first real VC. But when I asked Zale to ask him who he was, the surly prisoner said he wasn't Vietcong, he was a farmer. He had been working in a rice paddy when he was arrested. That meant he was a Class C prisoner—an unproved Vietcong suspect.

Zale asked the same question of the next four prisoners. Not one of them admitted to being VC. They all said they were peasants living in contested areas; that's why they had been arrested. Class C prisoners, all of them. One of these guys could be a VC district chief, I thought, and nobody here would know the difference. How could they know? They had no way of checking anything. There wasn't a piece of serious background information in the PIC files, no biographical data, no structural charts, nothing to make an interrogation either interesting or productive. All they had the ability to do was beat the shit out of these people, and then what would they know?

When I left the Nha Trang PIC I was angry and depressed. I understood all too clearly that in a little while the pressure would be on me. I would be in Region Three with a boss breathing down my neck to "make the PICs work." I was also pissed off at Zale, who seemed to get more frustrated and abusive as the day wore on. You just couldn't talk to Asians the way he was talking to them, with this badgering, commanding style of speech, bawling special police out in front of each other, making them lose face. You can't do that in Asia no matter whom you're talking to.

Over the next two weeks Zale and I visited Provincial Interrogation Centers throughout the country. Everywhere we went it was the same story. The PICs were just not producing intelligence. Reading through the interrogation reports, I saw over and over the same answer to questions. "I don't know. I don't know. I don't know"—which was exactly what we were hearing in the live interrogations. Zale, whose bluntness I was beginning to understand better, was often furious and did nothing to suppress his disgust. "What do you mean they're saying 'I don't know'?" he'd bark. "What kind of an answer is that? What the hell do you think you're conducting here?"

Visiting Tay Ninh, I stopped to see John Pinossa. "Not much coming out of the PIC here," he told me. "We can't check out a story even if we manage to squeeze one out of a VC. The police?

Orrin, as far as I can tell they're just marking time. Operations here are going nowhere." Only one situation was really interesting: there was a Vietcong agent under development who had initially been recruited by John's predecessor. The American had returned to the States a couple of months earlier, and now John was trying to restart the operation. The developmental was a nephew of a South Vietnamese military security services officer. Allegedly, the prospective spy was a midlevel Tay Ninh cadre. John wanted advice on how to handle this, and asked if I could do anything to check out the security officer and his friend. I promised I would do what I could, and that I'd come back to see him once I finished orientation and took up my position in Bien Hoa, the Agency's Military Region Three base headquarters.

After Zale and I had visited a good number of Provincial Interrogation Centers, Ted Coleburne asked me to write an assessment report for him. It was an assignment I had half expected, and one I was eager to avoid. I was the new man on the block, and despite the utter worthlessness of what I had seen, I knew there would be no point in hammering one of Coleburne's pet programs. At least not yet. That could come later, after I had figured out some way of making improvements. Yet how I might dredge up any reason at all to be optimistic about the PICs was beyond me. The centers were clearly a waste of time and money. In the end I settled for the noncommittal approach, explaining that I had observed Zale and had noted his attention to the need for improving interrogation techniques and his constant and determined effort to provide personal support and expertise with the objective of achieving more complete intelligence results on the local level—the best line of bullshit I could manufacture. The only thing decent about the report was its brevity, and the fact that it wouldn't upset anybody's applecart.

By now I had seen far more of the PICs than I wanted to. Strangely, perhaps, understanding what an awful mess they were made me even more determined to get to work and see if I couldn't do better. I also had the distinct feeling that I had to get away from Saigon Station; I had seen absolutely nothing there to suggest that the Agency brass had any real sense for what went on in the field or a single clue about how to make any improvements. But before I left for Bien Hoa, I did want to see the Provincial Reconnaissance Units and Rural Development training facilities outside Vung Tau. And I wanted to have a good look at the Agency's Phoenix school.

The next morning I was in the copilot's seat of a twin-engine Beechcraft flying toward the coast south of Saigon. At the Vung

Tau airport I was met by a Mr. Dao, assistant to Colonel Nguyen Be, the man who had originated the Rural Development program. Mr. Dao spoke excellent English, which he soon let me know he had perfected as an undergraduate in engineering at Duke University. He was the one, he said, who always met visiting dignitaries for Colonel Be and acted as guide and interpreter. I was not in the dignitary category, I told him. I was just a workingman who wanted to talk with the colonel and see the school.

Colonel Nguyen Be turned out to be a friendly, hospitable individual who took the time to have tea served and to describe for me the concept of the Rural Development program and the successes it had had training thousands of peasants to take back to their villages essential development and defense skills.

When Colonel Be's briefing was over, Dao and I left for the training camp. We walked through the entire area, getting a close-up look at the Rural Development trainees digging irrigation ditches, building dams, and tending model rice paddies. They looked like an active bunch, peasants from villages throughout the country who were here learning agricultural techniques. At least that was what they were supposed to be. But as Dao explained what we were seeing, I could not share his enthusiasm. Watching the work going on, it seemed to me as if this was another American concept imposed from above on the Vietnamese and probably not worth much in practice. After a while I couldn't resist turning to Dao and saying, "If I understand it, you're telling a peasant who has been growing rice for two thousand years how to run his paddy. Is that right?" Dao just laughed.

But there was something a lot more bothersome than that about the peasants out in the training fields. I had slogged through plenty of rural areas doing CID investigations during my first tour and I had met plenty of Vietnamese peasants. Vietnamese peasants were burned permanently dark and their hands and feet were as wrinkled as a grandmother's, really weather-beaten. By these criteria none of the people working here were peasants. Their skin was light and their feet and hands were as smooth as lilies. Wanting to get a close look, I started going up to the trainees and shaking hands, staring openly. There was no question about it, not a single one of these trainees had grown up barefoot. No peasants had ever had complexions like theirs, or feet like theirs. And none had ever had the Saigon cowboy-style haircut that every one of these young men seemed to be sporting.

What's going on here? I thought. Not that it took any special genius to figure out why healthy draft-age men from the city were training as Rural Development cadres in place of the peasants who were supposed to be here. They could only have bought their way in. But at the same time I found it hard to accept that obvious conclusion. "Mr. Dao," I said, deciding to see if a direct approach might get something from him, "I don't see any actual peasants out here, so why don't you tell me how you're really recruiting these people." Dao looked as if he had been poked with a cattle prod. I was sure this wasn't the kind of question he was used to getting from visiting dignitaries. But he wasn't so shocked that he dropped the pretense. "Oh, yes," he said after a moment, "they are all recruited in their home villages for a two-month training program here, including all the self-help projects and the military training." "Well," I said, looking him in the eyes, "these people all have white hands and feet. I haven't seen any black skin or wrinkles on any of them, like you see in the countryside." "Oh," said Dao. "Well, most of the trainees are out on exercises right now."

I dropped it there and asked Dao to drive me over to the Provincial Reconnaissance Units training camp, which was located in an isolated beachfront area, only about fifteen minutes away. As we drove in the front gate I met an American Special Forces sergeant who turned out to be one of the PRU instructors. It didn't take much to convince him to give me an ad hoc look around, which I thought might be more instructive than a more official tour.

My experience at the Rural Development camp had primed me to find something out of whack here too. But as we started our inspection it was obvious the sergeant was proud of the PRU training program. In fact the place looked a lot like the Fort Bragg Special Forces course. We saw barbed-wire exercises—teaching the PRU trainees Vietcong sapper techniques, bunkers used for practice attacks on VC positions, and sand-table exercises that seemed efficient and to the point. From what I could see, the place seemed to be professionally run. "How many of the trainees are ex-VC?" I asked the sergeant. (A large percentage of Vietcong defectors and deserters ended up in one or another of South Vietnam's armed services.) "About thirty percent," he answered. "The rest are former ARVN soldiers who have completed their service or who have been partially disabled but can still carry a gun."

From the Provincial Reconnaissance Units camp I went to the Phoenix school, located in a CIA compound on the outskirts of Vung Tau. The commander of the school was a U.S. Army major who explained in more detail how Phoenix sought to coordinate the resources of all the existing South Vietnamese counterinsurgency organizations to identify and mount operations against the

Vietcong infrastructure. District- and province-level Phoenix committees were made up of representatives of the National Police,
Special Branch Police, Military Security Service, Provincial Reconnaissance Units, Regional Forces, and local ARVN forces, together with an American Phoenix adviser, usually from the regular
army. Pooling their information, the committees would categorize
targets as Class A—significant political operatives, Class B—lesser
Vietcong personnel, and Class C—suspected Vietcong. The program had been initiated by William Colby, who had been CIA
director for the Far East, then it had been transferred to CORDS
(Civil Operations and Revolutionary Development Support—the
unified civilian and military command for countryside pacification
programs established under State Department jurisdiction) when
Colby himself joined that agency.

The first question I had for the major was whether or not it was
really possible to get the different Vietnamese agencies to share
information or to cooperate on operations in the field. My experience was that they would not do it, that the jealousies and conflict-
ing personal and social allegiances were far too pronounced to
allow cooperation on any level. "Off the record?" he said. "Off the
record, they don't have a shot in hell at it." My next question was
one that had become a sort of constant refrain for me, at least in
my mind. "Do the village or district offices of the National Police
or Special Branch Police have any data banks where they've identified legal, military, or political cadre?" "No," the major answered,
"the only thing they have is short lists of VC suspects." "How about
wiring diagrams? Do they have even sketchy wiring diagrams of the
VC political and military organizations?" "No, I've never seen
one," he said. "Not one."

I left Vung Tau on the afternoon courier flight to Saigon, looking forward to a steak dinner and a martini. Maybe two martinis, I
thought, reflecting on what I'd seen and heard. The more I considered it, the more it seemed clear that in Military Region Three I
was going to have to start from the ground up. The first thing I
planned to do there was inspect all our province offices and talk
with all Agency people handling the different CIA programs. I
wanted to see what, if anything, was working and usable and which
people could be counted on to contribute energy and intelligence.
By now I knew a good deal about what was wrong. I hoped a really
close inspection of the programs might give me some ideas about
how to set it right.

The next morning I reported to Ted Coleburne, who had scheduled a meeting for Zale and me with the director of the Vietnamese

Special Branch Police. There I was to be introduced to four Special Branch officers who would accompany me to Bien Hoa and assist me in establishing the Three Corps regional interrogation team, a concept that Saigon Station hoped would breathe life into the floundering Provincial Interrogation Center system. Coleburne's overall idea seemed to be that I would analyze the system and develop reforms and innovations that I and my special police assistants would then train the local PIC personnel to implement. Whether or not the concept would have any practical relevance once we got out there was anybody's guess. But at any rate it was something new and different from Saigon Station.

The meeting with Colonel Pham and his deputy, a Colonel Thinh, started off fine, with smiles all around and tea on the table. Then the four Special Branch Police walked in, four boys, not one of them out of his teens—my team of experts. I couldn't believe my eyes. Moving out onto Colonel Pham's patio to talk further, Zale seemed exuberant. I was speechless. My team of experts that was going to reorganize Region Three, the hottest and arguably the most crucial of South Vietnam's four military regions, were teenagers! As I stood there in shock, one of them came up to me and said in broken English, "You buy me Honda?" I stared at him. "We have car or Honda drive to Bien Hoa?" he said, louder. "No," Zale put in, all smiles. "Orrin, I'm making arrangements for you and your team to fly to Bien Hoa in a special plane. We'll have the Region Three chief of base and the chief of the Special Branch meet you at the airport."

I had never felt lower in my life. This was not something I was going to do, as I told Ted Coleburne as soon as I got hold of him afterward. "There is no way I am going out to Bien Hoa like that," I said, steaming. "I'm going to get in a car with my suitcase and drive out there alone. I am not taking those children with me. Do you think I'm going to get off an airplane and meet an Agency chief of base and a Special Branch colonel with these four snot-nosed kids who couldn't possibly do anything whatsoever in any kind of intelligence work? They know nothing! These are supposed to be my experts? This is terrible!" I was stumbling over my words I was so angry. "All right," said Coleburne, momentarily taken aback. "If you feel that way, then go out by yourself." He was upset. The idea had obviously been to make a big show with a hot new concept and a hot new team of experts. Give the fellas in the boonies a little one-upmanship from the central office. And now there would be no show.

The kids were not my last shock of the day; that happened at

Colonel Thinh's house where Zale and I had been invited for lunch to conclude plans on how to use "Orrin's new special team of experts." A few days earlier I had read an article in *Stars and Stripes* about a farming organization in one of the New England states that had presented twenty thousand chickens to South Vietnam as seed stock for chicken farms. It was a short piece that I had just glanced at in passing. But I remembered thinking what a nice gesture this was, especially considering how scrawny and sick-looking the typical village chickens were in Vietnam. Now, as we walked into Colonel Thinh's French-style villa in one of the Saigon suburbs, I heard the sound of chickens clucking and cackling. A lot of chickens. There on the left side of his enclosed entrance garden was a brand-new chicken coop, six tiers stacked up against the wall complete with feeding troughs and covered with wire mesh. The coop was packed with beautiful, fat white chickens— not the kind any Vietnamese had ever raised. Oh, my Lord, I thought, the New England chickens. These special police bastards have split them up among themselves.

2

THE MONASTERY

B ien Hoa, the CIA base headquarters for Military Region
Three, was only fifteen miles north of Saigon, but I was
told the ride invariably took forty-five or fifty minutes, even on the
new four-lane highway. A mile or two outside the capital my driver
and I hit the traffic: Vietnamese cars and trucks mixed in with
endless lines of U.S. Army trucks, jeeps, armored personnel carriers, tanks, the whole works. Much of the military traffic was on
its way to or from the Long Binh post, a huge base area just east of
Bien Hoa that was the supply hub for all of Military Region Three.
From the Saigon port, equipment and supplies of all sorts flowed
in a constant stream into Long Binh, from where they were trucked
and air-transported out to the rest of the region, including the
nearby Cu Chi camp of the 25th "Tropic Lightning" Division.
Long Binh was also home to almost fifty thousand American
troops, the Army's Second Field Force headquarters, the sprawling
25th Evacuation Hospital, and a smaller hospital for enemy
wounded. Next door to Long Binh, Bien Hoa contained ARVN's
Third Corps, while South Vietnam's air force headquarters and the
U.S. Third Fighter Wing were housed at the airfield.
   Despite all the military, and its own population of 100,000 or so,
Bien Hoa still seemed more like a bustling country town than a

city. Beyond the little suburban hamlet of Tan Hiep the highway
narrowed to a two-lane street where pedestrians crowded together
with bicycles, cyclos, buses, and cars in a chaotic jumble. Looking
up to the right I saw a big sign that announced "Military Region
Three Chieu Hoi Center," the holding area for Vietcong and
North Vietnamese defectors. And there they were, what seemed to
be thousands of them milling around behind the barbed-wire
fences or sitting at picnic tables under hundred-foot-long tin-
roofed shelters. Moving at a snail's pace through the traffic, we
passed blocks of ruins, the blown-out remains of a residential
neighborhood that had been in the path of the Vietcong attack
nine months before, during Tet. Then suddenly we were in town,
driving down the main street past houses that had a vaguely Arab
look to them and heading toward the market area and the Dong
Nai River that flowed swiftly along the city's southern edge. In
another few minutes we passed the market and found Le Van
Duyet Street, where the CIA headquarters occupied a two-story
yellow apartment building that sat behind an automatic steel gate.

To all the CIA's Vietnam personnel, this building was known as
the "Monastery," a nickname it had acquired under a former chief
of base named Bob Hall. Hall had been uncharacteristically (for
the Agency) puritanical and had declared the place off limits to all
females other than employees. Since the base officers lived in the
second-floor bedrooms, the prohibition had considerably disrupted
their social lives and led to a lot of grumbling—the nickname was
a lasting remnant.

Walking in past the Nung guard at the sandbagged guard post, I
was greeted by a pleasant-faced, plumpish young American woman
who identified herself as Susie, secretary to base chief Loren Snowcroft. Loren was in Vung Tau visiting the Phoenix school, she said,
"But we've got a room waiting for you upstairs. If you'd like, after
you get settled we can have a cup of coffee together. Loren ought
to be back by 1600."

Like all the second-floor bedrooms, the room Susie showed me
to shared a bathroom with its neighbor. In the bathroom packing
up some toiletries was a big rugged-looking army major who introduced himself as Jack Black. He seemed to be the only one around.
"I'm from Texas," he said, in a drawl that left no doubt about it,
"West Texas."

Jack Black turned out to be one of the most amiable people I had
ever met, and we hit it off immediately, the way westerners often
do. He was the kind of guy you could stand with face-to-face and
jawbone-to-jawbone and he'd tell you his whole life story. The kind

of guy who, if you asked him for the straight poop on something, would say, "OK, friend, you've got it."

As I unpacked we filled each other in on our service experience. He was just finishing his second tour in 'Nam, he said, and would be leaving in four days. His first tour had been with the Special Forces, and he had seen a lot of action. When that was up he had volunteered for a tour with the CIA. "I should never have come on board with the Agency," he said, "it's been a total waste of time."

With very little coaxing Jack told me he had spent his time with the Agency as deputy Provincial Reconnaissance Unit officer for the region, for the most part inspecting PRU camps and keeping an eye on their operations. It hadn't been a happy experience. "I'm sick of playing games for the colonel [the regional PRU adviser] with the goddam statistics," he said. "All the PRU are reporting false information about wounded, killed, and captured. They count the bodies at the village, they count them again at the district, then they count them at the province. It's a goddam geometric progression of bodies. I've told the colonel a thousand times, but all I ever get from him is 'Don't rock the boat.' He always says we'll be leaving soon anyway, so what the hell is the difference? I've fought it for a year, and now I'm glad I'm out of it."

When we adjourned downstairs for a cup of coffee with Susie, she laughed and said, "Yes, Jack's a happy man now that he's going home." Susie was the one who typed Jack's reports, so she knew all his gripes. She also sat in on meetings between Jack Black, the Provincial Reconnaissance Unit colonel, and Loren Snowcroft, taking notes while they argued about the reports. "Well, I feel I've done my part anyway," Jack said, "so now it's back to Texas for a new assignment. Whatever it is, it's got to be better than this."

At 1600 Loren Snowcroft, the chief of base, returned from Vung Tau. Already the equivalent of a full colonel in the Agency's ranking system, Snowcroft was only in his early forties. He was a big man with huge arms, an intellectual weight lifter whose age was just beginning to get him around the middle. Snowcroft was already balding, and his receding gray hair, glasses, and pipe conveyed a somewhat scholarly air, though from the first it was obvious there was nothing standoffish about him. The smile and handshake said immediately that he was not one of the Agency's Ivy League types.

After Susie's introduction we went into Loren's office to talk, where we were joined after a few minutes by George Tanaka, a California Nisei who was chief of special police operations. "Listen," Loren began, "we got a cable saying you were supposed to fly

in here with a special team of some sort. What happened?" When
I related the story of the four juvenile agents, Loren laughed out
loud. "It's just like those fucking idiots in Saigon to dream up
something like that," he said. "Sometimes I can hardly believe it."

But it wasn't only Saigon that gave him problems. The Bien Hoa
base was responsible for the Phoenix, Rural Development, and
Provincial Reconnaissance Units schools in Vung Tau (though
Phoenix had technically been switched over to CORDS and Rural
Development was in the process of doing the same). It was also
headquarters for a region that was in some ways the heart of the
enemy revolution. Along the Cambodian border between the Fishhook and the Parrot's Beak lay the main Vietcong and North Vietnamese base areas and headquarters, including the Central Office
for South Vietnam (COSVN), the headquarters complex that directed the war throughout South Vietnam. Three North Vietnam-
ese/Vietcong divisions operated in the region as well as VC main-
force battalions and an undetermined number of VC local forces
and "legal" personnel (covert Vietcong operatives who lived openly
as ordinary South Vietnamese citizens). Several of the ten provinces were always hot, and in places like Hau Nghia, Tay Ninh,
Long An, Rach Gia, and Can Giouc, mortar attacks on district and
province capitals were a regular occurrence. One reason there was
so much continuous pressure in this region was that the Hanoi
planners knew that if they were ever going to win this thing it would
be done through the Saigon corridor, right down the Saigon River,
or through Long An or Long Khanh, through the heart of Region
Three.

Yet despite the difficulties in the region, Loren explained, of all
his agents in the field, only one—two now with John Pinossa on
board—was an experienced CIA career officer. The other forty or
so were either military men on loan to the Agency or contract
officers (as I was), individuals who had signed on with the CIA
from other walks of life and who had not gone through the Agency's year-long training "down on the farm." Instead they had been
put through a special ten-week Vietnam orientation course, then
had been shipped over and plunked down in the middle of the
action. All in all it was a kind of pickup operation. (Though Loren
didn't say it, we both knew that CIA career people tended to de-
cline service in Vietnam. It was, after all, a war zone, and there
was a much better chance of getting killed here than in some other
posting.) "I'm grateful they sent you here, Orrin," he went on. "At
least you've got a professional intelligence background. But
frankly, I don't know what a regional interrogation officer can do

under these circumstances. We are not getting much information from the PICs."

I told Loren that I knew what he meant about the interrogation centers, that I had inspected quite a number of them with Robert Zale. I also knew what he meant about the contract officers. Of my twenty classmates in the Vietnam course at Langley, only John Pinossa had been a CIA career man. Of the rest, some were military people who were looking for a change of pace or a change of career. But most were civilians: teachers, engineers, stockbrokers who had got fed up with their jobs, or who wanted to see some action and for one reason or another had applied to the Agency.

For the most part they had impressed me as well-intentioned people who, unfortunately, hadn't the slightest relevant experience. Even including the former soldiers there was hardly a shred of intelligence know-how among them, and the Agency's ten-week course was not by the wildest stretch of imagination an adequate preparation. They had never learned even the basics of intelligence work—the surveillance, communications, interrogation, covert action, and other specialized techniques that go into the formation of a professional. And now these people were advisers to the special police and to the other CIA-sponsored security and pacification programs. And it had been the same with the previous graduating classes from the Vietnam training. Six hundred CIA officers of all levels in country, I thought, and most of them without a clue in the world.

"Tet was a disaster for the Vietcong," Loren was saying now, "even though the journalists don't think so. When they came out in the open we absolutely slaughtered them. So it's true we're making some progress. But I'll tell you, half the time we don't have any idea what's going on." As he reviewed the situation in Military Region Three my impression grew that sitting in front of me was a very bright man, an honest man, an open man, someone I could be happy working for. But Loren Snowcroft was also a confused man. He was facing a very complex situation and did not know how to get a handle on it, how to change it. He knew nothing about the Vietcong, even after eight months as chief of base. He knew essentially nothing about the Vietcong defectors and prisoners. He had never sat down and talked to one himself, and he was getting precious little from those who were talking to them. He knew he had no conception of the enemy organization that confronted him and it frustrated the hell out of him. They were out there all right; the woods were full of Indians. But how might one get at them?

After an hour or so Loren suggested that we continue the discussion in a more relaxed setting. It was getting on toward dinnertime, so we might as well move upstairs, he said, to the balcony off one of the back rooms where we could enjoy the sunset and a drink while we talked. Would I by any chance care for a martini? (For some reason the Agency seemed to breed martini drinkers. I myself had picked up the habit in the air force's OSI.)

Loren's balcony directly overlooked the Dong Nai River, which at that point was more than a thousand yards wide. It was a stunning sight, majestic, but at the same time absolutely typical. Little sampans paddled upstream against the swiftly flowing current, or floated quickly downstream. Along the banks Vietnamese were bathing, rubbing their skin hard to get clean. Men wore T-shirts and shorts, women pajama pants and white blouses, the children were naked. It was a tableau that no doubt had remained essentially unchanged for hundreds of years.

As George Tanaka, Loren, and I sat and enjoyed the scene Loren asked me in more detail about where I came from, my family, my children, my education, my World War Two background. He seemed especially interested in my experiences in Japan. George Tanaka spoke and wrote Japanese and had been stationed in that country a good while. What had I done there? I explained to Loren that my main duties with the Air Force Office of Special Investigations had been to liaise with the Japanese National Police KGB-GRU section and with the PSIB, the innocuously named Public Safety Investigative Board, Japan's FBI. I touched on the approach these organizations had taken toward the Japanese Communist Party and the various Communist front organizations. I also described some of the situations I had been involved in there, in intelligence and also as a criminal investigator with OSI from 1955 to 1964, and with CID from 1964 until my first tour in Vietnam in 1966.

Listening to my account of the PSIB, George Tanaka's ears pricked up. "You know Kajikawa?" he asked in surprise, referring to the PSIB's legendary director. "Sure," I answered. "Who do you think was Kajikawa's golf *sensai?*" In fact I had by chance become the great Shoichi Kajikawa's golf teacher after being summoned one day to see him ostensibly regarding a KGB case the Japanese wanted our help with. My partner and I had been shocked to find ourselves in the PSIB director's vast and elegant office listening to him describe a KGB agent who had taken to drinking by himself at a Japanese bar that catered to foreigners. Since Americans would be less conspicuous in the bar than Japanese, Kajikawa wondered

if we might help with the surveillance. It would, he said, be "so
pleasant" if we could. Then, without skipping a beat, he was asking
about my golf game and my "handi," my handicap. A week later
we were on the course together, and that had led to more sessions,
then more, and eventually to a warm friendship. It went without
saying what effect my luck as a golf instructor had had on my
relationship with the PSIB.

I found it easy enough to guess what George Tanaka, a Japanese-
speaking CIA major, had been doing in Japan: government to government contact. "Maybe," George said, laughing, "you could be
right."

George loved Japan, as I did, and he hated every minute he had
spent in Vietnam. "I have never," he said, "seen so many incom-
petent people in one place at one time." As George talked, and as
Loren himself began to fill out the picture at the base, I began to
sense why Loren was so interested in the details of my background.
The plain fact was that he was strapped for help, and here I was, a
warm body—but a warm body that might, given my background,
turn out to have some life in it. Judging from Jack Black's assessment and now George Tanaka's, it was easy enough to see that
morale was not good at the Region Three base, nor was there much
reason for it to be good.

By now Loren was going through his lineup. His deputy was a
do-nothing deputy: no help. His chief of operations was an alco-
holic: no help. George was so goddam disgusted with Vietnam he
was no help. Bill Hope was a first-rate reports officer, but all he
could ever get from the ARVN regional intelligence officer, the
G-2, was information on the enemy's order of battle. Then he had
Dick Daniels, the Census Grievance supervisor, trying to put all
these little nothings of information together enough to make a halfway reasonable report. Which he did, about two reports a month.
Then he had Susie, his secretary, and Dick Brigham, his chief of
support. Then he had the Provincial Reconnaissance Unit adviser
who didn't want to rock the boat, and he had a man in charge of
Rural Development who was being phased over to CORDS, so he
wasn't really his. And that was it for the Monastery.

Finally, there were the people out in the provinces. "You're not
going to believe what I've got out in the field," said Loren. "Sometimes I think I'm talking to the darndest bunch of dodoes the CIA
ever collected. Now don't get me wrong; most of them are good
guys. But they're just not capable. I don't know who IS capable. In
fact half the time I don't know what the hell I'm doing myself."

I enjoyed Loren's self-deprecating humor. But I also knew I was

watching a pretty good interviewer at work. The rapport, the gentle
but thorough probing, were completely natural; they were also effective. And I had noticed that when I mentioned the Japanese
Communist Party and the other Japanese front organizations that
I had spent years observing as liaison to the Japanese security services, Loren's relaxed, martini-drinking manner had tensed just a
bit. It occurred to me that the chief of base knew where he wanted
to go, even if he did not know how to get there. What he was asking
himself as that unbelievable sun slipped behind the river was if I
was a person who might be able to help him along.

In fact, Loren already had his plans laid out for me. First of all
he wanted a complete survey of each of the ten provinces that
made up Military Region Three, not only of the interrogation centers, but also of the other programs. I was to look at the operations,
evaluate them, and make recommendations, starting immediately.
"You might as well begin in Binh Tuy," he said, "then go right
around in a circle. That's the way the CORDS courier plane makes
its stops and you can take that everywhere."

The next day, Sunday, I spent the entire day reading the Region
Three intelligence reporting—from the PICs, the special police,
and the other programs. By the end of the day I had had enough;
it was exactly the same dreary stuff the other regions were sending
to Saigon—material I had waded through during my orientation
there. In effect there was no intelligence to speak of. The few
reports were derived from low-level information that had come in
from the Census Grievance program through "road runners,"
peasants on the payroll who said they had seen this or that. Just
reading through this material I could feel a kind of creeping leth-
argy sneaking up on me. All this hostile activity was going on,
organized and carried out by a massive Vietcong infrastructure,
and all we could get were these tiny little pecks and nibbles. I
wondered if maybe there wasn't some kind of Vietnam syndrome
at work that attacked everybody, even good men like Jack Black
and George Tanaka. Maybe the place was like a swamp, sucking
your energy into an endless, incoherent bog and never letting you
get anywhere. Sunday night I went to sleep early, thinking about
whether I too would get sucked down or if somehow I would be
able to figure out a way to conquer the damn thing.

Monday morning I awoke early, raring to go. The night's sleep
seemed to have restored my spirits and optimism, and I could
hardly wait for the CORDS short takeoff and landing (STOL) Porter aircraft that would take me out to Binh Tuy.

The Binh Tuy capital of Ham Tan was forty minutes away from

Bien Hoa. Beneath the plane I could see no villages or farms, just
what looked like an uninhabited wilderness of bushland and forest,
almost like an African veldt except that there didn't even seem to
be any wildlife. Into the distance the scrub brush and elephant
grass stretched out, a desolate, inhospitable landscape that made
you wonder if you were still in the twentieth century. Although
Ham Tan was a province capital, it certainly didn't look like any
province capital I had ever seen. There was no city to speak of,
hardly even a village, just half a block or so of huts and small
government buildings. The one street was utterly deserted. This
has to be, I thought, the sleepiest backwater in existence.

At the little dirt airstrip a jeep was waiting for me with the Binh
Tuy POIC—the Province Officer in Charge—who drove me directly to his office, a small house that sported a giant antenna on
the roof. Next to this building was a tin shack that turned out to be
the Provincial Reconnaissance Unit headquarters, and next to that
was a little place where a half dozen or so listless Rural Development cadres were hanging out. All the PRU and RD guys were
sitting around smoking and drinking tea, as if they hadn't a care in
the world and not a thing to do. At eight o'clock the heat was
already in the mid-nineties and mosquitoes droned in through the
windows. A phrase from the old movie, *Mr. Roberts*, suddenly occurred to me, something about going from "ennui to tedium and
back." This place looked like a definition of it.

The Binh Tuy POIC was a young black contract officer who
spoke intelligently and to the point. I told him frankly that I was
trying to evaluate the entire situation for Loren so that we could
come to grips with what in the world we were going to do. "So if
you don't mind, I'm curious about what you've got here." "Well,"
he said, "whatever you end up doing, it won't be in Binh Tuy.
There is nothing at all happening here. I sit here and answer the
phone if it rings, then once a month I pay off the RD, the PRU,
and the Census Grievance. Other than that there's nothing. No
Vietcong activity, no PRU activity, nothing. If they wanted to overrun my compound they could do it in a minute. But they don't.
There's obviously an accommodation here."

"What about the special police office?" I asked. "Could we visit
over there?" "Sure," said the POIC. "But you won't find out anything talking to them. They'll just tell you there's so little VC activity in Binh Tuy that they don't have any operations."

The Binh Tuy Special Branch Police province office consisted of
a single dirty room, about ten feet square. When I asked the police
chief what was going on he told me exactly what the POIC said

he'd tell me. When I asked if he had anything on the structure of local Vietcong forces he said no. "How about the structure of the province committee?" "No." "How about the district committee?" "No." "Well, how about the village next door? Do you have anything on the VC committee there?" "No," he said, with a sleepy look in his eyes, "we don't have anything."

Over lunch I asked the POIC about what was coming in through the Census Grievance reports. "A little," he answered. "But it's all worthless. The entire province is about the same, worthless. I've already asked Loren to close this office. In my opinion," he went on, "it doesn't make sense to keep anything going here. There's an accommodation between the Vietcong and ARVN; that's the beginning and end of it. All I'm doing is paying off the people in these programs. And I'm getting nothing for it."

After lunch I got back into the Porter STOL for the hop to Long Khanh, another province whose reports were minimal. The POIC here was Clint Parcells, a six two, two-hundred-thirty-pound retired army master sergeant who was now a contract officer with the CIA. I had heard that a short time ago he had barely escaped an assassination attempt, so the first thing I asked was about his run-in with the VC. "Well, it wasn't much," he said. "They set up a kind of flimsy roadblock with a couple of guys. But when I saw them I floored the jeep. I must have been going sixty when I went through it. They managed to put two or three holes in the jeep, but that was it."

Like Binh Tuy, Long Khanh was a relatively quiet province, a place that was kept out of the mainstream of the war by tacit understandings between the South Vietnamese army and the Vietcong. Clint Parcells seemed like a competent guy, but here too there was nothing going on. Even the PIC was empty. "Clint," I told him, "unless you can get some effective action going with the PRU, I see no reason to keep this office open, do you?" That, he thought, would be next to impossible. "Obviously they know the general location of the VC units," he said, "but no one is going to do anything in the form of major operations. I think you're right. It would be best to close the office."

Late that afternoon I was back at the Monastery telling Loren there was nothing to report from Binh Tuy or Long Khanh, no intelligence, no operations, no activity. "Just write it up exactly the way you see it," he said. "I'll need the documentation to support closing them down."

The next morning I was in Phuoc Long and Binh Long. Both of these provinces were notorious for Vietcong ambushes against

ARVN and American forces. Phuoc Long's capital of Song Be had earlier been overrun by a VC battalion that shot up the Song Be Special Forces compound in the process, and during North Vietnam's "Great Spring Offensive" in 1972, the Binh Long capital, An Loc, would be the scene of an epic battle. Nighttime in both these provinces was more interesting than daytime. American harassment and interdiction artillery fire boomed all night long, answered by sporadic mortar rounds lobbed into the capitals by the Vietcong. But other than the nightly fireworks nothing was happening in these places at the moment. It was another standoff, little or no ARVN action and little or no VC action.

Also little or no intelligence reporting. The Phuoc Long Provincial Interrogation Center held a number of Montagnards—ethnic tribal people—who were classified as Vietcong suspects. When I asked the PIC chief for copies of their interrogation reports, my interpreter read them and began rolling his eyes. "All they say," he announced, "is that these men are suspected of supplying the VC with rice."

This time when I got back to the Monastery Loren asked why our offices in these two provinces were getting nothing when it was obvious the Vietcong presence was strong. On the surface it did seem to be something of a mystery. But the fact was that although the VC were there in numbers, they had simply chosen not to involve Phuoc Long and Binh Long at the moment. For their own reasons they were lying low, perhaps building up supplies, integrating reinforcements, or using the areas primarily for transit or R and R. And since there was little enemy action, ARVN too was content to keep quiet, happy enough for a tacit accommodation—or perhaps an explicit one; who could tell? But whatever the reason, nothing was happening and no intelligence worth the name was being generated. Neither Loren nor I could see that we would lose anything by closing these province offices as well.

That made four of the region's ten provinces. I wondered what I might find in Tay Ninh, where John Pinossa was stationed. Obviously nothing had changed since I had visited him during my inspection tour with the marine captain just a week or so earlier. But John was a smart, perceptive guy and an extra week's orientation might have given him a better insight into what was going on in the province.

The little military airport at the edge of Tay Ninh town was protected by sandbagged M-60 emplacements and just beyond the airport I could see a couple of 105s pointing toward Nui Ba Den Mountain. The runway, a short corrugated-tin strip, was perfect for the Porter, which needed only seventy-five feet to land. Waiting for me at the end of the runway was John Pinossa, carrying a Swedish K submachine gun. It had gotten to be a habit, he said. He spent many nights in his bunker listening to incoming mortar rounds and rockets, even artillery, zeroing in from the VC fortified zones in Nui Ba Den. Always alert to the possibility of attack, he just felt more comfortable carrying the Swedish K; it gave him a sense of security.

This visit was going to be a little different from the previous ones. I wanted to spend a long day with John, and John wanted me to meet his special police counterpart, as well as the man handling Forcie (the agent's cryptonym), the developmental agent we had talked about when I was last there, the man we now had nick-named the Reaper.

At John's office we talked about the agent, in particular how to authenticate him—to verify that he was who he said he was and to ascertain whether he was a plant, a double agent. According to John, the Reaper was obviously an intelligent man and a good writer. There was no doubt he had access to province-level docu-ments. We did know he was going up to Nui Ba Den Mountain at night and now John was trying to wrap up the authentication.

So far it looked good. John had unearthed a defector who said he knew the Reaper and that he was indeed a trusted, long-term party activist and a top political officer, a man who received direc-tives, distributed them and made sure they were implemented. An unbelievable find—if it was true. The whole thing had initially gotten started because one of the Reaper's uncles was a high rank-ing ARVN military security service officer who had once fought for the Vietminh guerrillas against the French but had later defected. After years of trying, the former guerrilla had finally found a way to bring enough family pressure to bear so that his nephew re-sponded to an approach. The story was that the family bond be-tween these two had been enhanced with the recent death of the Reaper's mother. Whether that was entirely credible I didn't know. But more to the point, the Reaper had already passed information that had proven accurate, so it was clear that he was someone high up in the structure.

It seemed like a good bet, one with little downside risk. The Reaper knew nothing about us, nothing that he might make use of if he was in fact a double agent. And as far as his information itself was concerned, we would take it a piece at a time, evaluating it as it came in and watching out for a trap.

The Reaper looked as if he had potential. If he did pan out, he would be a highly significant asset. John, of course, was quite happy about it. (In fact the Reaper did pan out. He provided high-level and accurate information right through the last week of the war.) But the Reaper was the only thing in Tay Ninh that John was happy about. Here, as was the case everywhere else I had looked, there was no data bank other than a short alphabetized list of names. Just as Loren was facing an invisible enemy on the regional level, John was drawing blanks on his level; there was simply no information on the structure of the Vietcong organization—either in the province or in the districts and villages—that would allow him to come to grips with his target. In addition, he was frustrated beyond words by the police, both the National Police and the special police. According to him the special police—he was their adviser—sat around picking their noses. The Provincial Reconnaissance Unit did nothing unless led into it by their American adviser, and even then they were mostly interested in stealing chickens. Then there were the RD, the Rural Development cadres. These people, he said, couldn't develop a thing if their asses depended on it. The Provincial Interrogation Center—the PIC—was another winner. John swore that the Province Security Council, which oversaw the cases of captured Vietcong, simply sold incarcerated suspects back to their families. John's descriptions of all this were marked by very salty language and obvious feelings of helplessness and anger. I felt as if I were watching him thrash around wildly, trying to save himself from getting sucked down into the same pernicious bog.

As an intelligence professional, John at least had the advantage of knowing what should have been happening. He had a good overview of the Agency's programs in his province and could analyze the massive deficiencies, not that being able to do so reduced his frustration level any. But in most of the other provinces the CIA field officers were at a total loss, just stuck in the miasma. With little or no experience, with unbelievably inadequate training, the contract officers simply did not know what to do.

Larry Rather, the PIC adviser in Long An, was typical, though as a former beat cop in San Diego he had a good deal more on the ball than most of them. "Orrin," he said when I asked him to describe his problems, "I know I have to get out there and interrogate these people. But how do I talk to them? What do I say?" Larry would have known well enough what to say back on 28th Street in San Diego, but here he had no context to fit anything into, no background information that would give him a way of questioning a suspect intelligently. "If you have nothing," I told him, "all you can do is go on your gut feeling. Talk to him about his family. Be sympathetic. Where are you from? What did you do as a kid? What did you do for entertainment? How well do you read, write? Anything at all you can think of to help you understand this guy. Ask him about his friends, why he joined the Vietcong. Because they did? Because a relative did? Because the government stinks? Give him a beer. Give him a Coke. Do anything you can to get him talking. Even if you can't get anything operational out of him, at least you can get some background, start to get an understanding of these people."

Larry was more down on the special police than anyone I had talked to with the exception of John Pinossa, and Pinossa was livid. "These guys will not work together," Larry said. The interrogator won't tell the PIC chief if he's got anything, afraid that he might have heard something different from another interrogator and that they'll give him the shaft. They're jealous as hell of each other. Same with the PIC chiefs and the special police chief, same with RD and PRU guys. Same with all of them."

Over a period of two weeks I made the rounds of all the provinces, talking to everyone I could get my hands on, the Province Officers in Charge, PIC advisers, Census Grievance advisers, PRU and Rural Development advisers. I wanted to get some insight into each of these guys, to try to understand what their capabilities were as well as to evaluate the programs they were advising. And everywhere I went I saw the same things. Some of the field officers were good, doing their best to make something out of programs that weren't working; others had given up the effort, numbed by the corruption and apathy of those they were supposed to be advising; still others hadn't the foggiest notion of what to do, and hadn't had since they first arrived.

I also made it a point to interview the Phoenix advisers. Their job was to coordinate the various Vietnamese security organizations in order to identify, target, and eliminate members of the Vietcong infrastructure, preferably by capture; by capture—that was in William Colby's directive. From my earlier visit to the Vung Tau Phoenix training school, I knew that the chance of actually achieving a decent degree of cooperation among the jealous and feuding government agencies was minimal, and my talks with the Region Three advisers only reinforced this perception. "How are these guys doing?" I'd ask. "Are they working together?" "Working together?" The answer would be incredulous. "Are you kidding? They hate each other's guts."

So on the one hand, you could not get the South Vietnamese to

work together. On the other, even with the best cooperation it
would be difficult to capture the Vietcong cadres. How the hell
were you going to capture the Trang Bang district chief who was
living in a bunker in the Ho Bo Woods surrounded by a North
Vietnamese Army regiment? You couldn't do it. Of course you
could capture legal cadres—the ones living openly as ordinary civilians—but only if you knew these people's secret identities.
Which we didn't. I went into every single district-level Phoenix
office in all the Region Three provinces, and the first thing I'd ask
was to see a wiring diagram. "Please show me," I'd say, "a wiring
diagram identifying the structure and membership of the Vietcong
district party committee." And without a single exception the answer was, "Oh, we don't have anything like that."

At the same time, I knew that Phoenix was reporting large numbers of VC captured and killed (several years later in a congres-
sional hearing Colby announced that Phoenix was responsible for
killing twenty thousand members of the VC infrastructure). But
the more I learned about Phoenix, the clearer it was that the statistics were phony. Although I could never tell with any certainty
what percentage of the reported VC dead were actually the result
of Phoenix operations, one thing was beyond doubt: most of the
capturing and killing was done not by Phoenix but by the Regional
and Popular forces under the direction of the South Vietnamese
province chiefs.

These Regional Forces normally did quite a good job and were
involved in wide-scale fighting. They were made up of people who
were protecting their own homes and villages, people who hated
the VC or disliked the Communist philosophy, and who had a lot
of local support. They regularly inflicted heavy losses on the VC.
Half the time Phoenix would claim credit for the casualties, saying
that they had done the targeting. But that was ridiculous. They
were rarely successful. The local PRU team might set an ambush,
or get involved in a firefight, or would come across the casualties
of another engagement, and all of it went into the Phoenix hopper:
the guilty, the innocent, the enemy killed in action, the casual
bodies along the roadside. They'd carry them in and count them
up. And that was Phoenix, at least in Military Region Three at the
beginning of 1969. I found it hard to believe it might be any different in Regions One, Three, or Four.

As I began to understand this—and it wasn't difficult to understand; all the Phoenix advisers were telling me the same thing—I
also began to understand why Colby was making the reports he
was. For someone who wanted to go into the field and track down

the process of reporting, figuring out what was going on was relatively easy. But Colby did not attempt to do this and consequently he did not know what was fact and what was fiction. When he visited a province he would buy the province briefing. In Saigon he would get the statistics across his desk, period. And what did he —or anyone else at CORDS—know about how they were developed? The district Phoenix committees would write up their phony statistics on captured and killed and report these to the province level, which gussied them up further and reported to the regional level, which reported to Saigon. Just what Major Jack Black had described to me my first day in Bien Hoa. And CORDS in Saigon compiled and reported out these statistics as Phoenix casualties.

Somewhat later the Phoenix program became the center of a roaring controversy in the United States because it was supposedly assassinating everyone in sight. But it was not. Every one of the advisers told me exactly the same thing: "You don't have the structure of the cadre in your district?" No. "Or in the villages?" No. "Then how do you target on them?" "We don't target on them. The RF (Regional Forces) brings in the bodies." It did not take long before I had concluded that the vaunted Phoenix was nothing but a bust and a fake. Yes, the people were being killed—at least a lot of them were—but it wasn't Phoenix that was killing them.

As my tour through the provinces went on, I found myself getting more and more frustrated. In each area of the Agency's programs I looked, I saw the same thing: incompetence and corruption. And when I looked in the next province, I'd see the same thing again. The interrogation centers, my special concern, seemed irretrievable, just a horrible mess. ("You must make them work," Ted Coleburne had told me.) They were not producing. They had no way of producing, except by beating the hell out of suspects, and then there was no way to verify the stories. They were commonly considered the sites of the worst tortures—in particular the water treatment, where they forced water down prisoners' throats until their stomachs swelled up, or the torture in which they applied electric shock to the genitals and nipples (though I saw none of this during my inspection rounds). I was disgusted with them and in despair over how the PICs might be revamped. This was my frame of mind when one day I was visiting the Bien Hoa PIC, a place that was no better or worse than any of the others.

The four special police kids who were supposed to have been my "team of experts" were working there at the time; they had arrived in Bien Hoa by bus—not plane—shortly after I had and I had

gotten them assigned to the interrogation center so they wouldn't
be in my hair. Visiting the PIC along with my interpreter, as I did
from time to time, I was nosing around, looking into a cell here
and there. I also intended to look in on the four kids, who the PIC
chief had told me were in one of the interrogation rooms. When I
got to the room I started to knock, but I heard someone crying
inside. Instead, I just pushed the door open. In front of me I saw
the four kids and a girl, naked from the waist down. She was bent
over a chair crying while one of the kids busily inserted a broomstick into her vagina.

As I walked in, the four of them looked up in shock and embarrassment. The broomstick clattered on the cement floor. The girl
looked as if she couldn't be a day over fifteen. Oh, my Lord, I
thought to myself, what could she be, the goddam VC commander
of Subregion One?

Without a word I turned and stalked out of the room, heading
for the PIC chief's office. Hurrying to keep up with me, my interpreter was upset and nervous. "I don't think we should tell him,"
he said; "this is very embarrassing." "I don't give a shit what you
think," I answered. "I want you to translate what I say, that's all I
want from you. That's the point of your job. You make no decisions, no speculations, nothing. You just translate." I also decided
on the spot that I was not going to keep this guy.

When I confronted the PIC chief he handled it very coolly.
"Please let me take care of this," he said. "I know how to deal with
these things. I'll send one of my officers to Colonel Hien [the
Region Three National Police director] with a report. I don't consider it any better than rape." "OK," I told him, "you do whatever
is necessary on it," wondering if he would. In fact the PIC chief
did find some way of getting rid of those four, because after the
incident they disappeared, sent off to God knows where to be pains
in the ass to someone else. But to me the incident put the cap on
my feelings about the PICs. They were ineffective. They were sor-
did. They were a pile of shit.

Incidents like this stood out from the morass of interviews I
conducted and observations I was making, and they tended to crys-
tallize my conclusions, or at least to confirm my state of mind.
Another incident took place shortly after my encounter with the
kids in the Bien Hoa PIC, when Loren asked me to take the
monthly Census Grievance payroll up to Song Be since the Song
Be officer in charge was on leave for a few days. I received a black
satchel containing 118,000 piasters from the base finance officer,
then I took my translator and hopped up to Song Be on a Porter.

In Song Be I first went to see the CORDS sergeant who worked with the Vietnamese Census Grievance chief and was our contact. "Does the CG guy travel?" I asked.

"Are you kidding?" the sergeant said. "Who's going to travel around here? You'd get your ass blown off."

"Well, what can you tell me about him? I'm supposed to pay him. Does he go down to the districts?"

"No, he doesn't."

"Look, he's supposedly paying this money to people out in the boonies. Do they come in here?"

"Maybe a couple," said the sergeant. "Not many."

The Census Grievance office was a little hut with two desks in it. Behind one of them sat a little guy whose pointed face, long neck, and buckteeth made him look like a weasel, or an old-time Mexican bandito. When I asked through the interpreter how he paid the people, he gave me a long story about his many dangerous trips down the country roads. Then I asked to see his receipt book.

In response he took out a big ledger book inside of which I saw the columns for names, hamlets, and dates. To the right of the date column was a column marked "Payment Received," and in that column were the initials of the informants, all of which were in the same handwriting, which was also the same handwriting that had filled in all the other information. "Who are these guys?" I asked him. "Let's take the first one. This guy signed it?" "No," he said, "I signed it for him. He can't write." "What about the next one? Did he sign it?" "No," came the answer. "He can't write either."

"Well," I said, "it's been nice visiting with you." And I left, taking the bag with me. The Census Grievance chief didn't even have the guts to ask where his money was going. A thousand bucks a month more or less per province, I thought. What a way to milk the Agency. But like the four kids with the broomstick, this was just another piece in a comprehensively bleak picture.

I was sitting on Loren's patio after one particularly brutal day asking myself what I was going to do. Despite the immense frustrations, I badly wanted to achieve something. I thought back to my arrival in Vietnam—only a month and a half ago, though it felt like an eternity. I had been so eager, just champing at the bit. Man, I wanted to do it, first team all the way! But in everything I looked at I had struck out: Zero, zero, zero. I struck out on data banks. I struck out on operational leads. I struck out on effective case offi- cers. Sitting there in my drawers—the rest of my clothes were in a

pile in the corner, filthy with the day's collection of red sand—I
felt depressed. George Tanaka, sipping a martini in the rattan
lounge chair next to me, looked his usual blasé self. He had figured
out the place long ago; there was nothing to be done, and he, for
one, was not going to let it get to him. Loren was in his usual seat
too, but he had a strangely happy look on his face, as if he had just
gotten a piece of good news for a change. "I heard this afternoon,"
he said, "that an old buddy of mine has been assigned to us, Bill
Todd. You'll love him, very energetic guy. He'll be here as an
independent officer working strictly alone to develop agents. I
couldn't be happier that he's coming and I'm sure you'll get along
just fine. I'm expecting him any minute."

Almost on cue a red-haired bull of a man bounced into the room
and out onto the patio. His khaki pants and white sports shirt
revealed the heavily muscled physique of a lifetime bodybuilder,
and he shook hands all around with bone-crushing enthusiasm,
then spotted the martinis and grabbed one for himself. The man
could not sit still. And he couldn't wait to start asking questions.
Where should he start? What were the priorities? What was working? What access would he have to prisoners? "Whoa," said Loren,
"slow down a bit. Bill Todd, this is Orrin DeForest and George
Tanaka. Orrin here has been touring the provinces evaluating the
situation. Why don't we just ask him to speak out."

As Bill Todd sat down I began to review what I had seen, first
nationally, visiting the PICs with marine Captain Zale, then in
Three Corps. "When they capture a Vietcong," I told him, "there's
no way to identify him properly. The VC knows this, and that
means he's smarter than his interrogator. That's why they beat him
half to death, since it's the only way they have to possibly get some
information out of him. There are no files or data banks of any sort
in the special police offices identifying any VC structures. So, for
example, no one in the Tay Ninh PIC has any idea where the VC
was living, his unit, even his birthplace. The same is true in Saigon.
All they have there is an alphabetical data bank. If you submit a
name to headquarters by cable, they trace it through and it comes
back 'Nguyen Van Dang, Vietcong suspect, Hau Nghia province.'
Not very damn helpful.

"This leaves us with one huge question, and that is, How can
anyone conduct operations against the enemy when we have virtually no information about village, district, province, region, or
headquarters of VC units? The only possible source of information
is the Three Corps Interrogation Center under Major Dinh—that's
up near the air base. He does have a small data bank that he got

from captured documents, pretty much all order of battle. And
that's it.

"I have to emphasize," I told Todd, "that what I'm saying is not
different from what the province officers are saying. There's no
disagreement among us. Most of them are dedicated men who
would like to accomplish something. But when they get up in the
morning and look around at what they might do, they don't have
much in the way of possibilities. They all believe that the Census
Grievance information is fabricated; they can't resolve the travel
situation. All the government Census Grievance supervisors say
they can travel to the villages, but in fact it's rare to find all the
roads open. And you can bet the villagers don't visit the province
capitals very often. In Binh Long and Phuoc Long, for example,
no one can travel in the daytime except in protected convoys. But
the CG payoff lists only get longer anyway. As far as the Rural
Development cadres go, most of them do not stay in the villages at
night. They come into the district or province for protection. They
know better than we how dangerous it is in the boonies at night,
and no creature on earth is going to get them to stay out there."

By this time Bill Todd was looking at me thoughtfully. He wasn't
quite so bouncy. "Orrin," George Tanaka said, "what about the
special police? What have you seen there?"

"George, that's your bailiwick, so I'm hesitant to go into it, but I
will anyway. When I visited with each of the chiefs I asked how
many trained men they had in the province, how many in their
office, how many operations they were working on, and so on.
Usually they're evasive about their personnel. God, they might not
even know. About operations, they always talk in terms of the
number of arrests per month. In Tay Ninh, for example, they say
they arrested more than a hundred VC this month. When I ask
how do they know they're VC, it's always the wrong question. They
tell you that other Vietcong identified them, but you can see
they're making up a story. They squirm around and look at the
ceiling and suck the air in through their teeth like they do when
they don't want to answer something. They're nervous. They never
reach into a desk and pull out a file with evidence of the structure,
showing a suspect's position in an organization. Never anything
like that. I had a bad feeling with almost every one of them I talked
to.

"Most of our officers say it's always like that when they discuss
operations or potential operations. Especially when they want to
interview a cutout, God forbid they should ever ask to interview a
so-called informant. Usually there are two, sometimes four or five,

cutouts between the police and what they say is an informant. But they always swear it's too dangerous for the cutouts to make contact with our officers. And of course we're paying the police for the informants and the cutouts. So you tell me what you think is going on. We've got these problems in every province and district."

"Jesus," Bill Todd said, "you're painting a pretty dismal picture. What does Saigon have to say about all of this?" "Well," Loren put in, "let me tell you the latest from Saigon. Ted Shackley, the new chief of Station, is now personally making all assignments, at all levels. I no longer have any control. You want to know what else? He's got a new concept. He just declared that from here on out each province is going to have a six-man team. On the basis of Orrin's reports I was just about to close up half our province offices, but instead we are not only going to keep them open, we're going to beef them up. The first batch is coming in tomorrow to join Dick Mahan in Song Be. Six guys living in Dick's little shack up there waiting for the mortars every night and the good chance of getting overrun every day. If anyone can explain that, please do. Personally it seems pretty obvious Saigon doesn't know what the fuck's going on."

The next morning George Tanaka, Bill Todd, and I gathered in Loren's office early, eager to be in on the meeting Loren had set up with the new team. When they came in we could hardly believe our eyes; five guys led by a GS-14, a CIA colonel, all of them in full battle regalia: tiger suits, assault rifles, cases of grenades, an M-60 machine gun, an M-79 grenade launcher, blankets, tents, tarps— all of it brand spanking new. They looked like a young army about to launch an invasion—the most comical-looking crew of civilians playing soldier I had ever seen.

After a brief orientation from Loren they piled into a Porter and flew up to Song Be, a very dangerous place with almost no intelligence potential. The interrogation center there wasn't even full-sized. It was a minicenter with a few Montagnard prisoners, guys who had gotten in trouble with the local authorities who had arrested them and put them in there so they could shake them down for whatever they could get out of them. There was nothing cooking in Song Be. But that was where Saigon Station had decided to try out its new six-man concept. It was the clearest indication possible of how little they knew about what was going on in the field and how desperate they were to get something moving.

That night the new team strung up hammocks in Dick Mahan's place under his leaky roof. About three in the morning the mortars started coming in, targeted right on the house. Probably the Vietcong had seen them arrive and decided to provide a welcome. Fortunately, Dick was able to get everyone into his bunker, but at dawn the CIA colonel radioed for an airplane to get them out of there.

When they got back they were disheveled and covered by the red dust of Song Be. They looked a lot less enthusiastic than they had twenty-four hours earlier. They had had it, they said. There was nothing up there and they were going back to Saigon. Dick, of course, was still in Song Be. He was an old paramilitary type. He could live through that stuff in a bunker and it wouldn't bother him. But not these guys. That was the beginning and end of the six-man concept.

Actually, the team had chosen to arrive at an especially bad moment. That night the Vietcong also attacked the Song Be advisory team headquarters, inflicting serious casualties on the Americans there. Shortly afterward, Bien Hoa itself was attacked and we too spent nights in the sandbagged bunkers on the patio and in the rear of the Monastery where my room was. One night when rifle fire banged by my bunker, I thought at first that the VC had entered our part of the city and was assaulting the office. But it turned out just to be a guard at the Bien Hoa PIC clearing his weapon, or firing at the moon.

That was a night of action and everyone was nervous. A half hour or so after the guard missed my bunker the sky on the outskirts of the city was cut by a searchlight beaming down from an American chopper. A moment later the chopper's Gatling gun opened up, the barrage of bullets looking like a solid stream of light. Then other choppers appeared, one at a time, crossing the area and hosing the ground with their own fiery streams.

The next day we learned that the choppers had caught an element of the Vietcong 273d Regiment in the open just as they were starting an attack on the airfield. Almost all of the VC had died—the count was a hundred and fifty, the bodies torn to shreds by the six-thousand-round-per-minute fire. Other elements of the 273d had suffered severe casualties near the Region Three prison at Long Binh. Some VC commander had made a terrible mistake, one he had most likely paid for with his life. We were not the only ones who had problems.

3

INTELLIGENCE
JAPANESE STYLE

L oren didn't waste any time wondering what to do with our new man Bill Todd. "I want you to get out into the provinces," he said, "and do the same thing Orrin did. But don't be so long about it. Take three days, meet the officers in charge, tell me what you see." Loren was no dummy. We got along famously and I felt he trusted my judgment, but he also wanted some confirmation.

Three days later Bill came back with as pessimistic a report as I had been making, less detailed, but equally negative. Somehow, though, seeing it with his own eyes didn't seem to affect his energy or upbeat attitude. "Well," said Loren after listening to Bill, "what do you think we ought to do?" "I don't know," Bill answered. "I don't know what you're going to do. But I sure as hell know what I'm going to do. I'm going to start finding out about these Vietnamese." Bill Todd had wanted to come to Vietnam for one consuming reason: to test the Vietnamese. And no amount of disappointment over the Agency's field programs was going to deter him from that goal.

Bill, it turned out, had a Ph.D. in clinical psychology and was an expert in psychological testing. A combat marine in the 5th Division during World War Two, he had gone back to school after the war and got his doctorate. (Loren was also an ex-jarhead; the Agency seemed to have a predilection for them.) When Bill joined the CIA he was put to work with Dr. John Gittinger, a renowned psychologist who was developing a personality assessment test for the Agency's use. Bill Todd was one of Dr. Gittinger's first protégés.

After working with Gittinger in Washington, Bill had spent nine years in various Asian countries, administering the test. He had trained testers and test interpreters who worked all over the world, giving the assessment in a dozen different languages. He had gathered a raftful of documentation on the universal applicability of Gittinger's test, and now he was dying to give it to the Vietnamese, lots of Vietnamese. As a scientist with a scientist's curiosity, he was raring to do this. But as an Agency staff officer he was eager as well —because the Gittinger test, according to Bill, had specific operational implications.

As Loren predicted, Bill and I hit it off from the first. I liked him immensely; he was smart, observant, dynamic, funny, an astute judge of people. He was also one of the horniest men I had ever met, and a wild, unpredictable drunk. "Don't let him drink too much," Loren implored when he saw we were getting closer, and I didn't. Bill had arrived without a specified assignment, perfect to allow him to accomplish what he was after. He had also arrived under a cloud of some sort. "How come you're only a [GS] thirteen?" I asked him one day. "Well," he whispered, looking around, "I had some trouble in Hong Kong. But I don't want to talk about it, so let's just let it drop." "OK," I said, "it's dropped. But how come you can ask me all these personal questions and I can't ask you?" "Well, Orrin," he said, laughing, "you see, that's the way it works."

The one annoying thing about Bill was that he was always bugging me to take this test of his. But though I knew he was deadly serious about the test, I kept putting him off. The idea that a psychological assessment test might have some validity or might somehow actually be useful seemed silly to me, a bit of academic bullshit that had inexplicably made its way into the Agency's thinking. He was so persistent, though, eventually I gave in, mainly to get him off my back. "OK, Bill," I said finally, "you want to have your fun and games, go ahead and test me." Loren, though, kept refusing, despite the fact that he was getting pestered worse than I was. "That's all right, Loren," Bill would tell him. "I don't need the test. I know all about you anyway." Then a day later he would be at him again.

The evening I gave in I went to Bill's room prepared for an

ordeal. "You'll take it by yourself," he said when I sat down. "Then, after I score and evaluate it, I'll give you a verbal readout concerning your personality. Nothing derogatory, just a simple understanding of yourself, your capabilities, and how the tester might use the information to predict and manipulate your actions."

The test itself took about an hour and a half. It seemed like little more than a fairly comprehensive IQ test with questions asking for basic knowledge, others that tested recognition of spatial patterns, then digit span questions and analytical questions.

After Bill had scored my test he began interpreting it for me. "First I'll give you some brief information," he said, "then I want you to confirm or deny the results. OK? Number one, Orrin, you are sensitive to feelings, your own and those with whom you associate. You have a tendency to fantasize. For example, at school you probably spent a lot of time staring out the window and thinking of other things. You're what we call an 'internalizer.' You're able to withdraw into yourself and follow your own lead. You're basically a loner, but not, you'll be happy to hear, psychotic. Just the kind of guy who can get satisfaction reading in his room rather than needing a crowd around. You are also flexible; that is, you can tolerate ambiguity well—you naturally see more than one side of an issue, or a person. You're good in situations that call for insight and interpersonal awareness. You're less effective in situations that require doing things systematically, by the numbers. This is basically what we call a 'primitive readout'—some of the personality traits you were born with, not necessarily those you might have adopted over the years."

As Bill read off the list I was surprised to find that I agreed with one point after another. The assessments he was making coincided closely with those I had of myself. Not only that, but as he expanded on his readings it struck me that he might be right about there being a practical use for all this. Evaluations of our own employees could help us decide what sorts of tasks they had an aptitude for and which to keep them away from. And what if we might also be able to test some of the defectors or prisoners? Was there some way that having a concept of their innate tendencies might make it easier to get information out of them, or use them ourselves? Might we, for example, be able to select likely candidates for collaboration?

These and other half-formed thoughts flitted through my mind. But mainly I wanted to know more about the test. The personality assessment, Bill told me, was based on an evaluative system that his mentor, Dr. Gittinger, had developed for a modified Wechsler

Bellevue Intelligence test. What we got first was an IQ score—and with all the work Bill had done on various forms of the test he was sure that the IQ scores were accurate from one culture to another. Second, the assessment could identify three basic components of personality. Number one, people were either Internalizers or Externalizers. Internalizers are quiet, resourceful, private—good at setting their own standards and goals. Externalizers are physically active, aggressive, sensitive to external cues—good at working in structured situations. Number two, people were either Regulated or Flexible. Regulateds like to do one thing at a time, a task they can concentrate all their energies on. They are orderly and persistent. They pay attention to details. Flexibles are more intuitive, empathetic with others. They use their imaginations better. Third, people are either Role Adaptive or Role Uniform. The Adaptives are sociable; they want and need people. Uniforms are loners.

These three components, Bill went on, are innate predispositions, "primitive" in psychology jargon. But they are modified by an individual's response to his environment. An Internalizer who grows up in a social group that values Externalizer-type behavior will make an adaptation, though underneath he will remain an Internalizer. The same environment will reinforce and enhance an Externalizer's basic traits. The assessment system had the ability to distinguish between "primitive" traits and these developmental compensations, or "contact," traits. These in turn could be differentiated from an individual's "surface" personality—the appearance he or she strives to project to others.

I was impressed with the overview Bill had given me, but more with the accuracy of what he had told me about myself. Now that he had me hooked, Bill couldn't wait to use me to help him out with this massive screening he had in mind. "You see," he said, "I brought the test along in Vietnamese, translated. All the paperwork is done. Now I have to train the best interpreters we have, two or three of them, to give the test, so I can administer it on a larger scale. I'll train you to give the test too; you can use it on your own people."

Over the next few days Bill gave me an intensive course in grading and evaluating the test, not going deeply into the subtleties of Gittinger's system, but providing sufficient understanding so that a layman could use it intelligently. Then we were ready to start testing the base's Vietnamese personnel, to judge the capabilities of our own interpreters and translators. That, we thought, would give us a very good insight into who to put in what positions. Secondly, Bill was really eager to start giving it to Vietcong. "They're obviously just as smart as anybody else, maybe smarter, and I want to see what makes them tick. I want to know what their intelligence level is and their capabilities. Orrin, this test will enable you to get inside these guys. It will tell you that if you take someone and tell him to do a, b, c, d, e, f, and g, by rote, he's going to do it, because he's an Externalizer-Regulated-Adaptive, an ERA. He'll be prone to taking orders, he'll like working for a reward, and he'll be drawn to the task. You, on the other hand, you're an Internalizer-Flexible-Uniform, an IFU. You'd do it halfway, then you'd stop and think about it, and you'd start wondering why it should be done and whether you couldn't do it better some other way or if maybe you shouldn't be doing something else completely different. You'll be able to see who might respond to what kind of pressure, what their needs are, what kinds of tasks they like to do. You'll be able to see who's got a rigid mentality with room for only one loyalty and who can accept ambiguities easily, maybe work for two masters. This thing can give you a real leg up."

Over the next week we tested some of the base's Vietnamese personnel. First was "Chieu Hoi" Lan, our brilliant, beautiful administrative assistant and translator who worked primarily with Vietcong defectors. Then Mr. Lam, "Sonny," and Mingo, the three others we considered our sharpest interpreters.

I was really wondering how the Vietnamese might take to a test like this—something very far outside their cultural experience. But their reaction turned out to be almost exactly the same as mine. At first they were skeptical, but they took it anyway—their boss had asked them to, and they did have a sneaky curiosity about what it might be like. But then, when they heard Bill rattling off some of their personality traits, they were shocked. They couldn't believe that a test might enable someone to tell such things about them. Bill would say, "Well, on the basis of this segment of the test that's my assessment of such and such a dimension of your personality. Do you agree or not?" And Chieu Hoi Lan would answer, "Oh, my God! That's exactly how I think. That's how I do things. How do you KNOW that?"

So just as he converted me, Bill converted them. First he had them take it themselves, then he trained them to give the test in Vietnamese. And from that point on the test became part of the base's employment and promotion requirements. We gave it to all the Vietnamese employees in all the provinces—more than a hundred people.

As Bill and I continued to work together, we found that in many ways we complemented each other's thinking. We were both new

enough to Vietnam that we retained the determination not to give
in to the immense frustrations of the job. Despite the failures of
the Agency's programs and the apparently insuperable difficulties,
both of us were still eager to find some way of cracking into that
invisible target out there.

Both of us were also tired of living in the Monastery, with its
one-room quarters and severe social limitations. As a result, Loren
Snowcroft found himself under a certain amount of pressure to
give us alternative housing. "Loren," Bill would whine in what he
imagined was an ingratiating voice, "can't you see that Orrin and I
don't enjoy living in monasteries? I know you might not be aware
of it, but men occasionally do need companionship other than the
kind they can get from their boss. And men like that, Loren, they
don't function well if their lives go on without any solace for a long
period of time."

"OK," Loren said finally, "I know exactly what you're getting at,
in fact I'm way ahead of you. I've decided to give you my house.
I've been wanting to move back into the Monastery anyway. The
fact is, I'm lonely up there. Besides, I need to be closer to my work.
Half the time I'm here at night anyway. So tomorrow I'll move
down here and you guys can move into my place. How would that
be?"

We were elated. Only a block from the Monastery, Loren's
house was a large two-story white stucco affair that included a
screened-in deck off the second-floor bedrooms that looked out
over the beautiful Dong Nai and into the amazing sunsets. Perfect
for a little private relaxation or occasional social functions. Bill
decided to take the downstairs and convert the dining room into a
bedroom, while I took the upstairs—three bedrooms, including a
twenty-by-thirty-foot master bedroom with a big adjoining bath.
Overnight my outlook on life seemed to take at least a small turn
for the better.

I also hired a house "girl" to cook and clean, a young woman
who had worked for Ron Ferris, the base's chief of support, the
only other officer who lived outside the Monastery. Her name was
Lan, and while she didn't speak much English, she was a good
worker and had an attractive personality. In the normal way that
these things seemed to happen in Vietnam, Lan and I soon found
ourselves in more than just an employer-employee relationship,
and this too made life seem a good deal sunnier.

One day, a month or so after Lan had come to work for me, I
came home to find her in the kitchen cooking soup while a tiny
fourteen-month-old Vietnamese girl played on the floor at her feet.

The baby, she said in her sparse English, was To Thi My—her daughter. That was a surprise; it was the first I had heard she was married. "Well, where's your husband?" I asked. "He *di di mau*," she said. "He gone."

A few days later a skinny twelve-year-old by the name of Luu was slurping a bowl of Campbell's chicken noodle soup when I came back for lunch. As far as I could understand it, Luu was Lan's sister's daughter. Within a few days Get showed up, another skinny one who liked chicken noodle, and then Thanh, a boy this time, about eleven. These too, I was given to understand, were her sister's children.

Before long I had also met Tam, Thi, Da, Hong, and Hai—that made nine of them all together—all of them except little My were Lan's "sister's" children, or maybe her sisters' children. I could never quite get it clear, although I was pretty sure it couldn't be one sister unless she was pretty damn prolific and had the ability to produce children of the same approximate age who weren't twins. I had also been introduced to Lan's mother, a fifty-five-year-old matron who said nothing but smiled a lot, even though she had very few teeth to show and those that she had were black from chewing betel nut. She too was fond of soup. The whole thing was a laugh. It wasn't exactly subtle what Lan was doing. I had seemed to accept the first kid pretty well, and the second and third, so now I had been semiadopted by the whole one-pajama brood. My pantry closet began to swell with red-and-white Campbell's soup cans and my refrigerator with chicken and beef. As skinny as this crowd was there was nothing wrong with their appetites.

The fact was that I enjoyed the kids, and I enjoyed watching Lan deal with all of them, lovingly but with a firm hand. As often as not I would come home to find five or six of them in the kitchen or maybe playing on the upstairs porch. It was kind of a family affair; not an ordinary situation for Agency personnel, but I got a kick out of it and Loren didn't complain. Nor did Bill who lived under it.

Maybe one of the reasons Lan and the kids appealed to me was that my own family life at home had gone to hell long ago. My wife and I had been incompatible for many years, and although we still shared a house when I returned on leave, we had in effect been estranged for a long time and we both knew we were on our way to a divorce. My children, Cecile and Julie, had somehow managed to survive my long absences and their parents' problems and had emerged as independent young ladies. I missed them a good deal, but my marital situation, I knew, was a goner.

One day after the urchins had been coming over for a while I decided to have a look at how Lan and these children lived. I found the building, down one of Bien Hoa's nameless back alleys, walked in past the bar that occupied the front and into a room that had a curtain for a door. It wasn't more than twelve by ten, the middle of it occupied by a Vietnamese-style plank bed with mosquito netting over it while a broken-down table with two chairs were pushed into a corner. There were no windows. On the bed were two of the kids, asleep for the afternoon siesta. The rest were on the floor, also fast asleep. It was hard to step in there over the bodies, and hard to breathe in the stuffy hundred-degree-plus heat.

That about did it. By this time all these children had taken to calling me "papa." I was their security of course, and Lan knew that I had developed a real affection for them, and for her too.

In April 1969 I was due for home leave. Although since leaving the Monastery my living situation had improved tremendously, I had not made huge strides as the regional interrogation director. The intelligence coming out of the interrogation centers was still minimal and unverified. The Reaper, John Pinossa's agent, was giving us consistently good information on Vietcong intentions and capabilities. But developing him had been a fluke, a result of fortuitous personal connections, and I for one didn't see where any other spies might come from. The Provincial Reconnaissance and Census Grievance operations were as bad as ever, and we had not been able to do anything about the special police with their multitudinous cutouts and "highly sensitive" operatives—none of which existed as far as I was concerned.

At the same time, I now felt that at least I knew what some of the possibilities were. I had been in Military Region Three for four months. I knew every man we had in the field, what each was like personally and what his capabilities were. We had managed to close the Binh Tuy office and were on our way to closing others. Bill Todd and I had been through the testing program with our Vietnamese employees and with some defectors as well. So we felt we had some insight into certain Vietnamese personality patterns.

Bill and I had also discussed time and again what our resources were and how we might make use of them. Of these, the *hoi chanh* —the defectors—were especially intriguing. These were Vietcong or North Vietnamese soldiers who had chosen to take advantage of the South's *chieu hoi*—"open arms"—amnesty program. They turned themselves in, were given amnesty as well as a government identity card, then were allowed to begin new lives as South Vietnamese citizens. And while desertions from South Vietnam's army were always a problem, the number of desertions from the enemy had to be giving their manpower officers fits. From 1963, when the program was initiated, until 1975 more than 200,000 deserters were processed through the amnesty system.

Typically, when a *hoi chanh* defected he was "debriefed" on the spot by South Vietnamese army (ARVN) field interrogators looking for the VC locations and order of battle. Often the debriefings weren't gentle, but sometimes the Kit Carson scouts—defectors now serving as scouts for U.S. Army units—got them to go along and identify bunkers and camps. Once they were debriefed the *hoi chanh* would be sent to the province Chieu Hoi Center where they might be interrogated further, but where more commonly they would just sit around until their identities were confirmed and their official ID cards were issued. In the Bao Trai Chieu Hoi Center in Hau Nghia 800 former Vietcong sat around in the sun every day. In Tay Ninh there were another 450. Long An—600. Bien Hoa itself housed 1,300 in the barbed-wire compound just two miles from the Monastery on the road to Long Binh.

What that meant was that thousands of Vietcong sources were sitting right there, in our own front yard, day after day. By and large they were not eager sources; just because they had defected did not mean the *hoi chanh* had any intention of providing information on their former comrades. Nor did they want to involve their families, who had probably been supporting their work in the Vietcong for years. Consequently, their general approach was to try to get processed through the system quickly, say as little as possible, and lie if they did have to talk. But neither were they unfriendly; they had taken their amnesty and knew it might not be a completely free ride. I had talked with a number of them. I knew what the potential was, and I was also pretty sure I knew what it would take to get them to talk freely.

By and large these people had lived their revolutionary lives in the jungle on extremely sparse rations. They had subsisted— maybe for years—on meager supplies of smuggled rice, on jungle animals when they could get them, and on an occasional vegetable they might have managed to grow if they were able to stay in one place long enough. When they came out they were typically sick and emaciated, suffering from a variety of deficiency ailments. At the Chieu Hoi Centers they slept on cots in sideless tin-roofed sheds behind barbed-wire fences. They did not starve to death, but their nutritional situation wasn't great either. The Chieu Hoi Centers' food was neither bountiful nor appetizing.

I was sure that full cooperation from these people would be a simple matter of giving them a little tender loving care and some decent food—fish and chicken, maybe even some shrimp to go along with their rice, some salad, a Coke. Give these half-starved people enough to sink their teeth into and they would start talking a mile a minute about their former units—where they were, what they did, who was in them, how they were organized.

I hadn't started plumbing these waters yet, for one reason. Stories we might get from the *hoi chanh* would no doubt sound interesting; some of the stories we were getting from prisoners in the interrogation centers also sounded interesting. But there was no way to corroborate any of them. Without the ability to cross-check facts, names, and places you just couldn't buy the information. Reports based on such intelligence would have to go out, as they were presently going out, marked "Possibly True." In other words, of little operational value. What we needed was the ability to check —a system that would help us determine whether whatever we heard was true or false and would give us the background to interrogate people intelligently, prisoners as well as defectors. With such a checking system in place, it was clear to me the *hoi chanh* could be immensely productive sources. Even more intriguing than the *hoi chanh* were the Vietcong legal cadres. The "legals" were the heart of the invisible Vietcong empire, and also its most vulnerable link. During the day they lived normal lives and carried South Vietnamese government identity cards. Then bingo, the sun went down and they went to work. They attended meetings at night, they went into the tunnels at Cu Chi or into other safe places. They got the VC directives and resolutions; they provided their own input. They did the propagandizing, the civilian recruitment, the military recruitment, the assassinating, the commo liaison work, much of the supply work. They were a shadow government. The South Vietnamese government—the GVN—may have ruled during the day, but these guys ruled at night.

And these people were living right under our noses. They were the ideal pool from which to recruit agents. In fact they were the only pool. As I told Loren, it was virtually impossible to take a prisoner out of an interrogation center and feed him back into the Vietcong. Number one, he's been kept in a shit hole and roughed up, so he hates your guts. Second, his family has already been notified because the South Vietnamese cops want the money to bail him out. Third, he's appeared before the province security council, so it's well known he's a prisoner. Consequently, none of his VC friends are going to trust him. But the legal cadres were in a perfect position to be made into double agents. They were not suspected. They had open access to both sides. They had the ability to travel, to meet with us in safe houses. They were the one way to penetrate the Vietcong, exactly as the Vietcong had thoroughly penetrated the GVN. The trick was to identify and investigate them —to know who they were and what their backgrounds were, so that they could be approached intelligently. You had to be able to select the right cutout for each and offer him an effective incentive. Then, assuming your target went along, you'd have to know how best to service his needs as a double agent. But for that we needed an informational system, a data bank—in fact, the same kind of data bank we needed to interrogate prisoners and *hoi chanh* effectively. And that was precisely what we did not have.

But even though I had possibilities to contemplate, my mood was grim as I flew to San Diego for a two-week home leave in early April 1969. I had arrived in Vietnam five months earlier full of piss and vinegar, and in those months I had been able to do nothing more than define the problems and work out some of our potential resources. In terms of positive accomplishment, it wasn't much. I was not a happy man on that TWA 707 flying eastward over the Pacific. The Agency's programs were an undiluted disaster, and my personal efforts had not exactly made a dramatic change for the better.

The whole experience had been a frustration. I had gone to Vietnam with those first-team expectations. But what I had found were inexperienced people attempting to do a job that could not be done, at least not in the manner they were trying to do it. At home in the States, separated from the daily routine in Bien Hoa, I began to think about whether there was any point in my returning.

I hated the thought of going back just for the sake of going, to finish off my tour without getting anything done. Why subject myself to another year of life in that tragic country if there was no way to make a difference? On the other hand, maybe it would be better just to grin and bear it. If I finished the tour I would be in line for another assignment, with a good possibility of getting sent to Japan, my old love. I could put my Japanese-language background to work, hook up with old contacts, operate independently. It would be a great life.

If I went back. But there were other options. I thought about renewing contact with the San Diego district attorney, with whom I had interviewed regarding an investigator's job back when I had applied to the Agency, three-quarters of a year ago. The DA and I had gotten along well and he had told me that his plans were to open an office in El Cajon. He had wanted to appoint me chief investigator there, but the funds had not come through and the

Agency post had seemed more challenging at the time. Maybe he was in a position to hire me now.

One afternoon I was talking to my father, who had just retired from his job as a jet electrician at the San Diego naval air station. I told him about the problems in Vietnam and that I was contemplating quitting, although I hadn't yet made up my mind. He listened, then said he thought I ought to go back. As he talked I found myself thinking of Loren and Bill, and George Tanaka and Susie, some of the best people I had ever worked with. Could I just leave them hanging? Besides, I had never quit anything in my life. How could I do something like that now, at the ripe age of forty-seven? Somehow Lan and the kids also injected themselves into my thoughts. Lan was an extremely alluring woman—it would, I knew, not be easy to just give her up. Rather abruptly—my father was still talking, still giving me the benefit of his advice—I realized that I had made the decision to go back.

I knew that if I actually was going to return to Vietnam it would have to be on a new basis. There was absolutely no point in just filling a slot for twelve months. I had to go back with a plan of action.

I spent the next day or two thinking and remembering. For some reason, the observations I had made during my four months in country and the half-formed ideas that had been floating around in my head began coming together, impelled by the memory of my eleven years working with the Japanese security services. Suddenly the relevance of that training came into very sharp focus. And as it did I found myself thinking about my old friend Takahashi Yoshi.

Takahashi Yoshi was an intelligence operative with Japan's National Police; he was attached to the independent unit at Tokyo's Haneda airport. Haneda also served as one of the U.S. Air Force's primary airfields, and as an Air Force OSI special agent there I frequently partnered with Takahashi on cases involving the base's security.

One of the cases back in 1955 had involved a series of major thefts from the base exchange. As Takahashi and I narrowed down the list of suspects, we kept a close eye on all the Tokyo area hockshops and fences, hoping to establish the identities of our bad guys and get our hands on the stolen goods. Unfortunately, after weeks of surveillance, we had come up with nothing. As a result, I decided to bring in the prime suspects and put them on the lie detector. But after a full day of testing, the operator gave them all clearance. There was no doubt that they were clean, he said. Theirs were the best charts he'd seen in ages.

When the operator pronounced this assessment, Takahashi gave

me a quizzical glance, as if to ask if I really believed this stuff.
Then, though I had put my participation in the case on hold, he
and his Japanese partner went back to work, expanding their hockshop checks to other major cities and intensifying the surveillance.

Early one morning, a week later, the Japanese detectives walked
into my office to announce that they had broken the case and
arrested two of our original four suspects. Both of them had already
confessed. Most of the watches, jewelry, and other stolen goods
had been recovered from the Osaka hockshop that had received
them.

Takahashi explained that he and his partner had continued their
surveillance making good use of the "police box" system. In Japan
each neighborhood or rural area has its own little police station
manned by several officers who are stationed there for long periods
and get to know everyone and everything that goes on in their little
corner. They know all the residents, their relatives, their friends
and enemies, their cars, bicycles, what they do for a living, when
they come and when they go. All of this observation is unobtrusive
of course, but thorough all the same. If you were to put together
all the information of all those policemen in all of those boxes, you
would end up with a comprehensive knowledge of the entire country. In our situation, the police boxes had done a good job of
keeping tabs on the suspects in question and eventually Takahashi
had what he needed to break the case. Total information had been
the key, knowing everything possible about the suspects' lives.

The same faith in total information applied equally to intelligence work as to criminal work. On another case Takahashi took
me with him to National Police headquarters to talk with the chief
of the KGB-GRU oversight section. The size of the place had astounded me. At least seventy-five officers sat at their desks in the
section, and it appeared that there must be another several
hundred in the rest of the Foreign Bureau. All of them were
perched in front of little wooden desks, two to a desk, and each
desktop was covered with what looked like diagrams and charts. In
the big open room it sounded as if they were all talking at once.
When I asked what they were doing, the chief told me that each
team was assigned to a particular Japanese target, say a Mr. Hajimoto, who might in some way be connected with the KGB or
GRU. They were busily compiling data on everything that could
be discovered about their man, combining information from the
police boxes with their own surveillance and research.

"Eventually," the chief said, "when we put everyone's work together"—he gestured toward the room—"we get something like

this." And he pulled out a file on the Nisso Kyokai, the Japan Soviet Society. The file included a gigantic, detailed wiring diagram of the entire organization, with all the slots for committees, sections, and membership filled in, a complete Who's Who of the poetry section, the sports section, the musical section, and all the other sections. Mr. Hajimoto and all his colleagues were there, name, rank, and serial number. Most of the members of the society, the chief went on, were cultural figures of one type or another. They had joined because they were sympathetic to socialist ideals or because of a general interest in the Soviet Union or for social reasons or whatever. But a small number of individuals were members of the Japanese Communist Party, and examining the committee hierarchies and structures, one could see that these people were all in leadership roles.

In fact, the story the wiring diagram told was that through a small number of well-placed people the Japanese Communist Party was actually directing the Nisso Kyokai. Among other activities, the chief said, the JCP was able to orchestrate newspaper and magazine articles, making use of the Nisso Kyokai cultural people. Needless to say, the writing was all anti-American, violently opposed to the U.S. military facilities and to the Japanese American Security Treaty. In the same way the Japanese Communists controlled the Sohyo labor unions and various student organizations, which enabled the party to foment huge demonstrations against the bases or visiting American leaders.

What the National police also knew from their identification efforts and surveillance was the pattern of connections between Japanese nationals and the East Bloc intelligence world. From surveillance reports, I could see where members of the target groups had met with Soviet trade or cultural figures who were in reality KGB or GRU agents. As the chief walked me through the diagrams and charts, explaining how it all operated, I knew I was getting my first lesson in the who, what, where, when, and how of Communist front organizations.

A short time after my introduction to the KGB-GRU section I had transferred to the OSI's counterintelligence office. With criminal work no longer part of my assignment, my collaboration with the intelligence arm of the National Police intensified. And as my exposure to Japanese methods continued over the next two years, the lessons stuck and became ingrained. Like the police intelligence people, I developed a sixth sense about front organizations; I became attuned to what they did and how they did it.

Later, after I had been through OSI's intensive Japanese-language training course in Arlington, Virginia, I went to work as liaison not only with the National Police, but with the PSIB, Japan's FBI. There my knowledge of Japanese procedures had expanded and deepened. The overall result was that I had become imbued with the Japanese approach to intelligence, especially with their insistence on thoroughness. They were fanatic collectors of information, always exerting themselves to achieve a comprehensive understanding of a person and his activities before making any overt moves against him. The same was true of their approach to an institutional target. Those agents sat in the vast space of the Foreign Bureau and the PSIB office day in and day out, each working on his own little piece of a giant puzzle. Their goal was nothing less than total knowledge. Without it one had no more than random bits and pieces, tantalizing hints of an effort by a superbly organized enemy. But with total knowledge, the opposition's pattern of contacts, activities, and priorities emerged before your eyes.

That was exactly what we needed in Vietnam. The fact that a data bank didn't exist meant that we would have to develop it from scratch, build it up, piece together the enemy. And in the process we would be developing the information we needed to interrogate suspects meaningfully, to give us the advantage. It would be a massive, painstaking job, and it would require time. But I knew it could be done—all those *hoi chanh* were just sitting out there waiting for us to get at them, thousands of them. If we used them properly they could make that motherfucker of an invisible enemy visible to us at last.

4

EVERY SWINGING DICK

On the way back from the states I considered the best way to hit Loren with all this. Everything seemed pretty cut and dried. Loren would just have to be brought to see that there was nothing else to do. I'd put it as strongly as I could: this is the way we're going to do it, if we don't we might as well give up the whole thing. He ought to be amenable, I thought. He knows better than anyone that we're just spinning our wheels.

At the Monastery I collared Bill Todd first. Before my leave Bill and I had spent hours and hours discussing the problems, discussions that always centered on the lack of information and the need for a data bank. Now he completely agreed with the idea of developing one ourselves and attacking the Vietcong from an intelligence standpoint completely independent of the South Vietnamese. We both knew this would not fit in with any of the Agency's guidelines or even with the acknowledged understanding that we were only to act in an advisory capacity—especially now that "Vietnamization" had begun. What I had in mind would be unilateral and covert, a CIA do-it-yourself activity. Yet we felt we had no choice. All the other programs were worthless. If we wanted to get the intelligence and develop the agents, we would have to make it happen on our own.

Neither Todd nor I was quite sure how Loren would react to this. Our boss was smart, sensitive to the needs, and immensely frustrated. And he was a friend. But he was also an Agency GS-15 looking to become a 16. "Bill," I said, "come with me to Loren on this. You know me, I'll lay it on the line. I'll be outspoken about it. But I need your support, especially now." (Bill had just been appointed base chief of operations, third man at Bien Hoa.) Bill hadn't a moment's hesitation, as I knew he wouldn't. Without so much as a blink of an eye he said, "Sure, Orrin, I'm right with you." We asked Susie to lay on a meeting with Loren, preferably late that afternoon, in case he might want to extend the discussion into the usual social hour.

When we walked into his office for the meeting Loren knew something was cooking. I was just back from leave, so obviously I was planning to tear up the world, and now here I was with Bill Todd standing next to me, fairly bursting his seams. He looked at us and laughed. "Whatever this is, it's obvious I've got the deck stacked against me. I guess you want me to be all ears, is that it?" "Yes," I said, "and then I want you to concur. Because what I'm about to tell you is the only solution to our problems. Bill and I are totally convinced that the proposals we are about to make to you will give us the one method of turning this nonproductive office into something that functions the way it's supposed to. Frankly, it's the only reason I decided to come back.

"Loren, we all want to develop intelligence, report intelligence, and develop spies. We especially want to develop the spies. But under the present circumstances there is no way for us to even try to penetrate the Vietcong. We can't go into a single district and look for a penetration—not Trang Bang, Cu Chi, Tan Uyen, Duc Hoa, none of them. The system we have now with the interrogation centers, the special police, the RD and CG and PRU simply does not work. Not one CIA program works. And they will not work." "Yes," Loren said, "I know. Nothing except Forcie. And it bugs my ass day and night." "So what we need," I went on, "is to gather the information first. Once we have that, then we can go get the spies. But we have to do it ourselves, we have to do it our own way, by cross-checking from the very beginning. None of this cutout baloney from the police or these unverified stories from the prisoners."

Then I explained the concept to him. I told him about my experience in Japan, about the way Japanese intelligence had had everything down on paper: the entire committee structure of the Japanese Communist Party on a ward-by-ward basis, all of it down to the individual members. "That's exactly what I want," I said. "The only way we are going to crack this thing, the only way we are going to be able to target on an agent, is to have all that information. [That was Bill Todd's favorite word: Who are we going to TARGET on? We need to TARGET on someone.] We are never going to pick up an agent at random without knowing what we are doing. So we have to collect the data. We have to concentrate on Tay Ninh province, Hau Nghia, Duc Hue, Duc Hoa, Binh Duong, Bien Hoa, and COSVN, and get our data. Binh Long, Phuoc Long, Long Khanh, and Binh Tuy we can forget about. There's nothing going on in those places anyway. So forget about them and concentrate on the provinces that are important to us.

"We can start collecting the data at the Chieu Hoi Centers. We've got thousands of defectors, and each one of them is chock-full of information. We'll have to screen them all. It'll be a massive job, but we can do it. We can exploit them and build up a data bank arranged by Vietcong structure. If we start right now, in a few months we can have a card file so big we'll all be amazed."

Loren asked me to explain it further, and I was pretty sure we had him committed. He had seen right off that this would be a significant deviation from the standard CIA modus operandi, but it hadn't fazed him a bit. "This is what I want it to look like," I said. "Here is, let's say, 'An Tinh Village,' that will be a subject heading in our card catalog. Behind 'An Tinh Village' the first card will be 'Party Secretary.' Once we interview enough defectors and prisoners from An Tinh we are going to know who the party secretary is. We'll have his name, date of birth, place of birth, family members, close friends, and associates. We'll have something about his history: his first assignment—'village guerrilla' or whatever—his other assignments, right up to where he is now. All of it cited as to source of information. Then behind 'Party Secretary' we'll have 'Current Affairs Section,' with all the members listed on separate cards and all the information we can get on each one of them, also cited by source. Then the 'Military Affairs Section' with cards on the members, then the 'Political Section,' and so on for each of the sections right down the line according to the organizational hierarchy. And I want this for every village, district, province, and subregion that we're focusing on. Each new source we interview is going to tell us something; he'll corroborate what we have or give us something additional. So we might end up with eight different cards on the An Tinh secretary, each one giving us the information derived from an individual source. What we'll eventually have is the structure of the Vietcong on every level as well as identities and

backgrounds of the members. Not just a wiring diagram but a goddam super wiring diagram.

"That will be our subject file. We'll also keep personal dossiers—
201 files—on each of the sources. The case file numbers of each of
the sources who provided information on a particular subject will
be cited in the subject file. So we'll be able to see at a glance that,
say, the head of the Duc Hue civilian proselyting committee was
identified by sources A, B, and C, who had this, that, or the other
relationship with him during this, that, or some other period of
time.

"Loren"—I was getting excited by now—"this cannot miss." In
my mind I was picturing that Japanese KGB-GRU section, all those
guys working away on their files and diagrams in that giant room.
"We just cannot miss. We have thirteen hundred sources sitting in
Bien Hoa alone right now, with more coming in every day. If we
only get a hundred of those guys to talk it'll be a major victory. But
I think we're going to get every single one of them. One way or
another there's no question we'll get their cooperation. And we'll
begin to get authentication, one to the next, back and forth. Everybody who was in one of their sections is going to know everybody
else in that section plus people in other sections. And all these
section chiefs know one another. It might come slowly, but it will
come. We can build this thing. We're going to start with a partial
breakdown of a village party committee, then we're going to add
and add."

By this time Loren's eyes were practically glowing and he had
started saying "Uh huh, uh huh" as I hit each of the points. "OK,"
he said finally, "I think you're on the right track. Now how do you
intend to do it? Is this something that's going to cost the Agency a
million dollars, and cost me my job while you're at it?"

"Not at all," I said. "With your help I want to go to the regional
Chieu Hoi Center and set up some kind of an office. They have a
lot of equipment out there, CORDS has a lot of equipment, trailer
houses and furniture and other things. Put some of those trailer
houses up there for me, desks, typewriters, partitions. Let's set it
up so we can do initial screenings of four people at a time, or eight
at a time, with different interpreters. Chieu Hoi Lan can oversee
all of this, make sure it's running smoothly; she's tremendously
capable.

"So I need interpreters, desks, file cabinets, trailer houses.
CORDS has these big forty-foot trailers. I need a couple of them,
maybe three. Why can't you go to your friend Charlie Whitehouse
[director of CORDS at that time]? He'll do it for you. Inside the

Chieu Hoi Center, I need some kind of fenced-in compound for security. I'll want to rent two or three houses where I can interrogate sources after they've been screened. I can put them up at the houses to get them away from the Chieu Hoi Center, and have my interpreters handle the interrogations there. We're going to have to pay rent and we're going to have to feed them, but it won't come to very much.

"First we'll set our people up. Then we'll get the Three Corps Chieu Hoi chief to help us select defectors according to what he says they used to be. Of course most all of them will claim they were members of the Farmer's Association, or that they were suppliers, always the lowest level. You should hear them. 'Yes, I was a member,' they'll tell you, 'but I never knew anything. All I did was carry rice from the village into the boonies.' But you can bet your ass they weren't all farmers and suppliers. We've got lots of significant people in those centers, there's no question at all in my mind about it.

"I know that Bill supports me one hundred percent on this. We've already discussed it thoroughly, his ideas and mine."

"That's right, Loren," Bill put in. "If we had a card file on a village so that I knew who every swinging dick was in the party committee, then I could finally target on somebody. I could find somebody who had some contact with one of the chiefs, say the head of the military proselyting section. And once I found somebody in the Chieu Hoi Center who knows him, then I could check out the target's background, who he knows in the area, his family and friends, and we could find the proper cutout to approach him, a relative, or someone else he trusts. We'll have an idea of who might be approachable and why, what kind of lever to use. Of course we can't take the word of one source for anything. But sooner or later somebody's going to come through the system who will corroborate the first guy's information. Someone who knows the same military proselyting guy. So, you see, we'd have a start, we'd have something to work on. Right now we've got nothing, zilch."

"That's right," I said. "Nothing. We don't even know the strength of a village party committee or a district party committee. Loren, the special police don't even know how many people they're dealing with on these committees. I've asked all over, not just in Three Corps, but also in Two Corps. 'Come on guys, how many do they have in this committee? How many?' You know what I get from the police? 'I don't know.' 'Well, do you have any names?' 'Yeah, a couple that we suspect are on it.' 'Well how do you know

they're on it?' 'I don't know.' That's all we ever get from them, 'I
don't know.' And you know what? They're telling the truth: they
don't know. Because they never had a data bank. So that's what
we're talking about here, creating our own data bank."

"OK," Loren said, interrupting me, "you've sold me. Let's do it.
Let's start tomorrow morning and do it. I'll go see Charlie Whitehouse tonight and I'm sure he'll tell Rudy [the CORDS Military
Region Three Chieu Hoi Center adviser] to let us have whatever
we need." "All right," said Bill Todd, "that's terrific. Let's assume
that CORDS will go along; it's really no skin off their backs anyway.
But that still leaves us with a problem. Namely, what are we going
to do with your buddies in Saigon Station?" Loren hesitated for a
moment, then said, "Bill, fuck'em. I'm not even going to mention
it to them. We can do this with our own special police money.
We're going to scrounge most of the material. Everything's already
funded. We've got the desks, the typewriters, the people. You're
just going to put them to work on this project instead of letting
them go on doing what they've been doing, which has been getting
us nowhere. So what does Saigon Station have to know? They can
find out later, after you've got it up and running and we're getting
results. Now, Orrin, what's your first step? What procedures are
you going to follow?"

"I've been thinking about it," I said. "First I'm going to draw up
a screening form, then I'll do an interrogation form. The screening
form's the most important. That's what I want to have rolling
across my desk immediately, something that's going to tell me who
these *hoi chanh* defectors are. Name, home address, date of birth,
place of birth, position in VC, VC code name. I'll put these forms
together, then I'll train our interpreters about how I want them to
handle the defectors and use the forms. One thing I'll need is a
special interpreter for myself, someone who's going to be smart
enough to understand exactly what I want, then act as a leader for
the other interpreters. I've been thinking of Lam Number One. Do
you mind if I take him?"

"Mind?" Loren's eyebrows shot up three inches. "You know Lam
handles all the Forcie material. You've got to be kidding. But now
that you mention it, I think I might have exactly the person for
you. In fact I'm expecting him in on the courier plane later this
afternoon.

"Let me tell you about this guy," Loren said. "He's been working
for us down in Vung Tau, and we've been protecting him from the
draft. He's ethnic Chinese, bright, brought up in Hong Kong, as
articulate in English as the average American, maybe more so. I

hear he's a good writer too. But the officer in charge down there doesn't like him, thinks he's a wiseass and lazy. So I arranged for him to come up here. Try this guy out, Orrin. I think he's your lead interpreter, he's really good." "Great," I said, "I'll take him. I've also asked Mingo and Sonny and Dat if they would like to work with me on this. I hope that's OK. They've all said yes."

An hour later Tran Van Minh stepped off the courier from Vung Tau, the man I would know as Albert for the next six years, one of the sharpest, most effective interrogators in Vietnam. He was maybe five feet tall if he stretched, and he might have weighed ninety pounds or so dripping wet. He had a big smile plastered permanently on his face, and his English, which he spoke with an upper-crust British accent, was perfect. Although he was twenty-seven years old, he hardly looked a day over fifteen. He had a smart aleck, joking way about him, with a sense of humor that was constantly on display. I could see why the Vung Tau officer might have found him annoying. But his manner didn't put me off at all. He was sassy but he seemed ready to work. I liked him immediately.

The next day I had Saigon Station run traces on Albert, which turned up some interesting information. His mother lived in Hong Kong, where Albert had graduated from high school. His father, dead now, had been one of Ho Chi Minh's top financial officers after World War Two. But in 1946 he had stolen ten million piasters from the Vietminh finance section—a lot of piasters in those days —and fled to Hong Kong. Albert's old man hadn't been a Communist after all, just a crafty Viet-Chinese ready to play the game until he saw his big chance. Albert had grown up around money and had acquired at least one expensive habit himself: opium. Not that I cared, as long as he kept it under control. But it was something I'd have to watch out for.

I also asked Bill to run Albert through the Gittinger test, which he did late that afternoon. Bill was astounded when he came to me with the results. "Orrin," he stated, "you're not going to believe it. This Albert of yours tests out at over a hundred fifty IQ. He's brilliant. Not only that, he's an ERU plus—externalizer, regulated, uniform plus. He will love to be given projects, he'll work like hell to get them done, and he'll do them by himself. The man does not need people. [Most Vietnamese were not role uniform but role adaptive or role adaptive plus—intensely sociable people who badly needed company.] You put him in a room by himself where he can just work and he'll flourish, he'll produce like mad for you."

The next morning over breakfast Loren told me he had spoken to Charlie Whitehouse at CORDS and that Charlie had agreed to help. Rudy, his deputy in Region Three, would get us whatever we needed—trailers, furniture, and space at the Chieu Hoi Center. When I spoke with Rudy personally he couldn't have been more forthcoming, and later that day three big trucks maneuvered forty-foot trailers into place inside a little compound that had been created for me at the center. Within a couple of days the furniture was in place, including a large card file cabinet, and I had organized my staff—ten female secretary/translators and five male interpreters who would do the screening and interrogating under my direction.

While this was going on Loren set up a meeting for Bill, me, and Colonel Thao, the ARVN regional G-2, Colonel Hien, the regional National Police chief, the Vietnamese regional Chieu Hoi director, and Colonel Dinh, commander of the Corps Interrogation Center. Loren introduced things, laying out the general concept of what I wanted to do, then turned the meeting over to me. I knew all these guys and got along with all of them. Colonel Thao, the regional G-2, was an especially outstanding officer—dedicated, smart, and a straight arrow. The same for Colonel Dinh. Both these guys were incorruptible, and worked their fannies off all the time.

I told them that I wanted to screen all the *hoi chanh* we now had on hand and then I wanted to have access to all new sources as they came in. I told them that we wanted to set up our own intelligence-gathering program and that we hoped to develop agents. Of course, I said, we would share everything worthwhile with ARVN intelligence. We would feed them our reports directly or translate them, then ship them over—whichever they preferred. "The only thing I'd like is to have access to whatever good sources come in as soon as they come in, prisoners as well as defectors. We'll take these people just as soon as you can let us have them, get them into our own houses, and interrogate them." Colonel Dinh, I knew, had some intelligence—sketchy information on the enemy units operating in the region: he knew something about unit identification, maybe a few guys in the unit, the commander, executive officer, and several other key people. I knew he would love to have anything more he could get along those lines. We would go after order of battle too, I told him. We intended to set up files on all military units as well as political units and this too we would share. Dinh and Thao were enthusiastic, and the others were happy enough to go along. They, of all people, knew exactly how bad the current situation was.

A few days later I sent Mingo and Sonny out to rent houses where we could put up our sources and interrogate them. I also gave Albert twenty thousand piasters to rent a two-bedroom apartment down some little alley that he could live in as well as use for interrogation. I gave him some furniture, a typewriter, and pots and pans so that he could do his cooking at home. And I told him to get his girlfriend in there—I knew he had a girlfriend in Vung Tau and that he didn't know what to do with her. "I'll have our commo man put in a call to Vung Tau to have her sent up," I told him. "Put her in the back room, she can cook for you, whatever. I don't care about it." I wanted to fix this guy up with all the amenities, give him a kind of self-sustaining environment. After Bill's assessment I was sure he'd be happiest that way and that he'd work better for it.

By now I had developed my SOP (standard operating procedure) forms for screening and interrogation and I began training my interpreters in how to use them. I also brought in the Provincial Interrogation Center officers and special police advisers from all the provinces to brief them on the new setup and how I wanted things done. With the help of a blackboard I laid out what I was after in terms of our own data bank and I told them that in a matter of a few months each of them (in the provinces) would have their own smaller versions of the data bank. They would send me copies of their forms and whatever wiring diagrams they were able to get. Our secretaries would type cards from their sources, along with 201 files. So it would all be retrievable, a kind of manually operated computer system. I told them that Loren had okayed everything, and if they needed to hire more people, an additional secretary or translator, they should do it.

I explained in detail to the advisers and interpreters how a 201 file works, what we wanted in there, all the biographical data, plus whatever wiring diagram the source was able to generate. If the source knew only one section of the village committee, we wanted it there. Also any intelligence the person might report should be in there. What I was looking for, I told them, was the ability for an interrogator to go down to the subject file and the 201 file and review them before he talked to the next source from the same general area. Then the interrogator would have something to work with. He'd be able to say, "Do you know so-and-so or so-and-so? What about the propaganda section, who do you know in that? You say you were in the Farmer's Association, but two people told us you were really deputy chief of the cultural section, so why don't you level with us?"

The response from the field officers was enthusiastic. "Why the hell didn't somebody do this before?" one of them said. "What are we waiting for?" Larry Rather's response was typical, though a little more outspoken than the others (Larry was the former San Diego cop who had been so demoralized). "This is just what I was looking for," he said. "This is the kind of help I've needed. I don't know anything about the Communist Party. How am I gonna talk to somebody? I hate sitting there like a dumbbell."

I briefed them on the concept and organization of the data bank, then followed it up with descriptions on paper, one, two, three, four, five for the R-tested rote-memory guys. [By now Bill had put almost everyone on base through the Gittinger test. "I know who you are," I'd tell them, "you rote-memory guys."] I explained inter- rogation techniques to them, and over a period of time I trained them that the first thing they had to do was establish rapport with their source. To learn from your source you have to have some feeling for him, you have to demonstrate a real interest in him and his family. "Where's your family? What do they do for a living? How much do they earn? Are they making it all right out where they are? Does ARVN bother them? Does the VC bother them? Do the Vietcong come around at night and take rice from them? Are you Buddhist, or mainly ancestor worshiper, or what? What kind of a Buddhist?" Be interested, I told them, that's the essence of it. Does the guy really have a religious nature or is it just super- ficial? Talk to him about his brothers, his sisters. Get into the guy. Don't even ask him about anything that might be construed as intelligence. Get into him enough so you can decide whether or not he is being honest with you. Is he trying to be evasive, sucking the air in through his teeth? Or is he telling you, "Yes, I do have a sister in such and such a hamlet. Yes, my brother and his family live over in that hamlet." You'll be able to tell, to feel it.

"So the first job is to establish rapport and get a feeling if your source is really going to level with you. He knows and you know that you are not asking him anything sensitive, anything that's going to compromise his friends. But keep in mind while you're doing this that even this kind of personal information might be usable at some point. For example, it might help us decide if this guy might be a good contact to someone else, or if he's got a family member who might be the right person to make an approach to somebody, or it might give us an important piece of background information on VC thinking or procedures."

We trained our interpreters to tell the source exactly whom they were working for, that they were with American intelligence, not with the Government of Vietnam (the GVN) in any way. We had nothing to do with Saigon; we were not sending reports to the

special police (we weren't). We were completely independent and
we were just trying to understand things. Then follow it up with
the point that this American I'm working for told me that if he'd
grown up where you have, with your background, he would have
joined the VC too. We know how corrupt the government is. "Always lay that out for these guys," I told my people. "We know how
corrupt Saigon has been and how corrupt it still is. It's one of our
main concerns."

Basically, I'd say the same thing to the interrogation center and
special police advisers. "Level with your subjects. Tell them you're
an American intelligence officer and that this interpreter works for
you. He does not work for the GVN; he does not work for the
special police. He works for you alone. We do not send our reports
to the police. We want you to understand our position. Then give
them something good to eat. When it's lunchtime tell them you
have to go to eat your American-style food, but you're having
something special made up for them. Then bring them a real meal,
lay it on."

Rapport was the object, and a major road to that object was being
honest. The second was TLC—tender loving care. That was a
constant theme. "Don't be hard nose on any of these guys," I'd tell
the interrogators and advisers. "It's not going to get you anywhere.
You have to have some compassion for your subject. You have to
have sympathy for him. You have to be in the frame of mind where
you're saying to yourself, 'I want to talk to this fella. I want to
understand why he was a guerrilla. He's got a story to tell and I
want to hear it.' That's the way you'll get them thinking, 'I don't
mind talking to this guy, to tell him why I was a guerrilla. I'm not
ashamed of it; I'm proud of it.' And then they hear you say, 'Sure,
in your pants I would have been a guerrilla too. Against those
bandits in Saigon? Of course I would have.' "

In fact, this approach was something I felt especially strongly
about, partly because I really was sympathetic. Of course the atroc-
ities and assassinations the Vietcong perpetrated were unpardon-
able. But in general terms I wasn't at all sure that if I had been in
these villagers' places I wouldn't have been VC myself. But my
approach went well beyond this kind of consideration. I had been
convinced for a long time that the way to treat an Asian if you want
something out of one—man or woman—is with decency and respect. These sources of ours had usually been whacked around
pretty good by the police or South Vietnamese army intelligence.
When they found themselves in my system, I wanted them to be
treated differently, and I wanted them surprised by the treatment.

I had given quite a lot of thought to this TLC approach over the years. In a way I suppose it came naturally to me because of my own upbringing; my parents and grandparents, with whom we also lived, had always been affectionate, loving people. Some of that had no doubt rubbed off on me in my childhood. But it was also something I had become conscious of when I went to Japan and started to learn Japanese. If you want to see how the Asian mind responds to kindness all you have to do is get to know Japanese women. Kindness tears them up. It overwhelms them. Very small things: sympathy, interest, a basic decency toward them as human beings; they responded to this in an unbelievable way. It was easy to be cynical about it, to use the approach as a means to an end, but in fact many Westerners' natural orientation toward Japanese women was one of interest and friendship, in addition to the sexual motive. Thanking a waitress for bringing a *tokuri* of sake, for example, where what she was used to was a harsh grunt, if that. And the waitress, or the potential girlfriend, or the casual acquaintance would be smitten. It never failed, very likely, I thought, because Japanese men so rarely treat their women that way.

Strangely enough, over time, I began to realize that Japanese men were no different underneath. My work in that country put me in the company of detectives and intelligence agents, tough guys who walked around with frowns and macho swaggers. But behind that exterior—that *bushido*—was something very different altogether. And it wasn't that hard to crack. Simple consideration and decency, an expression of concern or a favor so insignificant that you might not even notice you were doing it, these were things that affected them deeply, and persuaded them to respond. There was some basic dichotomy at work within these men. They were hard cases, yet they also harbored a deep streak of sentimentality and affection that surfaced in response to friendship and warmth. The simplicity of it never ceased to amaze me.

Though different from the Japanese in many ways, the Vietnamese responded similarly when confronted with a little human sympathy. They were absolute suckers for affection. They couldn't stand it, couldn't say no to it. Many Americans did not understand this at all. And as far as the Vietnamese themselves went, they did not have the cultural distance to see it. Their own traditions of dealing with enemies emphasized brutality and cruelty. What went on in the South Vietnamese prisons was abominable. But it had absolutely nothing on the torture the North Vietnamese doled out to their prisoners, including Americans. My Vietnamese interpreters had to be trained in the art of sympathetic interrogation. And they learned, though sometimes slowly. But with time and the right kind of reinforcement they got accustomed to it, and I'd hear from them sometimes when they picked up a prisoner, "Oh, he didn't look so good, Ong Gia [pronounced "Ohm Yah"—"old man"—my nickname in Vietnamese]. Not good at all. They beat the hell out of him in the interrogation center." They'd be disturbed about it. And I'd think, smiling to myself, Yes, this interpreter is disturbed about it now. But six months ago he wouldn't have been disturbed. Six months ago he would have got in a few whacks himself.

My lead interpreter, Albert, was especially fast at picking up the idea. He was the biggest sucker of all and understood the power of the process. He knew that if he had one or two sources at his house the best way of getting to them was to feed them, let them watch television, maybe even take them out to a movie. Early on he came to me asking for money for three or four soccer balls. "Those guys at the Chieu Hoi Center don't have anything to do all day," he said. "I know we can score some points with a few soccer balls." So he got them, and from that point on his defectors had soccer games constantly. They were just fanatics about soccer. So when Albert brought *hoi chanh* to his house for interrogation, it was "Hi, Albert, how are you?" They knew him and liked him. And when Albert began asking where they were born and who their parents were, it was "Oh, sure, Albert. I was born in Trang Bang. My dad was so-and-so and my mom was so-and-so." Answer, answer, answer instead of nothing, nothing, nothing.

TLC would not have gone over well in New York City. Give a bad guy there a little loving kindness and see what happens. But it would work on an Asian almost every time. It disoriented them and brought out that deep desire for contact and communication. You could practically see it going through their heads: "These guys are feeding me like I haven't eaten in years. They're dealing with me honestly. They're not slamming me around or electrocuting my balls. Why shouldn't I talk to them?" TLC was a fantastic thing in the context of Vietnam, especially when you put TLC together with the ultimate interrogation tool—knowledge of your source and his background, the kind of knowledge the data bank began to give us in greater and greater quantities.

One morning shortly after we had the system up and running, Loren announced that he had asked all the province case officers to come in; we would be having a special visitor that day: Theodore Shackley, chief of Saigon Station, the head of all CIA operations in Vietnam. Several hours later all the base officers gathered in the

large conference room to hear the tall, eloquent Shackley address
us. It was not exactly a laudatory speech. Three Corps had, as we
knew, only one developmental agent (although Forcie had been
delivering first-rate information for months, he was not yet fully
authenticated—that process might take years). One Corps and
Two Corps had none, but Four Corps, according to Shackley, had
almost fifty developmentals. If Four Corps was doing so well, there
was no reason the others couldn't do well also. "What exactly is
wrong with Three Corps, Mr. Snowcroft? You people seem to be
batting zero out here." Perhaps the time had come, Shackley remarked, glancing sharply from Loren to the rest of us, to take a
good long look at our procedures.

I watched Shackley carefully as he said this, aware that the only
developmentals in Four Corps were those reported by the special
police. Four Corps, like One Corps and Two Corps, had no data
bank, and from my occasional meetings with the Four Corps interrogation chief (a classmate of mine at Langley), I knew that the
programs there were as bankrupt as they were elsewhere. The so-
called fifty developmentals in Four Corps were undoubtedly all
police fabrications.

At the end of the general meeting Loren announced that he,
George Tanaka, Bill Todd, and I would meet with Shackley privately in Loren's office after lunch. Apparently the Station chief
wanted a briefing on the status of the interrogation centers. Oh,
Lord, I thought, what do we do now? Tell him the truth? Loren, as
concerned as I was and aware that the centers were a favorite
program at Station, suggested that I skirt the situation as well as I
could. "Tell him we're working hard on them, Orrin, but explain
how difficult it is to take a prisoner out of a PIC and make him into
an agent. Try to cool it until we can start reporting intelligence
from the new system."

That was fine as general advice. But it was I, not Loren, who had
to actually brief Shackley, and skirting the issue was not easy. In
my description of how the special police ran the PICs I tried to
tread softly, but I could not hide the truth, nor did I really want to.
The special police, I told him, generally lack an understanding of
operations, so they aren't extremely effective interrogators, nor do
they have a great desire to work. While I was going through my
little presentation, choosing my words as tactfully as I could, an
expression of disdain spread across Shackley's face. Obviously the
man didn't believe a thing I was saying.

Trying to get the meeting back on a positive track, Loren interrupted to explain that we were starting a new program to screen

and exploit the defectors and we hoped to make some progress shortly. But when he stopped short of going into details, Shackley turned to me and asked, "What are the VC vulnerabilities?" "The only apparent vulnerabilities," I said, "are the legal cadre, but to this point we have not been able to penetrate the structure. We are working on it though." I was not any more inclined than Loren to discuss what we were doing at this stage. I certainly was not about to make any claims. "Well, what about special police operations in this region?" asked Shackley after a moment of silence. He was not going to leave the special police alone. It seemed clear to me, and I was sure it was equally clear to Loren, Bill, and George, that in Saigon the Station chief was being fed a strong, positive line about the police, probably by my old friend Ted Coleburne. Although Shackley had directed the question at me, I wasn't about to answer it and looked at George Tanaka instead. He was supposed to be the special police adviser, let him handle it.

Somewhat to my surprise, George took the bull by the horns. "Ted," he said, "the special police here always use three or four cutouts whom they never make available for interviews. So we really don't know how to evaluate them. I worked with Japanese intelligence for fifteen years, and frankly, there's just no comparison. I have never seen such incompetence as we have here in Vietnam." George was a good guy, though I never thought much of his decision to just hunker down and endure his tour in Vietnam. But this performance earned him very high grades as far as I was concerned.

Shackley just looked at George, his face registering dismissal of what he had just been told. He was hearing differently from people he trusted more, and that was all there was to it. As far as he was concerned, Four Corps was doing splendidly. We were just not living up to its performance. A minute or two later the meeting came to an end, and that was the last we saw of him.

That was not the end of the subject though. A few days later Steamboat Charlie Timmes showed up at the base for a little chat. Charlie Timmes was a retired major general who had been the MACV commander in 1963 and 1964 and had now gone to work as a kind of roving troubleshooter for the Agency. A grand old man, he had an encyclopedic knowledge of the country and its people. His vast acquaintance included every leading officer in the South Vietnamese army and every province chief.

"Orrin," Timmes said over lunch in the dining room, "you know that I'm a kind of liaison man for the chief of Station. I try to help him resolve problems, and right now the interrogation centers are bugging him. What he asked me to do was to come out here and try to clarify the situation with you, then give him a written report on it. So why don't you explain what your position is on them and tell me what you see as the major problems." "Charlie," I said, "let's talk honestly and off the record. I can't simply tell Shackley the god-awful truth; there is no way he'll accept it." "OK," Timmes said—he may well have heard this kind of thing more than once— "tell me the straight story, off the record. Let me worry about putting it in a way that Ted Shackley can accept."

I did. I came down as hard as I could on what I considered the dumbest setup imaginable for exploiting prisoners of war. Nor did I spare the special police in their treatment of prisoners or in the greed and corruption that stood behind almost everything they did. "Charlie," I said, finishing up the whole sad tale, "I know this Provincial Interrogation Center program was somebody's brain-child and that it has found favor in high places. That's why I don't like to sound entirely negative. But what I've told you is the truth, unfortunate as it is. I'm relying on you to write it up in a way that's going to get me off the hook with Shackley."

As soon as Timmes left I sat down with Loren and Bill, who were dying to hear what had gone on. When I described our discussion Loren seemed relieved. "I think you handled it well," he told me. "But I'd also like you to dictate a memo to Susie for the record, just in case Steamboat Charlie decides to slip us the green weenie and write something derogatory. After that, let's all have a drink and you can bring me up to date on where your program stands."

5

PAYDIRT

I n fact the program was already working like a machine. Once the trailers and houses were in place and everyone was trained and ready to go we had got right into it. Albert had been the first to go over to the Bien Hoa Chieu Hoi Center and tell the chief we were ready to start. "We'd like to talk to some of the comrades," he said. "Do you have any here who have admitted they're members of the party?" "Sure, I've got some," came the answer. "Go ahead and take them. They're all yours."

After spending an hour or so screening his first two sources, Albert felt they were cooperative and worth talking to. He immediately took them out of the Chieu Hoi Center to his house. By chance it turned out that they were from the same village and knew each other. While one of them took a nap in a bedroom, Albert started talking to the other, feeling his way toward establishing a good rapport before he started the interrogation.

By the time I looked in on him Albert was pretty sure he was getting a straight story. The guy had been a VC local forces platoon leader who had defected only a few weeks earlier. He was fairly knowledgeable about order of battle in his area, about small-unit tactics, and about the level of VC effectiveness. "How is your recruitment going?" Albert asked. "Is your unit up to strength?" "No,

we're down," he said. They were down, we knew, well down, still
suffering the aftereffects of Tet. The guy wasn't trying to mislead
us. "How many did you originally have in the platoon?" "Well,
originally we had about fifteen." "What about now?" "When I left
we were down to six." "Come on," said Albert, uncapping another
bottle of Coke (one empty bottle was already on the desk, next to a
big bowl of Vietnamese peanuts), "don't kid me."

By that afternoon Mingo and Sonny were also interviewing people at the houses we had set up for them. On the Honda 90 motor-
cycle I had bought so I could get around fast, I'd go out to the
Chieu Hoi Center to watch the screenings. Then I'd pop in at the
houses to listen to the interviews. I'd come in, pat the VC on the
shoulder, shake his hand, ask him how he was, make sure he knew
he was dealing with an American. "Where's he from, Mingo?"
"He's from Can Giouc." "Oh, hey, that's a hot little area, isn't it?"
—Mingo translating—"Well, it used to be," said the VC. "It's
pretty quiet now." It was an honest answer; Can Giouc had indeed
been quiet for a while. So this guy too was probably leveling.

Sonny and Mingo were good—enthusiastic about the work, perceptive, and thorough. But they were not up to Albert's level. Albert was a great talker who could make friends quickly and would
soon be kidding his sources about anything that came into his
head, including girls. "Maybe I can arrange to get you a piece of
tail," he'd say. "You know, get you a pass from the center, fix you
up at a place I know right down the block from here. What do you
think?" And the guy's eyes would light up. Even if he was being
recalcitrant and surly, still he might not have had a girl in the last
five months, or maybe the last five years if he had been a real
bunker dweller out in the jungle. And these guys were just as normal as any other red-blooded male, even if they had been hard-
core for a decade with a father who had fought in the Vietminh
against the French. Wave something they really wanted in front of
their faces and they'd grab at it. The rapport would be established.
That was the key. Then the guy would get friendly and the information would start flowing.

When that happened Albert would get excited. "Ong Gia," he'd
say to me, reporting on an interrogation, "I know goddam well he's
telling me the truth. He's telling me about VC policies and intentions in Can Giouc district. What their capabilities are. And it jibes
with the information we carded last week when Mingo had that
other guy from Can Giouc. Look, here's the file. Right now their
capabilities are nothing. They can't do a thing. The American
Ninth has simply kicked the shit out of them. This guy says they
had about eighty percent casualties and they're just hanging on by

the skin of their teeth." All this delivered in colloquial American in Albert's high, squeaky voice with the clipped British accent.

So things just fell into place. Of course we could not truly authenticate anything yet. One or two or even three sources telling us similar stories about Can Giouc did not constitute authentication. But that would come, I knew, as the data bank grew. Meanwhile I could write a report for Saigon Station that would be graded "probably true" rather than "possibly true." And that same day Sonny might have a cadre from Rach Gia, right next to Can Giouc, who talked about the difficulties they were having recruiting, that they couldn't recruit anybody there either. I would write a report on that as well, indicating that VC recruitment problems apparently were common to the entire district.

I went over all the interrogation reports carefully, watching for discrepancies and for signs of truth. A source would say he came from such and such hamlet and was a member of the district militia, that he started five years ago as a hamlet guerrilla, then was made a village security section guerrilla. Well, that was the way they progressed, as we knew. They were tested all along the line, then advanced. "Then later I joined the party." "Well, why did you join? What did you have to do to join?" And the source would explain why he joined and what he had to do. And a day later in another interrogation report a different source would be describing how he joined the party, what the procedure was. And it would be similar. Our understanding was growing.

We also found, somewhat to our relief, that the VC code names gave us little trouble. Each Vietcong had a nom de guerre, Hai Duc, for example, who was a COSVN sapper captain. His real name was Phuong Van Duc, but they called him Hai Duc—"Number Three Duc." Or Ba Tung, whose real name was Thai Van Tung. Most often they left the first name (which comes last in Vietnamese usage) the same. But since individuals were commonly known by their first names rather than their last names (Mr. Tung rather than Mr. Thai) we usually could find out who was who. For some reason that always escaped me, the Vietcong always thought that by someone's calling "Number Three Duc" they were deceiving us.

Sometimes, though, they did have a real code name. Tu Duc, for example, was a proselyting chief and his real name was not Nguyen Van Duc or some equivalent. In fact his real name never was known. But surprisingly enough we often came up with the real names even of these people because most of the sources knew true names as well as VC names.

As we started gaining experience with the *hoi chanh*, we found we could accurately distinguish the significant sources from those who really were just suppliers or Farmer's Association members. We began looking for the hotshots. Working at the screening center in a trailer, the beautiful and industrious Chieu Hoi Lan soon had a list of fifty people who she thought were good prospects. "Ong Gia, we've got to get this guy and this guy and this guy. We've got to get them right now." So they'd bring them in and screen them, then ship them out to the houses for interrogation.

I developed a real appreciation for Albert's artistry at interrogation and reporting. This skinny, ugly, little pipe-smoking guy was absolutely brilliant, not only with defectors but with prisoners. He had a knack, a way about him of calming them down. He'd tell them, "I'm a draft dodger myself and these Americans are taking care of me. I'm not going into ARVN to fight you guys. You don't have to worry about talking to me, or to the old man either. The old man's not going to tell anyone in the GVN, not a word. He just wants the information, that's all." Albert could sell anybody a rotten piece of sausage, convince them right down to the wire. And of course we *would* protect a good source from the government.

I would walk into Albert's house while he was talking to a source. He would be able to type out a report in narrative form as he was conducting the interrogation. And on review the report would be near perfect. I would not even have to rewrite it before I submitted it to our reports officer. Given the landslide of work that had begun to engulf me, this was a talent I was grateful for.

My own days were taken up checking the progress at the center and at the houses. Then I'd go back to my office and pore over the screening and interrogation forms that were rolling across my desk, trying to decide what to do with this source or that. Who was worth pursuing? Who had given us his all and could now be returned to the Chieu Hoi system? I wanted to be extremely careful. The amount of information that had started to come in was staggering, but I did not want to miss any bit that might turn out to be significant.

Meanwhile Albert was producing twice as much as the other interpreters in number of reports as well as in discrimination and substance. He just had a gift for putting this kind of material together. After a while the other interpreters started asking his opinion on one thing or another. I might pop in on him at his apartment at eight-thirty in the evening and there he'd be, working at the typewriter. I'd pop in at eight in the morning, and he'd be at the typewriter—a true ERU workaholic.

At first I was so surprised I suspected that maybe he was making things up, giving me partial or total fictions. So I started taking some of the sources over to another interpreter after Albert was done. But invariably the other interpreters would get the same story. Everything would check out. I did that now and then with Albert, and with the others too. Albert of course suspected that I was checking on him and asked me once, "Ong Gia, why are you looking over my shoulder?" "Albert," I told him, "we don't have a data bank yet; we don't have another way of checking on what your people are saying. I have to be satisfied that it all checks out. And I have to be satisfied that you're not playing any games with me." He accepted that.

After the first month or two, I was convinced that we indeed had our hands on an extremely powerful tool. I asked Albert, Mingo, and Sonny to begin concentrating on Cu Chi, Trang Bang, and Go Dau Ha in Tay Ninh—all of them focal points for the Vietcong. "Don't worry about Long An or Binh Duong," I told them. "They're important, but I'm going to start others working on them. Just target these places."

Considering our limited manpower and all the information coming in, it was obvious we would have to start focusing our efforts. In addition, one or two of the Province Officers in Charge were beginning to generate good results themselves. Clint Wilson, a staff officer who had just taken over in Hau Nghia, was especially effective. He had eight hundred people in his province Chieu Hoi Center. Following our model in Bien Hoa, he put a trailer out there, assigned two case officers and several interpreters to the job, and started building up data—sending copies of their forms into our central data bank and incorporating all the intelligence and wiring diagrams we were able to send him on his area. A few of the other province officers were also doing well, despite their lack of intelligence experience. And Loren's monthly staff meetings with the Provincial Interrogation Center and special police advisers were more and more devoted to follow-ups and training on the data bank, how it was working, what we were generating from it, how the field people were integrating their work into it, and how they could do it more effectively.

As we concentrated on Trang Bang along with several other districts we found that the documentation on two villages, An Tinh and Loc Hung, was proliferating far faster than anybody might have expected. Almost before we knew it we had developed relatively detailed wiring diagrams of the Communist Party structure in those areas, diagrams that showed exactly which section was which and who were the people in those sections. Again, at this stage we were not yet confident that the information was fully accurate. But the amount of intelligence coming in drew our attention. Watching the card catalog expand every day, it was clear that these places were swarming with legal cadres, Vietcong masquerading as normal South Vietnamese citizens.

That news itself wasn't exactly a shock, though seeing the party organization come to life under our eyes was a bit sobering. Radio Hanoi, we knew, referred to Trang Bang as a district controlled by the revolution. That wasn't exactly true, but they liked to brag about it. And within the district, An Tinh was known, again according to Radio Hanoi, as a "model revolutionary village." It was, they said, "our village."

As a result, An Tinh was a place I really wanted to go after, on the theory that if we could crack the hardest nut we could crack the rest. Major Ngo, the GVN district chief in Trang Bang, was a smart, honest individual, a real pleasure to work with, and as the card catalog grew we began meeting with some frequency. We were both sure that once we had enough information, we could bring the world down on the 101st North Vietnamese Army regiment based in the Ho Bo Woods just outside An Tinh and its neighbor, Loc Hung. The village secretaries in these places and all their key committees had to be intimately involved in the job of keeping the NVA regiment supplied and informed. If we could crack the village committees we stood a good chance of being able to pinpoint the regiment. If we were good enough, and careful enough, we could learn their MO: where they moved, when they moved, how often they moved. And once we knew that, we could let the furies loose on them.

So as our knowledge of Trang Bang filled out I kept a close watch for a likely agent there, a person in the right position to give us the information we needed. At the same time, we were making great efforts to get reports completed and sent to Saigon and Washington explaining what the war was all about in Military Region Three. We increased the number of intelligence reports coming out of Bien Hoa base fairly quickly from a couple a month to a point where the province of Tay Ninh alone was sending in a couple, Hau Nghia another two or three, and Long An two or three, while Albert was doing eight or ten by himself.

Most of these reports concerned VC status, intentions, and capabilities. Could they overrun the Cu Chi base camp? Would they try to? Did they intend to cut Highway #1? If so, when and where? When could we expect the next assault on Trang Bang district? We were also learning about the functions and procedures of the party committees, most of them manned by legals. Members of the Cu Chi district military proselyting section, for instance, liked to go to Cu Chi market to develop agents, recruiting South Vietnamese soldiers right there. On any given day all sorts of ARVN officers could be seen sitting around the market drinking coffee. A Vietcong military proselyting agent, a legal cadre who lived nearby or perhaps had a shop there, would strike up a conversation and over a period of time he would get to know the officer. Step-by-step he'd develop a relationship. Then when he saw a chance he'd insinuate a question, "Gee, there's that much fighting going on up there in Dau Tieng [or some other place]? How many guys do you have up there anyway? Are you going to have to go up yourself?" He knew exactly what to ask and how to ask it. Of course, once he found somebody who looked vulnerable, he'd throw him a pitch, and then he'd have somebody new in his network.

As we also learned, the information the Vietcong developed through their South Vietnamese army contacts and agents was remarkably detailed. This battalion, that battalion, how many personnel they have, where they're located, how many are on leave, when they go on leave, how often they go on leave, what their full strength is on Monday morning, on a holiday. This was the kind of thing the VC intelligence people were busy piecing together in the Cu Chi tunnels from reports they would get from the legals each night. And this was what we were finding out from our own sources who might have been former proselytizers or intelligence analysts or commo liaison people.

The information we were getting by now was beginning to form a fascinating picture of what made the Vietcong tick. Interestingly, in 1969 and early 1970 what we were discovering about their military capabilities was mostly negative. It was a time when they were not capable of doing much. They had been hit hard by Tet and were struggling to retrench and reestablish their pre-Tet levels.

Meanwhile the work of building up the information bank and filling in the slots bit by bit went on relentlessly. If we were not able to get three or four different sources confirming our data, we knew we were not on the right track. We had to know from several sources, for example, that the VC Trang Bang district chief's name was Ba Be, that he was still alive and healthy and working in the tunnels under the Ho Bo Woods. One might tell us that Ba Be's bunker was right on the edge of the woods near the little river that runs down that side, that the district MI (military intelligence) section was about fifty yards south in bunkers where they were holed up most of the time. But we had to have intelligence like this confirmed beyond doubt before we could take action. And so the work went on.

The main point of this whole effort was to develop a spy. That was the objective, to get an authenticated spy, someone who really was who our sources said he was, and who filled the position they said he filled. Once we knew that for sure, we could target on him: figure out his vulnerabilities, decide how to make an approach. It was not an easy process. Everything about the potential spy had to be verified, from his family background to his position, to his access to party directives, to his MO. Then we had to have an angle or find just the right friend or relative to make the contact, then that person had to be recruited. And all this was slow, painstaking work.

Of course at the same time we continued to pick up information of all sorts, adding to our picture of the previously invisible enemy. For example, why were such large numbers of defectors coming in? What made them defect? As we were to see, at different periods there were different reasons for defections—which lasted right up to the very end of the war. But in 1969 and 1970 thousands of Vietcong and NVA were coming over for the most part because of intense American military pressure. The Chieu Hoi Centers were full of people whose units had been overrun two or three times and who had just decided they had had it. Some of the North Vietnamese defectors came in saying they were simply not going to die in the South. (The North Vietnamese slogan "Born in the North to Die in the South" conveyed the fatalism so many in the NVA felt.) Probably ninety percent of those we interviewed had been drafted. They had not volunteered out of a burning passion to save the homeland and drive out the foreigners, nothing like that. They were just inductees. Back in their homes they had known that as they came of age they'd go into the army. Their older brothers and friends had disappeared into the South; now they would too. And the longer they stayed in South Vietnam, the more some of them concluded that there was no way they were ever going to get home. They started saying to themselves, "I've been sent here to die," and the conviction grew on them. They got no R and R leave, no sick leave, nothing of that nature. They had no contact with their families, often they could neither send nor receive letters. They recognized that they had just been shipped as fodder into a great killing ground and that their government's attitude was if you survive, fine; if you don't, that's fine too. They were simply ready to hang it up.

Quite a few *hoi chanh* also talked about the B-52 bombings. They had survived the attacks (though often with ruptured eardrums) but had witnessed the horrifying results: the concussions that killed many of their friends, or buried them alive in their bunkers. The B-52 strikes had paralyzed them with fear, and their descriptions were dramatic—the bomb path that began a mile away and walked toward them, wham, wham, wham, wham; the ground under them shaking harder with each explosion; then pitching and rocking.

While the Northerners talked about missing their homes and about their unhappy sojourn in the South, the Vietcong defectors often complained about the Northerners who were filling up their units, taking the places of their dead friends. Times were hard for the Vietcong; their units were short on food and ammo and they were finding it progressively more difficult to recruit. In many of the contested villages that had been fertile ground for the Vietcong, village boys wouldn't even talk to the recruiters and would hide when they came around. As a result North Vietnamese fillers began to play an ever greater role in the Southern revolutionary forces. We learned, for example, that the Trang Bang district unit, equivalent of a company, had a full strength of sixty men. But the unit had been decimated, and by 1969 almost half were NVA fillers. And many of the Southern Communists, whose territory it was, were fed up. They were fed up with having North Vietnamese on their backs, having a North Vietnamese as their company commander or platoon leader or squad leader. But most of the problems and stresses could be attributed to one primary cause—the aggressiveness of U.S. forces. American units would sweep through the Ho Bo Woods to mop up after a B-52 strike and they'd bury four hundred or so people. And that kind of thing would happen in place after place. All during 1969 and 1970 we kept getting reports of severe enemy casualties. The VC couldn't tie down battalion after American battalion as they did in 1966, '67, and into '68. And as they became less effective, their demoralization grew.

Within a few months after we were up and running, we began producing fairly detailed intelligence about enemy troop strength, losses, and North Vietnamese integration into VC units, among other subjects. We also started finding out about the National Liberation Front—the NLF. In June 1969, the NLF announced the establishment of the Provisional Revolutionary Government, the "sole legitimate representative" of the South Vietnamese people, as the propaganda had it. But what we were discovering was that the NLF itself, let alone its new creation, was simply a skeleton organization. As the NLF heading in the card catalog filled out, we began to see the pattern. We would identify committees that apparently duplicated the Lao Dong (Communist Party) committees. There would be the same structure, the same sections and hierarchy. But whereas a party committee might comprise eight or ten or even fifteen people, the counterpart NLF committee would have a chief and only one other person, or perhaps no others. Even the key units—the current affairs section or the military affairs section—would have no more than one or two warm bodies. The only section that was staffed at all would be the entertainment/culture/propaganda committee—the traveling troupes of actors and musicians that sometimes included well-known performers. But other than that, the National Liberation Front was a paper organization, a magician's conjuring trick. And normally even the illusion only existed at the province level; rarely did we turn up even a paper committee in a district or a village.

Moreover, as our bank provided us with an increasing number of identities, we could see that several members on every NLF province committee were Lao Dong, Communist Party men. So even this poor skeleton of an organization was controlled by the party—in exactly the same way the Japan Soviet Society was controlled by well-placed members of the Japan Communist Party. Except, of course, that the Japan Soviet Society at least was a full-fledged organization, even if it was a front. The NLF didn't have that much dignity.

As this understanding dawned on us we were taken aback, even shocked to a certain extent. Of course we had known that the revolution in the South was controlled and supplied by the North, that is, by the Hanoi Politburo. Yet with all the worldwide information that was being cranked out (and believed) about how the NLF was a real, autonomous entity, a separate South Vietnamese nationalist movement, I don't think we were quite prepared for the full truth of it. But when you looked at the structure of the thing you could see precisely how it worked, and it was total baloney. We'd interview twenty-five or thirty cadres from a district and each one of them would tell us the same thing: The NLF? It was a laugh.

As we found out about this, we turned our attention away. There was no point in developing anybody inside the NLF. They knew nothing about what was going on. They only received propaganda material to pass out in those areas they supposedly covered. We surely didn't need any spies there. The PRP (People's Revolutionary Party, as the Lao Dong, or Communist Party, was known in the South) was the name of the game. They received the directives right down to the village level. We were looking for someone who was in the party at a decent level; that was the individual we wanted as a spy.

Although the Lao Dong controlled Vietcong activity, that did not mean that most of the VC were Communists. Some of the regroupees from the North could talk to you ad nauseam about dialectical materialism, the oppression of the workers and peasants, the worldwide struggle against imperialism, and so on. But the fighters for the most part wouldn't know dialectical materialism from a rice bowl, as one Phoenix adviser put it. You'd mention a term to them, ask them about it, they'd look at you blankly and say, "Huh?" They didn't know anything about it. Nor did they know much about the Communist Party. What they did know was their political officer, and they would go to some lengths to stay out of trouble with him. "No, no," they'd say, "I never wanted any problems with that guy." So while ideology was not a motivator, party discipline unquestionably was. All the Vietcong cadres understood that the Lao Dong had the control, and that it was the party political officer who was the key man.

Other information we were able to provide during this period included targeting data for the B-52 Arc Light bombings of enemy base areas in Military Region Three and across the border in Cambodia. Many of our sources had been in Cambodia with their units or in hospitals, and from our debriefings we were able to specify coordinates, especially in Mimot, the site of Hanoi's Central Office for South Vietnam, COSVN, and north of Mimot along the Mekong River. By the spring of 1970 we had become quite good at this; we were able to identify enemy units, approximate numbers in units, and quite exact coordinates. Our sources would come in from one of these areas and they would draw us maps. (Vietnamese, expecially those who had been guerrillas for any length of time, tended to be excellent map readers and map drawers.) Sources could (and did), for cxample, point out precisely where COSVN was located; they would draw it, indicating trees and streams and other specific features. And they could tell us precise distances—from this point here it is twelve klicks due north to the COSVN alternate headquarters below where the Mekong makes a U-bend, or five klicks west to a trail terminus and rest area, or twelve klicks southeast to a certain supply dump.

Often they knew the region intimately. They had been chased from one side of the border to the other by American actions and they had had a bellyful of experience moving around frantically in an attempt to avoid bombing raids. We were able to take the maps they drew, transpose their drawings onto our own detailed maps, and come up with precisely located targets, which we then sent in by cable, providing a "box" of coordinates for the bombers. These included the Ho Bo Woods, the Straight Edge Woods near Go Dau Ha (which the B-52s just blew away), and Mimot, as well as other North Vietnamese Army and Vietcong bases on both sides of the border, from Parrot's Beak up to Fishhook. Despite the domestic furor over the "secret bombings," that sector of Cambodia was, exactly as the United States government said it was, almost entirely a sanctuary, supply center, and concentration area for North Vietnamese units. The targeting requests we received through the commanding general of U.S. Second Field Forces at Long Binh included explicit instructions that civilian populations were not to be endangered. We were to limit ourselves strictly to military targets. It required care to comply with those instructions on targeting inside Vietnam, but on the other side of the border there was very little civilian population and almost nothing in terms of innocent peasants. Any Cambodians in that area were likely to be Khmer Rouge, and no one had any compunctions about hitting them along with the VC and NVA.

We were also able to report the consequences of Arc Light strikes, as well as provide targeting for them. Within weeks of a significant series of strikes, we would be interrogating a new batch of defectors for whom those strikes had proved the last straw. One interesting fact was that most often they knew when the bombers were on their way and they knew the general direction of the attack, although not the exact target. From our own headquarters we were aware that Russian radar trawlers located in the Pacific beyond the Philippines tracked the bombers, checking speed, altitude, and headings, and relayed the information to the North. Commonly, the targeted base areas would receive word an hour or so ahead of time. But still the VC and NVA units couldn't run fast enough. And we learned too about their evasive procedures; if, for example, they thought a strike was heading for Mimot, they would take off to the northwest, toward the secondary complexes. Of course we included that in the targeting information.

With all the information gathering and analysis we were doing in the months after setting up the system, I barely had time to look around. Working twelve or more hours a day I oversaw the interrogations and pored over the forms and reports coming in from our own operation and from the provinces, trying always to focus the effort more effectively and identify operational leads and potentially significant sources. I was always strapped for time and so was not happy when one day a cable came in from Saigon Station asking me to fly down to the Phoenix school in Vung Tau to give a class of new Phoenix advisers a lecture on how best to utilize the Provincial Interrogation Centers to obtain intelligence for their program.

My first impulse when I read it was to make a paper airplane out of the cable and toss it out the window. This PIC thing just would not die, however fervent my wishes. And the centers were not only a worthless pain in the ass, they were also a minefield. Whatever Charlie Timmes's report to Ted Shackley had been like, the PIC program was still considered a hinge of Agency–special police co-operation. And, in the Vietnamization phase we had recently entered, all the emphasis was on expanding the Vietnamese role in operations, exactly contrary to the direction I was taking in Bien Hoa. Bad-mouthing Vietnamese capabilities and running down a highly visible Vietnamese-led program in public was an excellent way to get persona non grata'd out of the country. I did not want to go down to Vung Tau in the worst way, as I told Loren. "You have to do it," he said, "you have no choice. They want you; they feel you're the most knowledgeable about this. But you will have to smooth it over a little. Don't lie to them, but try to give them some hope. Just don't blow the PICs out of the water." "But, Loren, really," I began, "what the hell am I supposed to say?" "Tell them about the design," Loren answered, his face deadpan. "Tell them about the wonderful concept, tell them where the PICs are located, tell them any damn thing. Just don't go overboard."

At the Vung Tau airport the officer in charge picked me up, a little bald-headed fat guy. "Oh, Orrin," he said, "you're going to enjoy this. This is really a fine group of officers." I knew that, he didn't have to tell me. Almost always the Phoenix advisers were very fine officers, and after a short time on the job they became very frustrated officers. My idea was to address these officers in a leisurely manner. I was the last speaker of the afternoon and I was supposed to be on for an hour. But I would try to go on late and leave early, using the excuse that I had to catch the last courier back to Bien Hoa.

In the lecture room of the Phoenix school there were twenty-five or thirty captains and majors waiting for me. And in the back of the room sat one of Ted Coleburne's staff officers from Saigon, there to listen to and report whatever it was that I said. I started, as I had planned, to talk about the interrogation centers in a general way, describing their history, the concept behind them, the special construction, and so on. But the Phoenix officers weren't dummies, and before long some loudmouthed major butted in with

"For Chrissakes, Mr. DeForest, you're not telling us very much. How the hell do the goddam things work?"

He was right, of course, so I decided to shove it, just go through the process for them, though I'd still try to keep it relatively low-keyed. "Well," I said, "when prisoners are picked up or captured, they're usually beaten by ARVN field intelligence to get immediately useful information. Then they go into the interrogation center. But as you know, or as you will soon learn, most of them are categorized as 'Vietcong suspects.' There are very few captures of Class A or Class B prisoners, so usually they do not have much information. When you visit the centers you will find that conditions are harsh; they're not the most conducive to gathering intelligence. I believe that is a mistake and that we ought to correct it. Consequently, when you are out in a district or a village, you are going to have to start working on penetrating the local party committee yourselves. That's what Phoenix needs to do, and that's the direction we're taking in Bien Hoa."

Beyond that I wasn't interested in discussing our program. I did not want some partial report getting back to Saigon Station about an unauthorized, unilateral operation going on in Region Three, so I evaded most of the questions. Nothing worthwhile could come out of a more detailed description of what we were doing, and with the Station guy sitting in the back of the room I did not want to come out flatly and say that Ted Shackley's PICs were no good. So the general tenor was "get out there and give it your best shot. Talk to them, get some rapport established, give them some cookies and a Coke. Anything to get them talking." And that's all I could tell them.

Given my performance in that lecture, I was a little surprised when a few weeks later our good old jarhead Captain Zale in Saigon sent a cable asking me to lecture the special police trainees on the techniques of interrogation. Resigned, I took Sonny along as an interpreter for a presentation to about a hundred cadets at the Special Branch training compound in Saigon. But when I got up on the podium, I found myself looking out at a hundred zombies sitting there staring off into space. They didn't move, didn't hear a thing. They just stared at the ceiling, or out the window, or sat there deeply enmeshed in their own little world with their eyes glazed over. There wasn't an ounce of enthusiasm or interest in the whole crowd, and not a single question, during or after. The special police trainees didn't care in the least about "techniques of interrogation." What did it matter how you might establish rapport with a prisoner or authenticate a story? Just slap the dogshit out of him, that's the whole ball game. Pour water down his throat, he'll start talking. It's an old Asian custom.

Toward the end of 1969 I was so loaded down with intelligence I couldn't get out from under it. We were getting reports out as fast as we could type them. The bank was growing by leaps and bounds, with more and more authenticated information. The subject files on Cu Chi, Trang Bang, and other focal spots were burgeoning. I knew I needed to be able to step back, spend more time going over records carefully to identify operational leads, and especially to look for that opening, for a spy, for someone to develop.

So it came as tremendous news to hear at the end of the year that I would be getting some help. Lou Bishop, a contract officer who had already spent two tours in Vietnam, was being assigned to the Bien Hoa Provincial Interrogation Center, which meant, of course, that I could grab him myself. The cable announcing Lou's arrival also included a partial bio; the full 201 file would be sent later. The bio revealed that in civilian life Bishop had been a teacher; he had an M.A. in English. With all the information waiting to be reported, the thought of having a good writer on board made me want to shout for joy.

My first impressions of Lou Bishop were positive. He was quiet, soft-spoken and bright; he had a self-effacing manner and seemed as if he'd be an easy person to work with. When Bill tested him he came out as well above average intelligence, but also a real loner, a double plus loner. When I asked what he had done in Four Corps, his previous assignment, he said he had assisted the regional interrogator and had also worked as a special police adviser. "In essence," he said, "I did nothing." This was obviously not a person gilding the lily or building himself up for a new boss. "I knew the special police were lying to me about everything. We couldn't check anything; we certainly never authenticated anything. You know what happens when you send the traces in to Saigon, what you get back? That's the kind of checking we could do."

Over the next month or two I found that behind his retiring manner Lou was indeed sharp and perceptive. He picked things up quickly. He was also quite a good, fast writer. Before long he understood what I was trying to do and how I wanted it done. He grasped the entire concept of the data bank and the interrogation techniques. And he was good at them himself. He was capable of working on his own, initiating ideas and implementing them independently. In a short time I knew I had found not just another employee but a deputy.

In early 1970 Loren Snowcroft left the Bien Hoa base to become
CIA chief of Station in Taiwan. He made his G-16, a promotion he
had not been at all sure of, given Ted Shackley's earlier unhappiness with him. Still, by the time Loren left, base reporting was up
to twenty a month. With the continued growth of the data bank,
more effective interrogations, and the deepening of our understanding and knowledge, even more productive times were ahead.
Loren was leaving the base in far better shape than he found it.

We had a lovely farewell party for Loren, then Bill Todd and I
drove him to the airport. "Well, Orrin," he said, "now you can fight
with the new guy about where you go from here. You do have to
stop by and see me, though, on some of your travels. You know I'll
want to hear how things are coming along." On that note Loren
Snowcroft left and the new man, Don Gregg, came in. There was
no transition period; Gregg hadn't wanted one. I could appreciate
the new chief's wanting to start with a clean slate, but the abrupt-
ness seemed strange. "I talked to him on the telephone," said
Loren. "He'll be coming out after I leave. The guy doesn't even
want to sit down and chat with me I guess." Loren took it as a kind
of slap in the face. And it was unusual that a new man wouldn't
want to have even a brief orientation from his predecessor. Bill and
I wondered what kind of person we were about to welcome as our
boss. All we knew about him was that he had been chief of operations in another Asian country—the third man—so this was a promotion. Oddly, the grapevine was silent; his reputation had not
preceded him. Don Gregg was a mystery man.

6

ROLL UP

When Don Gregg arrived at the Monastery the first thing
he did was make a tour of the offices to introduce himself. Tall, slim, and gray-haired, he seemed amiable enough, but
aloof. After a few moments I had the clear impression I was talking
to one of the Agency's Ivy Leaguers (or what I considered an Ivy
Leaguer), proper, but certainly not the buddy type, not a man with
much warmth in his personality. He had heard about me, he said,
though when he didn't say anything more I wasn't quite sure how
to interpret the remark. He probably means it as a compliment, I
told myself. I knew Loren had left him a letter in which he described the data-bank operation in enthusiastic terms. But after
another word or two Gregg rather abruptly excused himself and
went back to his office, leaving me feeling that interpersonal skills
were not my new boss's strong suit.

The next week or two was more of the same. When we passed in
the hall he would say good morning or ask how things were going.
And that was it. There was no attempt to sit down and get an
understanding of the interrogation program. There was no attempt
to create a relationship, not even a working relationship, either
with me or any of the other base officers. Lou's opinion confirmed
mine. The man was, we thought, seriously insecure, his standoffish

manner largely a matter of self-protection. He adopted the role of detached manager rather than hands-on chief executive officer primarily, we believed, because he simply did not know what to do. He had no experience in Vietnam, was not conversant with the problems, and thought it best to let those who were carry on, rather than get involved himself. Maybe because I was used to Loren's earthy egalitarianism, Gregg's manner put me off, though I also understood that his was not the worst possible style of management. He didn't seem to be a man who was likely to take risks or make great commitments. But by the same token neither would he allow his inexperience to lead him into great mistakes.

Pretty soon I had concluded that the relationship between me and the new base chief would be one of live and let live, and once I had accepted that it didn't seem all that bad. But Bill Todd was a different story. One morning I was picking up my correspondence in Susie's office. A few steps down the hall was the radio room where we had a direct phone line to Saigon Station. When I came in I had noticed that Bill was on the phone there. Another phone that hooked into the same line was on Don Gregg's desk, and as I shuffled through my cables Don stormed out of his office and down the hall. "Goddammit, Todd," I heard him say, "get off that telephone. I've got to use it." I was a little shocked: Gregg was usually so restrained. Then I heard a half-garbled, angry "you and that fuckin' test." He was really pissed off and I couldn't imagine why. Bill was upset too. He was chief of operations, the number three man, and he didn't appreciate the treatment. In his office a few minutes later he told me, "Orrin, I am not going to be around very long. That guy is after my ass for some reason and I don't know what it is."

Whatever it was, Bill was right. Within thirty days he was gone, transferred to Saigon base to work on drug trafficking. What the problem was between him and Gregg I never did find out, though what it meant for me was that a good friend and ally was no longer around. With George Tanaka having finished up his tour, Loren leaving, and now Bill gone, I felt like the last of the old guard. I wondered if I was on the block too, and I began to suspect that maybe I was.

Before Bill left we did an overview of what his findings were on the hundreds of tests he had done of the Vietnamese. "What we've come up with," he said, "is that by and large they are Internalizers —I's—unlike, for instance, the Japanese. They're reflective people, thoughtful people, people who fantasize a lot, who probably dream of things they'd like to have or they'd like to be. I'm sure they fantasize like mad about the goodies they see on television. They like to divorce themselves from reality to an extent. You'll find a lot of I's, also a lot of R's, Rigids—they like to do one thing at a time. Once they're involved in something they will concentrate on it and do it more or less systematically. And they'll want to finish one job before starting to think about something else.

"Another thing, when you're dealing with defectors, you're dealing with I's, more than likely with IF's and IFA's. F is flexible, they're capable of seeing the other side, and they're looking at the other side. The classical defector is an IF. People who perceive that maybe their situation is wrong. ER's, on the other hand, can go along for years in a straight line and they don't see anything outside of it; they don't perceive, for example, the values that might lie behind their supposed enemy's thinking or objectives. They won't engage with what might at first seem an alien idea, like political freedom; they'll figure it's a waste of time. But an IF is going to mull it over. He might have it in mind for years, he might fantasize about what it could mean, and eventually he's the one who is going to say, 'Screw it, I'm leaving.' So the IF is your potential defector; it's the ER who's your stoned hard charger. We are also seeing a lot of A's here. These guys need people; they really like being part of the social life."

Bill Todd's departure was a loss, especially after Loren Snowcroft's. But there was not much time to mourn. Just before Gregg came I had acquired two more houses, making five now, and even those weren't sufficient to handle all the interrogating. Things had just gotten too big and the data bank was snowballing. We had processed almost all the region's *hoi chanh* by this time, and from the provinces every decent new source was coming in to Colonel Dinh, who then shipped them over to me. We were overwhelmed. Reports flooded in from Hau Nghia, Long An, and Binh Duong—the provinces where advisers were following the procedure. The advisers who didn't weren't good at the procedure, or didn't like it. In Tay Ninh, for example, the adviser who had taken John Pinossa's place was an ex–Special Forces sergeant who had developed a dislike for me and didn't hide it. "Fuck your procedures, Orrin," he told me, and he didn't use them at all. But he was an exception.

In the data-bank trailers I had ten women working and one man, Mr. Thiet, a chubby little guy who supervised the typing, the filing, and the research on requests from the province case officers. Lou now had Buffalo Number One and Gekko Number One, two interpreters, working for him, while I had Albert, Mingo, Bang, Sonny, and Tien Number Three. There were seven interrogator/interpreters altogether, all of them fairly well trained and some of them on their way to becoming case officers in their own right.

Reviewing the forms that crossed my desk, I'd watch for sources who might be useful operationally, either by making contact with an old Vietcong friend, or by cultivating a mutual friend or a family member who might be a better contact, or perhaps in some other way. When I found a likely candidate I'd have Chieu Hoi Lan test him, to see what his intelligence level was and whether he was the kind of guy we could put to work with some assurance that he would follow through. If he was an extreme loner (a U double plus or triple plus), we'd have to be wary of him going into a shell if he were under pressure; if he was an extreme sociable (an A double or triple plus), he would be prone to waver on the job, be likely to have his mind on his friends and family, be highly susceptible to their influence, and might not take on something he thought they wouldn't like.

By now the data bank contained more than twenty thousand cards, the preponderance of them on the Hau Nghia and Tay Ninh districts of Trang Bang, Cu Chi, Duc Hoa, Duc Hue, Go Dau Ha, Bien Hoa, Tan Uyen, Di An, Rach Gia, and Can Giouc, and also on the Binh Duong districts of Tri Tam, Ben Cat, and Phu Hoa. We were concentrating on Cu Chi and Trang Bang. These were the tough areas—the Saigon corridor, an arrow pointing directly from COSVN to the capital.

Among the subject headings swelling the catalog were the tunnels of Cu Chi. Originating back in Vietminh days, the tunnels formed a vast, complex underground network used by thousands of people as headquarters areas, supply depots, quarters for troops, and jump-off points for certain kinds of missions. The entire Vietcong Subregion One military and political sections were down in the Cu Chi tunnels. Other tunnel complexes ran along the Saigon River and honeycombed the Ho Bo Woods. The Vietcong and the Vietminh before them were like gophers; they had tunneled everywhere. You could enter these tunnels on the outskirts of the Cu Chi market and walk all the way to Trang Bang district underground—more than ten kilometers. From time to time, VC teams would pop out from camouflaged holes right inside our 25th Division's Cu Chi base camp and shoot half a dozen GIs before disappearing into the ground. From various sources we were able to get detailed diagrams showing how far the tunnels extended, where one system hooked up with another, and where many of the outlets were. One prisoner we took showed us the entrance to the Subregion One security section bunkers that sat on a vast complex dug to a depth of more than thirty feet. There were troops down there, he said, but they were below any area that could be affected by most bombs. They had a dozen escape routes that spread out like a fan and could get out under any circumstances. Another source drew a complete picture of the Subregion One hospital complex, located right on the Saigon River. The hospital went down fifty or sixty feet and included large tunnels with wards and surgeries, all of it lit by a generator-driven electrical system. When we got that drawing, Albert looked at me and said, "Ong Gia, you know what's going to happen if we turn this in." I did. The place would be bombed. The hospital was one diagram I kept in my files without reporting.

But the rest of it we mapped and turned over to Colonel Thao and to the 25th Division commander. We even put in a strike ourselves on the security section. But do what we might, the tunnel system was never put out of business. The 25th would find the holes, go down with their tunnel rats, kill people, put explosives in, bomb them. All of it was done methodically. But regardless, large parts of the system survived and continued to be used.

The tunnels were fascinating, but they were never one of our primary targets. There were too many other things to do. Trang Bang, for example. The data bank was probably most complete on Trang Bang. We had hundreds of defectors from there; the American 25th Division had been through the area a hundred times on sweeps and operations and had brutalized the 101st NVA. They had overrun the military intelligence section, overrun the Trang Bang current affairs section, and had chased most of the VC units way up into the Ho Bo Woods. One result of these operations was that beaten and discouraged VC would walk into Trang Bang city, put their hands up, and announce "Me *hoi chanh.*" As a result, we had a lot of sources coming through.

With all the new people we were processing, by the middle of 1970 I was in a seven-day-a-week job. Even then I could not begin to keep up with the flow of intelligence; I needed more case officers badly. Lou was working just as hard as I was, concentrating on Subregion Five while I took Subregion One, and as time went by I was more and more impressed with his work. Every morning he would come in to review situations he thought were possibly significant. "I'm interrogating this guy now, Orrin," he'd say, showing me the file. "What do you think, should I pursue it?" I soon recognized that Lou's tentative manner was in fact a learning style, that he was consciously building knowledge and experience, becoming more sure of himself all the time.

Lou was so capable that all I'd have to do was give him hints about directions to take or things I wanted him to do, but as effective as he was, his manner never became forward or assertive. Consequently I almost fell off my chair when one day he rushed into my office exclaiming, "Hey, Orrin, look at this. This is pretty damn hot stuff!" He told me about a source he had been working with, a defector from Subregion Five, a cultural officer from the regional headquarters, the equivalent of a captain. "He's a pretty damn sharp guy," said Lou. I've already been talking to him for two or three days and he's totally cooperative. He's happy as hell to be out and wants to solidify his position with us. He's identified everybody in Subregion Five headquarters. I'm really going after this one, Orrin. I've got some great leads. The guy says he has a good friend who's still in—a security officer. He says he can contact him. How about *that!*"

Lou was so excited he was taking the interrogation reports down to the data bank himself while his interpreter kept talking to the source. So even while the interrogation was going on, Lou was busy confirming everything he could from the card files. Boy, did he want things to check out. And they did; he was able to confirm most of the information with three, four, and sometimes five sources.

Lou's source, the VC captain, had had it with the war. He had come to feel that the fighting was almost over and that Saigon was going to win. Now he wanted to help. To an outsider this kind of decision and this kind of willingness might have seemed odd, but after having screened thousands of defectors I knew that it wasn't. On the contrary, it was a fairly typical behavior pattern. Here was a cultural officer, a long-term Lao Dong member, a regroupee who had spent years in the North. But once he was in the right frame of mind, he could just say, "Fuck it, it's all over." It was common; the Vietcong were susceptible to that way of thinking. But it did give you something to reflect on. The Japanese, as I knew so well from my World War Two experience, would die before thinking of doing such a thing. But then, after it was all over, they were your buddies. My B-29 crew had slaughtered them, and they had slaughtered my friends. But after the war I had Japanese friends whom I would trust with my life, without an instant's hesitation, true buddies. And that was the kind of thing the Vietnamese were capable of doing midstream, without waiting for the war to be over.

According to the captain, his friend who was still in was smart, but high strung and itchy. He thought the friend might be developed. And he knew he could reach him through the friend's old aunt, who had raised him. The captain himself knew the auntie well; they themselves were distantly related. He could pay her a visit and tell her that he wanted to talk to her nephew the next time he came in.

According to the captain, his friend visited his aunt every couple of weeks. The party allowed cadres to contact and visit their families, though they were a lot more careful with young guerrillas who might have been sucked in by the recruiter and were not whole-hearted volunteers. (They were right to be careful; thousands of those young kids defected.) But the friend was a sophisticated officer, a man who had been in the party for a long time. He could go back and forth almost at will.

After doing all his homework on the case Lou decided to go ahead with it and have the captain make an approach through the friend's aunt. She was an old woman whose husband was senile and had been unable to work for several years. She struggled to take care of him and support the two of them by hawking fish at the village market. So Lou gave the captain 25,000 piasters to give to the auntie, the first of what would be monthly payments if the friend would co-operate.

When the captain met his friend, the aunt had already taken the money and was on our side. Starting with that advantage, the captain explained that he was not working for South Vietnam's government, but for Americans. These Americans, he said, were super guys who took care of him very well. They had gotten him out of the Chieu Hoi Center and had given him a house and more money than he ever dreamed of (which wasn't much). You can trust them, he said. They don't want you to do anything or to jeopardize yourself in any way. All they want is information. They can set up a dead drop and you can put something in it once a week or so, just whatever you see that might be interesting. Meanwhile your aunt will have something for herself for the first time in her life. She and the old man won't be starving to death for a change.

When the friend agreed, as we suspected he would, the captain was sent back for the second step. He was to tell his VC friend that everything sounded all right, but that it wasn't enough just to agree. The Americans were asking him to do something to establish his bona fides, something that would indicate to them that he really was going to cooperate. The captain was to explain to his friend that this was just one of the Americans' normal procedures, something that was always done in this kind of situation. They wouldn't go forward without it.

The friend's answer, as the captain reported it to Lou, was un-believable. "Well," he said, thinking about it for a moment, "I can blow up the Long Khanh ammo dump. Would that be OK?" It wouldn't be hard. He could put some plastic in there, set the timer, be five miles away before anything happened.

And that is exactly what he did. He said he would blow the dump at such and such a time on a particular date, and he was as good as his word. Late that day Lou met with Colonel Thao, who knew nothing at all of this situation, and asked for a report on activity in Subregion Five that day. "Boy," said Colonel Thao, "they blew the shit out of something in Long Khanh. Gigantic explosions in the jungle." "That's interesting," said Lou. "What do you think it might have been?" "Well, I don't really know, but a little while later we picked up a radio intercept requesting an emergency supply of ammunition. What do you think happened out there?"

As a demonstration of intention, this wasn't half bad. A day later the friend left a letter in the dead drop. "I blew it up. Are you happy now?" This was fantastic. This was a daring guy. From that moment on we called him the Mad Bomber rather than his formal crypt, Piano. So now we had an agent in place; he was being handled by our source, who, in turn, was being handled by Lou, who, in turn, was reporting to me. The Mad Bomber was the first spy we developed. Lou had managed the whole thing flawlessly. He should have been promoted on the spot; but though I requested it, he wasn't.

We serviced our spy's dead drop once a week. It was in a hollow at the bottom of a tree trunk on the outskirts of a little hamlet. During the day our handler could go up there to buy some bread or something, fool around in the market a little, then go off into the brush to collect or leave messages. Occasionally, if something unusual came up, the handler would set up a live meeting at the aunt's house. The aunt herself was having a ball with her monthly twenty-five thousand p, burying most of it in her backyard and no doubt feeling comfortable as hell.

The Mad Bomber was an actual spy, a party member—that was the key. If you don't have a party member you don't have a spy; you just have another human being. Only a party member has access to directives. In his position, the Mad Bomber had access to all Vietcong directives in Subregion Five, whose security section was directly subordinate to General Tra's Security Section in COSVN, the heart of enemy operations. Subregion Five included Long Khanh, Bien Hoa, Binh Duong, and parts of Phuoc Long and Binh Long. The chief of the subregion had all the province, district, and village structures under his direction, including local forces, which were coordinated with the main-force units, both command structures subordinated directly to COSVN.

From here on in we knew about everything that was going to happen in those places. We'd get it practically verbatim. The Mad Bomber would read the directives, write them down, then leave his report in the dead drop. And his information matched exactly with what the Reaper in Subregion One's Tay Ninh province was telling us, to the extent that the two jurisdictions overlapped. All the COSVN resolutions would be reported from both agents in detail, including both military and political intentions. North Vietnamese units, although they were directed by COSVN, would not do anything in the region without the concurrence and cooperation of the Subregion Five commander, so we knew about them as well.

We would get the material, write up the report, hand carry it to the base reports officers, and keep a sanitized copy—with no names or crypts—in our files. The reports officer would look at it, evaluate it, rewrite it to the extent necessary, then send it encoded to Saigon Station. We might also give Colonel Thao a sanitized version of material that pertained to military activity in his area that would affect ARVN troops. And Colonel Thao would call in the air strikes and artillery strikes, even ground action on occasion. It was very effective. We were kicking the shit out of them, which created more defections, which led to more information. And on it went.

Shortly after Lou developed the Mad Bomber, our boss, Don Gregg, decided to have a staff meeting in Vung Tau, including all the base officers and a couple of key personnel from each of the provinces. It was to be his introductory party, a chance for him to meet everybody and exchange a few words in a holiday beach setting. At the staff meeting, Gregg suggested that it might be a good idea if the interrogation program focused on a few especially important areas. That surprised me a bit, because Don had just not seemed that interested, but this remark indicated that he had indeed given the problem some thought. I was happy to tell him that we had already focused the effort, and though we were having success in several areas, at this point Trang Bang district was the most likely field of opportunity, not only for identifying the Vietcong infrastructure but for developing operational leads.

When the meeting was over, the twenty-five or so of us who were there went down to the beach to swim, lay around in the sun, and enjoy an early-evening barbecue. It was an immensely relaxing interlude. When it got dark we went back to the Phoenix school bachelor officers' quarters where we were staying. After a shower I took a couple of the others for a tour of the city, where I had spent eight months in 1966 as a criminal investigations warrant officer.

Vung Tau, the designated R and R center for Two Corps, Three Corps, and Four Corps, was a place I knew well.

With Vietnamization in full swing Vung Tau seemed slightly less jammed than it had when I was trying to police it, but just slightly. There were still more than 400,000 U.S. military personnel in South Vietnam, and a healthy percentage of them seemed to be carousing in Vung Tau's streets. As usual, most of the activity was centered in an amazing three-square-block area that contained, if I remembered right, three hundred and fifty bars, ten barbershops (where you could even get a haircut as well as the real house specialties), five or six large hotels (most of which were not hotels), an unknown number of back-room opium dens, and a variety of other entertainment opportunities for GIs with a three-day pass and a thousand bucks' leave pay in their pockets. The first time I laid eyes on Vung Tau I had found myself wondering what the Roman army or the Mongol army had in the way of playgrounds for their troops. No doubt they had been spirited places, but it was hard to believe they were anywhere near as rowdy as Vung Tau.

That evening, like every evening, Vung Tau's small streets were lit up and awash with GIs. The shops and restaurants were packed, and so were the bars—the Blue Goose, the Korean Bar, the Kim Bar, the Melody Bar; they were all still there and still doing a land-office business. So was the Grand Hotel bar. Stopping in for a beer, we sat there and took in the scene. To me it seemed as if time had stopped. There were the same boys I had watched four years ago, sitting around the tables, each one with a girl on his lap, playing around, a hand here, a hand there, the girls giggling and kissing them, the boys drinking their beer and laughing as if there were no tomorrow.

I had always thought of the place as a kind of half-crazed fun house, a demented Disneyland where the soldiers came to let out the frustrations of war. In Vung Tau nothing at all would surprise you. GIs would be parading up and down the streets, getting their haircuts, their oral sex, getting into fights with one another, or with an Australian soldier, or with a barbershop girl who perhaps hadn't been paid. As a CID officer I had early on thrown up my hands and surrendered—except of course for serious crimes. What were you going to do? You had to have a sense of humor about it. They were all just out of it, out of it and having such a good time it was comical to watch them, a comedy of errors every night.

On April 29, shortly after we returned from our Vung Tau inter-lude, the Cambodian incursion kicked off. Although the American and South Vietnamese cross-border attack created surprise and shock in the United States, in Vietnam there was nothing secret about it and certainly nothing shocking. Cambodia's central and northeastern provinces had long before been turned into a base area and supply conduit for Vietcong and North Vietnamese troops operating in Three Corps, and the decision to disrupt the enemy's logistics in order to alleviate pressure on our own troops was a simple matter of military common sense. For the past year, our operation had been providing B-52 targeting information on the Cambodian sanctuaries from the lower part of Laos all the way down to the border of Chau Doc in Four Corps.

The only problem with this incursion was that the coming blow had been telegraphed in a dozen ways. The South Vietnamese army was so thoroughly penetrated that it would have been impossible to keep the secret under any circumstances. As a result the North's army and Vietcong forces had already taken evasive measures: essential COSVN personnel had been moved to temporary bases deeper inside Cambodia, near Kratie. There was, as we knew, little hope for any surprise or even for any significant engagement with the enemy. Nevertheless as American and ARVN troops attacked through border areas, we were instructed to debrief any sources who had information on the effects of the fighting.

As the weeks passed, sources did begin to come in. For the most part what they reported was the destruction of supplies. Aware of what was coming, North Vietnamese and Vietcong forces had indeed fled early, successfully avoiding any large-scale fighting. But they had not had time to take their stockpiles with them. As a result the incursion had succeeded in destroying rice caches, ammunition depots, and weapons factories, in addition to the deserted bases. So while from a combat point of view the operation was not much of a victory—not many casualties were inflicted—the damage done to the Communists' logistical support system was extensive. Our assessment was, in fact, very much as Kissinger and Nixon announced, that the Cambodian incursion bought somewhere in the neighborhood of a year's time. And this was borne out. During the following year there was reduced Vietcong and North Vietnamese activity in the border areas. Tay Ninh, Binh Duong, and Hau Nghia saw lower levels of action, due primarily to the NVA's need to regroup, reestablish supply lines, and rebuild reserves that had been lost.

While intelligence requirements stemming from the Cambodian incursion demanded time and effort, I kept the thrust of our effort focused on Subregion One, in particular Cu Chi and Trang Bang. With so many sources coming in from those areas it was inevitable that eventually we would get a break, and in the summer of 1970 we got two. The first one was interesting. The second was the answer to a case officer's prayers.

The prisoner Tu Duc was a tough little rascal. He had been captured by the Trang Bang Regional Forces who had hit a Vietcong area we had identified for them. Another captured VC had fingered Tu Duc as the chief of the Trang Bang military proselyting section and he eventually admitted it. This was a fairly big deal; in Tu Duc we had our hands on a very successful long-term member of the party, a senior officer.

Tu Duc was not a defector, and he was not very cooperative. But he was facing a major dilemma. He knew that as soon as we released him he would be sent to the ARVN interrogators. And for him that would be a death sentence. They would ask us if he had been cooperative. We'd say, "Not really," and those boys at the National Interrogation Center in Saigon would take it as a challenge; they would beat him to within an inch of his life, at the very least. Tough bastard though he was, Tu Duc wasn't eager to face that fate. He wanted to delay his departure as long as he could. But the only way he could do that was by providing intelligence, something he was very reluctant to do. For him, then, the trick was to make it appear that he was cooperating while never giving us anything too valuable, but also holding out the possibility that more was coming. It was a delicate game, and he played it well.

Interrogating Tu Duc was a show, particularly with Albert, one of the world's great bullshit artists, as the interpreter. "Don't you see," Tu Duc would say after some convoluted, evasive answer, "I'm trying to cooperate with you?" "Come on," Albert would answer. "Who do you think you're talking to here? Look, you don't want to say a lot? OK, but you've got to give us something. You know that and we know that, so why don't you just do it." "Really, Albert, I am trying to cooperate with you guys, but you ask too many questions. You confuse my mind."

Tu Duc's tactics were good, but information dribbled out, as it had to. He told us how the Vietcong did its military proselyting inside the southern army. But when it came to naming specific agents, well, yes, he did have a few agents, but he knew them only by code name. (It was a bunch of shit, of course.) "Tell us about Ba Be then," I said, naming the Trang Bang party secretary, Tu Duc's boss. We had identified Ba Be and profiled him in the data bank from various sources. Tu Duc was so surprised we knew about Ba Be he almost lost his composure. "How's Ba Be getting along? And how about Nam Viet and Phan The?"—two members of the current affairs committee, the district's "politburo." "How do you know them?" said Tu Duc, letting his defenses down for a moment. He was shocked we knew who these people were, and we earned his respect. Realizing that we already knew a lot about these guys, he was willing to talk about them, and we learned a lot from him, but he still managed to say nothing too damaging.

We kept Tu Duc in Albert's apartment during the interrogations, and there he got the usual TLC treatment. Tu Duc was a full-time revolutionary, but his wife was a legal cadre who worked by day in An Tinh, Hanoi's "model revolutionary village" and spent her nights in the tunnels. She too was in the proselyting business, though at a much lower level than her husband. Once we had established a talking relationship with Tu Duc we told him we would be happy to bring his wife in and set her up in the apartment with him. We told him we didn't want to talk to her in any way (we didn't; she had nothing to tell us); we just thought it would make things more comfortable for him to have her there. The fact was it would also make him more reluctant to leave.

Tu Duc could see our game easily enough and at first he resisted the temptation. But two weeks or so into the interrogation his willpower broke down. He told us exactly where his wife would be at what time and asked us to bring her to him. That afternoon Albert took a couple of soldiers and went into An Tinh, something you could do during the day, though God help you if you tried at night. When they found the wife, she was stunned, even more so when Albert told her that Tu Duc was in Bien Hoa living in a private house and that she could come and stay with him.

Surprisingly, even with Mrs. Tu Duc there, Tu Duc himself did not open up much more. He did talk to us; he had to. But there were lines he wouldn't cross, and talking to us at all was creating obvious emotional stress for him. So much so that sometimes I thought he would be better off making a martyr of himself in Saigon. When it was clear to me what kinds of things he would talk about—that is, anything other than direct operationally useful information—I began to concentrate on getting a thorough understanding of An Tinh from him. This place was the real nut. Its strategic location, its relationship with the 101st NVA regiment, its revolutionary fervor, and its standing as a model of Vietcong control all combined to make An Tinh an outstanding target. And frankly, it irked me that Hanoi was so arrogant about it with their "our district" and "our village" bullshit.

An Tinh was a village of some 3,900 people who lived in five separate hamlets. Over the following weeks of in-depth discussions with Tu Duc, we were able to piece together a complete profile of the place: its history, sociology, geography, economy, and political life. We learned where most of the families in town lived, what relations were like among them, who worked where, who traveled at all—say, to Saigon—and who didn't, fact after fact. Aspects of Vietnamese rural life that we knew about in a general or half-intuitive way before now opened up to us in detail and nuance. It was like a graduate course in Vietnamese peasant society, taught by a highly knowledgeable and articulate (if slightly reluctant) native informant.

At the same time we learned a great deal about Loc Hung, the neighboring village to the north, also a hardcore Vietcong stronghold. And when Tu Duc understood that we were fairly well versed already on some particular military subject, the district security section, for example, or the tunnels, or the use of the Saigon River as a supply route, he could be pushed to fill in gaps in our information. So we kept on him, milking everything we could, watching to see if at some point he would not just break altogether and decide to come over.

It was while we were still actively interrogating Tu Duc that our second big break materialized. Every intelligence case officer, like every cop, knows that hard work can uncover leads and create results. But he also knows that more good information comes from walk-ins than from any other source. A witness you didn't know about decides to come forward, someone who participated in a crime makes up his mind to confess, a foreign national with secrets to sell makes a contact, or an agent decides for one reason or another that he wants to defect. Like everyone else, I knew all this. But that didn't prepare me for the call that came in one day from Colonel Dinh, commander of the Corps Interrogation Center. He had just gotten a call from the district chief in Trang Bang. A man who identified himself as the party secretary of An Tinh Village had just turned himself in. Did I want him to pick up this guy and bring him over?

Within a few hours we had the purported village secretary established in a house I kept for VIPs. He was in his mid-thirties, handsome, with a pleasant smile, absolutely nothing that would indicate he had been, until half a day earlier, the most powerful individual in the Vietcong village organization, a man in the direct chain of command that led from the Hanoi Politburo to COSVN right down to the districts and villages. If indeed that was who he was. I let Albert talk to him for a while, to break the ice, then I went over to introduce myself. "His name's Ba Tung," said Albert. "He's scared to death of what the government will do to him, but he says he had to defect." The story Ba Tung told amazed both of us.

One of his commo liaison people, Ba Tung stated, was a beautiful young girl, just fifteen years old, not only extremely attractive, but one of the best workers he had. She had been a special favorite with him. Three days ago she had been raped by a VC village guerrilla. Although the guerrilla threatened to kill her if she said anything about it, he himself had not been able to keep quiet about his "triumph" and had had the poor judgment to brag about it to some of his friends. Inevitably word had gotten back to Ba Tung. "When I went over to her house to talk to her family," he said, "she admitted she had been raped, then broke into tears. The family was very upset. She was so young, and you know what this kind of thing means to us. So that night I had two security people take the guerrilla down to the river and shoot him."

The next day Ba Tung had visited his father and told him about the incident. The father, formerly a high-ranking political officer in the Vietminh, was a famous man in his day. But now he was in his seventies and had retired to his little farm where he raised a few vegetables and looked after his family, as a Vietnamese grandfather does. "You did the right thing," said the father when he heard the whole story, "but you also made a terrible mistake." "Oh," said Ba Tung. "What's that?" "The guy you shot," his father answered, "that guy was a nephew of the Trang Bang district chief of security."

Albert and I looked at each other. If this was true, and it sounded too incredible to have been made up, we could imagine what must have gone through Ba Tung's mind when he heard that. The security cadres were the really bad guys, and we tracked their activities as well as we could, which often wasn't very well. The district cadres handled security for the entire party committee, and for the area. They did thorough background investigations for candidate party members. They also handled assassinations of government hamlet chiefs or policemen, and often the assassinations were horrible. One of their favorite methods was to hang their victim in a tree and split his abdomen open while he was alive. Then they'd leave a note attached to his shirt explaining who had done it and why. It was the kind of thing that had a lasting effect on people who saw it; you didn't easily forget a sight like that. Another thing the security section did was to guide sappers on demolition missions and minelaying expeditions. A security cadre was a knowledgeable and capable comrade. He (sometimes she) was disciplined, loyal, and flinched from very little. For the most part they had been trained by regroupees who had spent years in the North at the party's schools, which themselves had been set up on Russian or occasionally Chinese models, and which taught first-rate procedures and techniques.

When Ba Tung heard what he had done, he knew instantly that the district security chief was already planning his revenge. "Absolutely," said his father. "The only thing you can do is become a *hoi chanh*." And he did it. The next day Ba Tung walked into the Trang Bang district headquarters and gave himself up. Here you had a strong Communist, the son of a leading Communist, and yet family came first. The father wanted to save his son, and the son listened to his father's direction. The Trang Bang district security chief too, another loyal Communist, felt that his duty to avenge his nephew and the family honor came above anything else, certainly above party discipline.

"Ong Gia," said Albert, "it's true. The family would come first in this situation and the father would make the decision." With one part of me, the part that had been taught to think like a Vietnamese, I knew it was true. But the other part couldn't help marveling. Meanwhile Ba Tung sat and smiled at me, very amiably. Oh, said the smile, sorry for my past ten years of sin. Let's be friends now. God only knew what he had been responsible for—the village secretary of Hanoi's model village. But here he was, smiling like a Sunday-school teacher on a picnic. "The test," Bill Todd had told me, "the test says they can defect. They are loyal, yes. But they are also susceptible to blowing it off. All they need is the right stimulus at the right time."

But though I knew how it worked psychologically, and though I had seen it happen so many times, it still amazed me. If a Westerner were to do something against the principles he'd held for years he would have to rationalize it, figure out some justification for it. He'd agonize over it until he had convinced himself that he had done it for some good and sufficient reason. And if he couldn't successfully rationalize what he had done, the decision might torment him for years. But not a Vietnamese. When it's over, it's over. "I'm on the other side now? OK, I'll do what I can to help them." That explained the success of the Kit Carson scouts—former VC who scouted for U.S. Army and ARVN. They'd pick someone up in the field and not infrequently they could turn him right around to go get his former buddies. Bomb the base camp, surprise the ambush. It was difficult for us to understand, but it happened.

Ba Tung was not afraid for his father. His father would not be
blamed for what his son had done, and the Trang Bang security
chief would not dare go after such a famous man. But we did pick
up Ba Tung's wife and children, for whom he certainly did fear. As
he had done just a short time earlier for Tu Duc, Albert went into
the village during the day, while the hard cores were in their bunkers sleeping, and extricated the family. We put the wife and children up in the same house as Ba Tung, all of them eating like
gourmet kings. The interrogation program was beginning to look
like a Vietcong family leave center.

Ba Tung was overjoyed when we got his wife and kids out. Every
morning I'd stop in to talk to him. I'd shake his hand and ask how
things were going, knowing they were a million times better than
he ever dreamed they might be. He loved it. He couldn't believe
his luck. First of all, he thought he would end up in the hands of
ARVN; he'd never put any stock in the amnesty program. He had
been a village secretary for Christ's sake, the key man, and he
didn't have any illusions about what the ARVN or the police might
do to him. Instead he had landed with us, and we were treating
him like royalty. Albert bought him a set of new clothes—slacks,
shirt, sandals. He and his family were eating, really living it up.
Pretty soon he started pinching me on the arm whenever he saw
me, a sign of affection among the Vietnamese.

By this time I was convinced that Ba Tung was telling the truth,
not only about why he came over but about the nitty-gritty of who
was who and what was what in An Tinh. I could sense that the guy
was straight, and it didn't hurt that everything we checked in the
data bank turned up aces. And once Ba Tung got settled, the information just came flooding out. "Ong Gia, you're not going to believe all this," Albert said one day when I checked in on him. He
was more excited than I had ever seen him. "Just look at this. We
got the entire structure of An Tinh village, right down to the last
man. He knows every single person in the village by name, practically everybody in the district. He knows half the guys in Loc
Hung."

I looked at Albert's notes. There was the entire structure and all
of the people in the village and much of the district. Unheard-of
information. In the village section he had seventy-five to a hundred
people on the political and military committees plus another
twenty to thirty in the guerrilla militia. This was a lot, more than
we had estimated. But An Tinh had a dedicated bunch of people,
mainly I thought, because of Ba Tung's leadership. And now we
had Ba Tung.

As we went through the process of checking out and integrating

Ba Tung's information we realized we had a fairly comprehensive picture not only of An Tinh and Loc Hung, but of Trang Bang district as a whole. One interesting facet of the information was the numbers. As we pored over the committee structures and the way the local population was tied into the Vietcong organization, Lou Bishop and I found we could make a decent estimate about the size of the enemy effort. Then, if we extrapolated to other districts we could put together guesstimates on overall numbers.

In Trang Bang alone, we believed, a minimum of eight thousand to ten thousand people was actively participating in the VC effort. And that would be a minimum. Every able-bodied person in An Tinh helped the Vietcong, right down to the twelve-year-old runners. The same went for Loc Hung. That number included sympathizers as well as formal members, but only sympathizers who were actively working for the Vietcong—the suppliers, the loaders, the people who every night were walking down the trails carrying the wounded to medical care or delivering rice and ammunition to the fighters. In our estimation these people had to be counted, because without them the Vietcong would not have been able to function. They were the logistical force, performing the same functions our logistical personnel had to do in order to keep the front-line combat soldier out there. They were, for example, the buyers, peasants who would go to the market, buy a two-hundred-kilo bag of rice, put it on their little cart with a buffalo pulling it, and take it all the way into the Ho Bo Woods, though it might take them all night to make the trip. Multiply that by ten or fifteen guys and you have two to three tons of rice making its way into the woods each night.

Including people who worked at this level in Phu Hoa, Cu Chi, Duc Hue, Duc Hoa, and Go Dau Ha, we might be talking in terms of fifty thousand to sixty thousand Vietcong. And that was without counting the rest of the region: Binh Long, Phuc Long, Long Khanh, Binh Tuy, and Long An. These weren't particularly active places, but there were a lot of Indians out there. Then we looked at each other and said, "My God, you know what we're looking at here? We're looking at a hundred thousand members of the Vietcong in Region Three, let alone the North Vietnamese Army." If we multiplied that by the other military regions on a rough population basis, we were looking at 400,000 to 500,000 people in late 1970, early 1971—that is, after Tet.*

---

* General William Westmoreland's estimates of enemy troop strength became the subject of a controversial CBS documentary which accused him of conspiring to present

. . .

But Ba Tung's information allowed us to do considerably more than estimate numbers. With identifications and addresses of almost all the legal cadres in An Tinh, we were ready to roll up the place, just go in and arrest them, exactly as the Phoenix program was meant to do. And this was precisely what I had in mind.

After I planned the An Tinh roll-up operation I flew to Hau Nghia to go over it with Clint Wilson, the officer in charge, and Colonel Bartlett, the senior province adviser. As I walked in to the meeting neither man knew what I had brought with me to show them. But they did know I had been interrogating Ba Tung, and they were eager to hear how I was doing with him. "Pretty good," I said. "Right now I've got identifications on about fifty legal cadres in An Tinh. I think we can go right out and capture them. The secretary says it'll be easy." Colonel Bartlett's face tensed up and his eyes opened wider. "I don't think," he said slowly, "it's going to be very damn easy in An Tinh village."

I explained to Clint and Bartlett that I wanted to meet with the province chief to fill him in and get his formal approval. My plan was to go in with American choppers, pilots, and chopper crews carrying the Hau Nghia Provincial Reconnaissance Unit company. We could set right down in front of the houses and capture the legal cadres. Ba Tung, I told them, swears that at six or seven in the morning they will be home, which is when we'll arrive. We could even get some illegals who might be in from the boonies visiting their wives and kids.

Thirty minutes later the three of us were sipping tea in the office of the province chief, Colonel Nguyen Van Thanh. This was the first time I had met Thanh, though by reputation he was honest and gung ho, unusual for someone in his position. When I told him what our objective was, he said "Sure, you can do whatever you want. Just tell me exactly how you intend to do it." "Well," I said, "my boss, Don Gregg, wants me to use the PRU in choppers.

---

lower figures than were justified by the intelligence data. Westmoreland's subsequent libel suit against CBS was one of the most highly publicized events of the war's aftermath. The truth was that Westmoreland just did not know. He didn't have the information to base his numbers on. He said 280,000, but extrapolating from our data bank there were that many people in the party alone. CBS was talking in terms of 600,000 or 700,000. But I believe there were even more. Sam Adams, one of CBS' chief sources, was a CIA analyst in Saigon Station who had been given the job of trying to figure out the numbers on the basis of captured documents. But when the Agency wouldn't buy his estimates, he quit. Adams called me during the trial and I generally agreed with his figures.

So one man will go in there in a light helicopter and mark the
houses with orange smoke. We've already identified the houses
from air photos. We know exactly where they are. Then we'll set
down, put a chopper in the front yard and another in the backyard
of each house—we'll use Hueys, with eight or ten PRU in each
one. I'll be in the command chopper with our source, Ba Tung, in
disguise. When the PRU rounds up the people from the houses,
we'll have him identify them." "It'll sure as hell surprise me," said
Colonel Thanh, "if he actually picks out any VC. Do you know
what you're getting into here? An Tinh?" "Well, I said, "we just
want to give it a shot, see what happens. We have no idea what we
might stir up. But Ba Tung says they won't come out of those
houses shooting. They have their wives and children there. But if
they do, we have plenty of protection. We'll have the chopper
gunners sitting on both sides of the houses. The PRU will have
M-79s and they'll be right outside the front door. So if there's any
indication of a fight, we'll just blow them away and get out." "OK,"
said Thanh, "when do you want to do it?"

We picked up the PRU from the Bao Trai airport at six o'clock
the next morning. It was a bit precarious because the area was hot
and VC snipers used to like to get down in the bush around the
runway and cause a little hell. But we didn't think they would take
a chance with so many choppers coming in. One could take right
off and zap them. Although I would be in the command chopper,
I intended to stay well in the background and observe. Felix Rodriguez, our lead pilot, would mark the houses. Then as soon as the
smoke went off, the other chopper pilots would set down immediately and dump the PRU. They'd round up the people; get them
out of the houses and scoop them up. With twelve choppers we'd
be able to hit five houses at a time and still keep a reserve for
emergencies. Although I had offered to take Clint, Colonel Bartlett, and Colonel Thanh along, all three of them declined the invitation.

From the command chopper I watched the CIA's hotshot pilot
Felix Rodriguez in his Loach light helicopter zoom in to mark
the houses. With orange smoke swirling into the morning sky,
the Hueys sat down next to the first targets and PRU troops hit the
houses. There was no shooting. By the time I was on the ground
with my man Albert and Ba Tung, the houses had been emptied
and the people were lined up—husbands, wives, children, cousins,
grandparents, whoever was living there. Then the PRU marched
them by Ba Tung, who was wearing dark glasses and a big fake
mustache, a stupid comic disguise, but good enough so that no one

could tell who he was. Out of the first batch he identified four, three men and a woman. By the time he was finished we had taken twenty-eight cadres, without a single shot. Many of the women and some of the men had tears in their eyes. They didn't know what had hit them.

I watched Ba Tung during the whole operation. I hardly could believe what he was doing. He could have picked out three, or seven, or ten—we would have been happy with anything we got. But he turned over almost a third of the entire village structure: twenty-six legals and two bunker dwellers who were in for the night. Among them was a Subregion One security cadre, a couple in the military section, a couple in the finance section, and an assortment of current affairs personnel and Farmer's Association members. They were all village level except for the security cadre, but the number was staggering. For all intents and purposes we had broken An Tinh, at least temporarily.

Loading everybody into the choppers, we flew back to Bao Trai where we didn't even turn the blades off, just dropped the PRU and continued on to Bien Hoa. There the four Hueys carrying the An Tinh VC put down on the CIA pads across from the Dong Nai River, directly in front of the Monastery. The truck I had ordered was waiting for us, and as the prisoners climbed down from the choppers and walked over to it I noticed Don Gregg standing out on his balcony watching the procession. I looked up at him, and as I did he started clapping his hands in a solitary, but meaningful round of applause.

7

THE N-10 TERRORISTS

When I walked into Don Gregg's office a few minutes later his first words were "Orrin, are these people real?" "Well, yes," I said, "I think they are. As soon as we have a chance to do some checking and talk to them we'll find out for sure." Gregg was not a demonstrative person, but I could see exactly what he was thinking. It was the same thing I was thinking: Damn! The entire 25th Division of the U.S. Army couldn't capture twenty-eight Vietcong.

While I was talking to Gregg in the Monastery, the VC were being distributed among our five houses where conditions were now crowding up considerably. Before long, though, we had brought in enough bedding and had mustered an additional group of Nung guards to keep watch. Then we began the interrogations.

The approach was to confront each one of the prisoners with the intimate knowledge we had of the An Tinh committee sections and to play one off against the other—not a difficult thing to do given the circumstances. "Now, who do you work for?" the interrogator would ask. "Do you work for this guy, or do you work for that guy? We have information you work for this guy." We knew he did and we faced him with it. Shocked and angry as they were, inevitably the answer would come. "Yes, I do work for so-and-so. Yes, I am a

military proselyting cadre. OK, yes, I do have sources." Every one
of the twenty-eight identified himself properly and to one degree or
another began to talk. Running through their minds was the
thought that if they weren't cooperative we would let the special
police know, and then they might be putting their families in danger. They were, after all, from An Tinh, Hanoi's model revolutionary village. We knew that was what they were afraid of, and
although we were actually playing a straight game we didn't go out
of our way to alleviate their fears.

As a result of these interrogations, information snowballed even
more. In a short time we had generated fifty or sixty new identifications. The Subregion One security cadre was a special find; from
him we got IDs of the entire security section, including the half-
dozen executioners, the ones who carried out the subregion's assassinations and other terror assignments. These were the people
you really didn't want to meet, VC Rambos and hit men, exactly
the guys Ba Tung knew would have been after him for killing the
security chief's nephew. We got all their names.

We also got the location of the Subregion One security section
bunker. And a week later, after checking our drawings against aerial photographs, we went into the An Tinh hamlet of Suoi Sau
with the hope of wiping the bunker—and its inhabitants—off the
map. To do this job I took a company of Regional Forces, much
better troops than the PRU we had used for the An Tinh roundup.
Colonel Thanh, the province chief, had gotten over his initial skepticism and was now even willing to use his own resources (Clint
Wilson, the officer in charge, thought that Thanh's Hau Nghia
Regional Forces were "the best damned troops in the country"). In
addition to the Hueys carrying the Regional Forces, I promoted
eight Cobra gunships from the U.S. First Cavalry. If we could get
rockets down onto the bunker we could at least blow it to hell.
There was also, I knew, a good shot at grabbing some of the security cadres the attack might flush out.

Since the security section tended to operate at night, we anticipated that if we hit the bunker at six or seven, they'd be home
having breakfast. The Cobras could come right over and put their
rockets in, blowing the top off the complex. Then, if we were lucky,
the cadres would come crawling out, right into our arms.

That morning at 0700 the attack went in, once more led by Felix
Rodriguez, who darted ahead in his Loach to drop smoke. With
precise timing the Hueys set down with their characteristic flap,
flap, flap in predetermined positions, 150 to 200 yards from the
bunker. My own chopper put Ba Tung (disguised again), Albert,

and me onto the edge of a cleared vegetable field where we could have a good view of what went on, yet still be a little apart from the action.

The Hueys had just put down and the Cobras were lining up their runs when Albert, Ba Tung, and I started walking slowly toward the bunker. Suddenly from a line of bush on the far side of the little field a girl stood up, her hands held straight up in the air. Instantly Ba Tung slapped Albert on the back and pointed her out. "Grab her," he shouted above the noise. "That's Tuy Hoa."

Tuy Hoa was a name we knew. She was the deputy secretary of the SR 1 security section, a female rascal. A tough little monkey, as we found out later when we interrogated her, your typical hard-core security agent and assassin. As Albert and I walked over toward her, Albert covering her with his M-16, Tuy Hoa stood there, her hands up and not moving a muscle, absolutely rigid. I didn't blame her. Behind and a little off to the side sat our Huey, the door gunner gripping his M-60 with his finger fastened on the trigger, scanning the brush and scared shitless. That's the picture Tuy Hoa had seen when she put her hands up. She was sure the gunner was about to blow the whole area up just for good measure, as he might well have. He certainly wouldn't have waited to ask questions if he thought there was something in the bushes that looked just slightly wrong.

When we reached Tuy Hoa, Albert pointed his M-16 at her and told her to squat down. Then he asked her her name, and when she gave a phony response, he barked, "Bullshit! I want your real name right now. I know what it is. But I want you to tell it to me, now!" "Tuy Hoa," she said, looking into the M-16. "You mean Tuy Hoa, deputy commander Subregion One security section?" "Yeah." "OK, you're coming with us back to the chopper." Tuy Hoa looked at him, her face almost white. "I don't want to move," she said. "We're in the middle of a minefield." What I heard, of course, was Vietnamese. When Albert turned to look at me his eyelids were blinking. "Ong Gia," he said, "there are a few mines around here, maybe more than a few. She says we're in the middle of a field." I felt my bowels threaten to give way, and as I fought to gain control over them, I heard myself say, "OK, we're going back exactly the way we came in."

By the time we got back to the chopper with Tuy Hoa, the Regional Forces guys were moving by us around the field. Thirty yards away, I sensed rather than saw a piece of earth move, and in a blur of action a man in black popped out of the hole and was cut down by the nearest RF before he had a chance to swing his rifle around. The next moment, as if that were a signal, the Cobras swooped down and plastered the place with high explosives.

One after another they came in and unloaded their hardware, explosion bursting on top of explosion. When the smoke cleared, the earth that covered the bunker had collapsed into it, forming a crumbled depression almost forty yards long by ten wide. Everything from the bunker was scattered all over the place, debris settling to the ground in the aftermath of the explosions. But nobody came out. When the RF went over the place, they found nothing, not a single body. I knew they had been down there. Tuy Hoa was in that field for some reason: either coming back from a job, or leaving, or just taking a leak. But she wasn't there by accident, and that meant the place was in use. But we also knew that there were tunnels leading from the bunker deep underground to escape routes. The others must have heard the choppers coming in in time to get down into the tunnels and bug out.

Despite the miss at Suoi Sau, Colonel Thanh's enthusiasm for operations launched from our data-bank material wasn't dampened in the least. Even if we hadn't gotten the whole security section, we had managed to get Tuy Hoa, the deputy chief, and we had knocked out the bunker. Colonel Thanh was satisfied that our information was good and he was eager to keep things hot for the other side. Next on the agenda would be Loc Hung, An Tinh's sister village, just as staunch a revolutionary hotbed as An Tinh itself.

After discussing the kind of information the data bank had available on Loc Hung, Colonel Thanh and I decided that an operation against Loc Hung market might yield some interesting results. Like An Tinh's Vietcong, those in Loc Hung were so secure they had gotten used to operating almost in the open. Since we could identify many of the village's legal cadres, it seemed that a raid on the market area during the midmorning marketing time might be able to catch a bunch of them at once. In addition, Loc Hung market was where the NVA 101st got most of its supplies, and with a little luck we might be able to grab some of the North Vietnamese supply cadres.

This time we took Nam Van, a COSVN military proselyting cadre, and Hai Duc, a COSVN recon company commander. These two were defectors with such skills that I had decided to keep them around even after we had milked them of all the information they had. Eventually, I thought, something had to come up where we could use them. Hai Duc, the company commander, was an especially accomplished officer, an expert at reconnoitering

fire bases and laying out minefields, also at the art of setting ambushes and then disappearing—the Vietcong's stock-in-trade.
These two were not the only specialists I had collected, and this
operation did not particularly call for their kinds of skills, but I did
want to keep them involved in some way, especially Nam Van, who
had been swearing he was going to help us but as yet had done
nothing concrete. So I took these two, along with Ba Tung of
course, and Nguyen, another one of my specialists, a former recon
sapper in the Cu Chi military intelligence section. Nguyen was
kind of a goofy kid, but likable. "Well," he'd say, laughing in a kind
of bumpkin way, "I don't know if I can do that, but, hey, I guess I
can try." One of those kind of guys. And he was a talent with
mines.

We also took three companies of Colonel Thanh's Regional
Forces—a whole battalion—bringing them into Loc Hung by truck
and helicopter in a precisely timed movement that sealed off the
marketplace at 10 A.M., just when most people were coming in to
do their shopping. It was a bit of a dicey situation. We had lists,
and we had Ba Tung along to make identifications, but our understanding of Loc Hung was not nearly as complete as it was of An
Tinh, and we did not know what to expect from the North Vietnamese units billeted in the nearby Ho Bo Woods, some of whose
officers we hoped to catch in town.

But as the Regional Forces quickly deployed around the central
village area it appeared we had caught them completely by surprise
and that the show of force was sufficient to discourage any hostile
action. In short order we rounded up fourteen or fifteen hundred
people in the market and began marching them in single file past a
little school building where "our" Vietcong informants could see
them through a window while keeping hidden.

Among the first fifteen or so who marched by was one of Hai
Duc's former soldiers, a member of the hundred-man sapper recon
team attached to COSVN. By the time we finished the parade, we
had identified and arrested eleven more, including several Trang
Bang district-level cadres, though none were leaders. We put the
twelve into a chopper and flew them back to Bien Hoa, installing
them in the already overflowing houses. It wasn't a bad haul, and
Colonel Thanh seemed happy enough with it. But I had thought
we would get more, especially illegal cadres. It was funny; a couple
of weeks back we would have felt lucky to capture twelve Vietcong.
But after the An Tinh raid twelve didn't seem like anything special.
On the other hand, Loc Hung village wasn't going anywhere, and
the information we were likely to get from this group would expand

our knowledge of the place considerably. I knew that Colonel
Thanh didn't intend to leave the village in peace, and neither did
I.

With the Loc Hung and An Tinh raids under our belts and with
our targeting capabilities growing more accurate and more comprehensive almost daily, I began to think of the entire war effort in
rather different terms than I had previously. More than a year and
a half ago I had told Loren Snowcroft that once we started, the
data bank would grow so fast it would shock us. Now, looking at
the card catalog cases expanding along the walls of the data trailer,
I could see that the prediction had been warranted. Our subject
file on An Tinh village was thick with entries. So was our file on
the NVA 101st and the Vietcong's H-1, H-2, and H-3 battalions in
Subregion Five. By now we had succeeded in documenting these
units' complete order of battle, identifying almost all the officers
and men. We knew who they were, names and backgrounds of
both North Vietnamese and South Vietnamese. Other subject files
were a lot less complete, but in much of the infamous Iron Triangle
we had turned an invisible enemy into a visible one. (In mid-1971
we had more than thirty thousand cards in a catalog that would
grow to a hundred thousand by the war's end.) We knew the Ho
Bo Woods intimately, as we did the Saigon River, and Tan Uyen
district. We had cracked Cu Chi and Trang Bang. In lighter moments I liked to call An Tinh "my village."
    But the ironies of our effort were too stark to miss. General
William Westmoreland had left Vietnam in mid-1968, his "search
and destroy" strategy largely discredited. Since then General
Creighton Abrams had been busy presiding over the slow withdrawal of American troops. We were, I knew, years too late with
our intelligence.
    I couldn't help but think how different things might have been
had we had our data bank available for the U.S. forces during the
height of the American effort, and what a failure it was that we
hadn't. It was infuriating to think about the good people in Saigon
Station enmeshed in corrupt special police programs with their
multitudinous cutouts and fabricated agents. The failed and brutal
PIC program, the unbelievable Census Grievance program, the
Rural Development peasants who weren't peasants, the do-nothing
Provincial Reconnaissance Units, the phony Phoenix program—
these were not just wastes of money and energy. Put together they
represented the broad failure of American intelligence in Vietnam.
Data banks and detailed wiring diagrams and the real spies such

information makes possible were not exactly startlingly new, groundbreaking intelligence devices. On the contrary, they were exactly the kind of thing I thought I would find when I first got off the plane in Tan Son Nhut. And yet they hadn't been there.

Good, exploitable intelligence would have obviated the need to invent the bastard strategy of "search and destroy." Had I only had our system up and running earlier, I thought, we could have provided much of the targeting the army needed. For instance: The North Vietnamese 101st is presently located in the such-and-such quadrant of the Ho Bo Woods in bunkers at the following coordinates. If they know you are coming they will move along the following routes into this second quadrant. If you hit bunker areas XT6490 and XT6897 you've got them. That was what was needed, and that was what we had to offer—but I was filling my file drawers years too late.

Instead of having intelligence this concrete at their disposal, American soldiers in Vietnam were sent out cold, to search and destroy. And that really meant search and *try* to destroy. It meant you got your point men shot up or blown up, and got a company or two tied down by three guerrillas. Then, even if you did find any Vietcong, chances were you'd lose them, because you didn't know where they'd run to. It is one thing to debate the appropriateness or inappropriateness of strategies in analytical studies and history books, but for the GIs who fought the war it was the failure of intelligence that contributed the lion's share to the hell they went through. I fought in World War Two and knew the soldiers and marines from that era well. They were magnificent soldiers. But the American fighting soldier in Vietnam was, if anything, the braver man. The war he had to fight—with its endless patrols on mined trails through menacingly hostile jungle and bush, with unexpected death waiting around each turn—forced him to be.

With the twelve new sources from Loc Hung, the twenty-eight from An Tinh, as well as others who continued to come in through regular channels, the houses were now packed to the rafters. It wasn't only that we were overloaded with sources. We desperately needed to centralize our administration and data bank. The operation was spread out all over the place: Lou and I with our offices in the Monastery; the screening and data-bank facilities with all the typists and researchers in trailers at the Chieu Hoi Center; five houses with prisoners, interrogators, guards, cooks, and my little group of specialists scattered around Bien Hoa. It was a logistical nightmare.

As a result, I started looking for a permanent home, sending Mingo to scout around the city to see what he could find. In the end, Mingo came up with three possibilities: two apartment houses and an old hotel. I went around to look at them myself and talk to the landlords, thinking that once I had a decent location lined up I'd make my approach to Don Gregg.

At just this time a new officer came on base. In his mid-forties, tall, slender, and good-looking, Jack Martel arrived to take over as Don Gregg's deputy and executive officer. Unlike Gregg, Martel was instantly popular, a sensitive, amiable man who was as mentally sharp as he was good at making friends. In short order Don Gregg had turned over to him most of the hands-on management of the Monastery's programs.

My own relationship with Jack got off to an especially good start. He had taken the time to do some homework on Bien Hoa before he arrived and was already aware of the data bank's existence, if not with many of the details. Coming in just in time for the An Tinh roll-up, he was as amazed at the success as we were. "You mean you went out and captured twenty-eight VC?" he said to me. "Hell, the whole U.S. Army never did that." "Well, we did, Jack," I said, trying to sound nonchalant. "But remember, these were legals, the easy kind. All we had to do was know who they were and where they were."

Soon after Jack took over I was dealing with him almost exclusively. I filled him in on the developments since Loren Snowcroft's days: our relationship with Colonel Thao, the G-2; with Colonel Dinh at the Corps Interrogation Center; our budding relationship with Colonel Thanh, the Hau Nghia province chief; and Major Ngo in Trang Bang district. I explained where we were now on the roll-ups, and the direction we hoped to go. Jack was a good listener and soaked up the history, but with his quick mind he also went right to the heart of the matter. "Orrin," he said, "it sounds terrific, but where are the spies? We need those spies, Orrin. What are you doing in that area?" He had read the Mad Bomber file and the Reaper file and liked what he had seen. "Jesus, they look good," he said. "But what else do you have going?"

In fact Lou and I did have a number of operational leads we were working on. I told Jack about them, but also explained how overloaded we were. "I don't necessarily want to burden you with this," I told him. "I know I should go directly to Don Gregg. But the fact is that I have to have a building; I have to be able to consolidate everything under one roof. I've got people coming out of the windows at my places, and it just isn't allowing me to get done the things that ought to get done. I need something like a hotel or an apartment house." Jack's reaction was immediate. "Orrin," he said, "I think you ought to have it and I think you ought to have it right now."

"OK," said Don Gregg, when Jack and I went in to see him the next day. "Why don't we all go and take a look at what you have in mind?" I could hardly believe my ears. Even though I knew Jack was on my side, I was surprised. I just hadn't known what Don's reaction might be. At the very least I expected him to start talking about what a bureaucratic problem he'd have with Saigon Station about it. But there was no discussion, just "Let's go over and have a look."

What I wanted was one place in particular, a vacant apartment house on old Highway #1 that could comfortably accommodate about sixty sources at a time plus fifty or so employees. The building included fourteen good-sized apartment units plus enough space inside a walled courtyard to bring in the trailer that housed the data bank itself. Although one of the other possibilities my scout had come up with was somewhat larger, the layout of this building was ideal. Walking Jack and Don through the building, I explained how the rooms could be divided to house the sources—each unit could have its common room, sleeping rooms, and inter-rogation rooms. I showed them where we would put the adminis-tration area, offices for Lou and myself, and other offices (dropping an unsubtle hint) for any new American case officers who might be assigned to help us with the mass of intelligence, and especially with operational leads. We also looked at the building from the point of view of external security—where we could put guard sta-tions, how we could install barbed wire on the walls that ran around the entire building.

As we discussed the barbed wire, Don Gregg suddenly asked how much all of it might cost. When I told him the rent was only $5,000 a year, he said, "Orrin, I think you should have it immediately." I practically came unglued. Maybe I had misjudged Gregg's aloof-ness.

By this time I had moved my own residence from the house Bill Todd and I had shared to a large French villa at 15 Cong Ly Street. The place had eight bedrooms, a back patio, and a large grassy front yard that spread out behind brick walls, providing privacy from the street. Almost every night Colonel Thao, the G-2, would come over to drink a beer, talk a while, and unwind from his day. Initially, Thao and I had regarded each other with as much suspicion as friendliness. On the surface our relationship was amiable enough, but anytime our interests failed to coincide, Thao knew I would not hesitate to leave him uninformed, or even put him off track. I, in turn, had no doubt he would screw me at a moment's notice. Yet we also knew that, as high-level intelligence officers, each of us could be extremely helpful to the other, that the relationship had to be cultivated.

Once the data-bank program was under way and producing, though, things changed. Thao became convinced that I was doing something substantial for the cause and he began to show himself a real friend. And I began to discover that the man lived up to his good reputation; he was absolutely honest, worked fourteen or fifteen hours a day seven days a week, and drove into Saigon every other Sunday to see his family. He knew he was fighting for nothing less than his country's life and he had dedicated himself to the struggle. But even Thao had to find a way to relax, and that's what he would do late each evening over a beer on my patio.

Thao was not the only one to come by the house for a beer or two. Lou frequently stopped over, as did friends of mine from the provinces who might happen to be in Bien Hoa. I had also gotten to know a group of Vietnamese pilots from the Bien Hoa air base, including Colonel Nguyen Van Tuong, who was arguably the world's hottest F-5E fly-boy. They visited frequently, as did Albert, Bingo, Buffalo One, Gekko One and Two, Tiger One and Two, and some of my other interpreters. Nor was it unusual to find one of the VC or NVA sources sitting down and having a beer or a soda with them.

That was how Albert found himself on the patio one evening with Ba Tung when the former An Tinh secretary nonchalantly dropped another bombshell. "Albert," he asked, sipping his Coke, "how would you like to capture the commander of the COSVN N-10 Sapper Battalion?"

When Albert told me, my jaw dropped. "A battalion commander? What kind of battalion commander? You've got to be kidding." "No," said Albert, "he's dead serious." After reflecting on it for a moment, I didn't doubt that Ba Tung knew exactly what he was talking about. There was nothing accidental about his having "forgotten" this intelligence for so long only to have it occur to him over a Coke one evening. He had obviously been keeping this as his ace in the hole. It was his way of ensuring an extension in his stay. Ba Tung knew that as long as he kept giving us information he would not end up in the National Interrogation Center in Saigon. This was a perfect strategic move on his part. Whatever kind of operation it turned out to be, it would take time to resolve, and maybe I'd believe he had more where that came from.

According to Ba Tung, the N-10 Sapper Battalion had its command post in a bunker complex outside An Thanh hamlet (part of An Tinh village), less than a mile from the government's Trang Bang district headquarters. The bunkers were in an area of scrub brush and jungle about a mile square, right in the middle of An Thanh's cultivated fields. For all the sweeps and search-and-destroy missions that had gone through the hamlet, no one had ever touched the bunkers. It was known that mines were scattered throughout that little patch of wilderness and people were understandably reluctant to examine it too carefully.

Ba Tung knew it well, however. He had been born only a hundred yards from the bunkers. A tall banyan tree that had been in Ba Tung's backyard still stood there. There were no tunnels under the sapper headquarters, Ba Tung told us, only the bunkers themselves. Eight or nine people in the N-10 staff were usually there, keeping in touch with the sappers in Saigon by messenger and with COSVN by radio. The sapper commander, a colonel named Nam Cuong, was almost always in the complex.

The N-10 was not exactly a new name to us; we had had reports on it, though not much in the way of details. Our understanding was that this battalion operated in Saigon and was responsible for most if not all of the bombings and terrorist assaults in the capital. I had assumed that their headquarters unit was in the Cu Chi tunnels or out in the Ho Bo Woods somewhere.

But Ba Tung had explicit details. The N-10, he said, had been operating in Saigon for years. They had done the famous Brinks bombing on Christmas, 1964, which killed two American officers and wounded almost sixty others who were living in a hotel converted into officers' quarters. They had also done the Rex job, blowing up another American bachelor officers quarters, and they had destroyed several smaller American and ARVN billets. The murderous Tu Do Club bombing, which left thirty-seven dead, including half a dozen GIs, was also theirs. I had experienced the Tu Do bombing firsthand: in Saigon for my orientation, I had been walking with John Pinossa along Tu Do Street, a couple of blocks from the club, when an explosion shattered the air. John, an expert on demolitions, had remarked, "Uh, oh, that was one big hunk of plastic." Through the years, the N-10 had blown up many of Saigon's smaller police stations, often using sappers who would ride by on a bicycle or motorbike and lob a grenade inside. It was the N-10 too that had targeted Secretary of Defense Robert McNamara for assassination on one of his trips to Saigon.

Ba Tung knew a good deal of the N-10's background and procedures because of his friendship with Nam Cuong, the battalion
commander. According to Ba Tung, Nam Cuong was a tough bird
—aggressive, intensely proud of his accomplishments, and frustrated by what he considered COSVN's overly cautious use of his
men. He was also a talker, with few people to talk to. Ba Tung, An
Tinh's village secretary, had been Nam Cuong's confidant, the
senior party member in the area, a man he could share his loneli-
ness with and his triumphs. As a result, Ba Tung had spent many
an hour in the bunker with him. He was a walking history of the
battalion.

As Ba Tung related it, for the most part the N-10 recruited their
sappers in Saigon, with the help of the Saigon Party Committee.
From there they were sent to COSVN across the Cambodian border where they were trained in demolition. They became expert
with TNT, plastic, grenades, detonators, B-40 rockets, and other
tools of their trade. Back in Saigon they were set up as sleepers,
legals who held jobs and seemed no different from any other citizen. When they were activated, it was usually one at a time. With
sixty sappers in the company, each might go for long periods of
inactivity before being called on to do another job. As a result,
there was little chance of anyone's cover being blown.

The Saigon officer in charge of N-10's sappers was a nineteen-
year-old girl by the name of Nguyen Thi Kieu. A highly trained
demolitions expert herself, she was the point of contact between
N-10 headquarters and the sixty Saigon agents, and she oversaw
their missions. Nam Cuong had told Ba Tung that Nguyen Thi
Kieu had done the Tu Do Club bombing herself.

The day after Ba Tung gave us all this information, I arranged
for a chopper to fly him, Albert, and me to see the area and take
photographs. As we flew over, Ba Tung's description of the bunker
complex materialized under us. An Thanh hamlet's fields were a
patchwork of manicured rice paddies, and there, right in the middle, was maybe two thousand square yards of bush and jungle.
Now that we knew what to look for, the overgrown rectangle appeared strikingly out of place; it seemed amazing that no one had
noticed it before. There was the banyan tree, and next to it what
seemed to be the remnants of an old house. Though the bunkers
themselves weren't visible, the area Ba Tung pointed to seemed to
stand out slightly from the rest of the patch in contour and vegeta-
tion. The trails he had described were right where he said they
were. I was sure our aerial-photo analysts would have enough to
make a close determination of what was down there.

Once they were developed, the photos confirmed Ba Tung's report. The maps he had drawn matched perfectly, and the analysts identified a complex of three bunkers just to the south of the banyan tree. When I talked to Jack Martel and Don Gregg about drawing up a plan of attack they were both excited.

My approach this time was to bring in Colonel Dinh (the Corps Interrogation Center commander from the beginning.) When I described the situation to him in his office he almost fell out of his chair. "These bunkers are where?" he said. "That's not even a mile from the Trang Bang headquarters! This is hard to believe."

But hard or not, he believed it, just as Albert and I did. The main problem, I told him, was to bring troops in through the minefields that surrounded the bunkers. But I thought I had a solution. One of the specialists I had been collecting was a young NVA sapper by the name of Truong. Truong had come in several months earlier after having experienced one too many B-52 strikes. His hearing was partly destroyed, he had seen many of his friends blown up or buried, and he had only escaped death himself by what he considered a miracle. "Nobody's going to make me go through that again," he declared when we interrogated him.

We had debriefed Truong for intelligence on sapper activities and capabilities—what they do and how they do it—and he had provided detailed accounts of such things as how to switch claymores around, how to detect mines on a trail, how to get under barbed wire without breaking it, how to prepare whole-body camouflage, how to reconnoiter a fortified base, how to use satchel charges, and other fine points of his profession. As young as he was, he was obviously a master of his trade. He was best, he thought, at planting and detecting mines. I was so impressed by his knowledge that I had kept him around with my growing team of specialists, not knowing exactly where I might use him, but sure that he'd come in handy sometime. All we had to do now was persuade him to walk down the trail in front of the South Vietnamese troops and deactivate the N-10's mines. I had already asked Albert to start working on him.

Once Colonel Dinh was over his initial shock, his enthusiasm for an assault on the bunker complex matched mine. If we managed to capture whatever records they kept, and if we could get some live prisoners to interrogate—maybe even Nam Cuong himself— the gains could be enormous. Dinh would have played a role in cleaning up terrorism in the capital, an accomplishment that would greatly enhance his already strong reputation and position.

When Colonel Dinh arranged a meeting with Colonel Thanh, the province chief, we went to Hau Nghia together. There we first saw Colonel Bartlett, the Agency's province adviser, and Clint Wilson, the officer in charge. Their initial reaction was the same as mine and Dinh's had been: incredulity. "I just can't believe it," Bartlett said. "I couldn't agree with you more," I told him. "But everything this rascal Ba Tung has told us up to now has been true, and you know what we've been able to do with it. Here we've also got the aerial photos to back it up. Unfortunately, I haven't been able to confirm any of the identities in our data bank, but the N-10 has been so secret that I'm not particularly surprised. The only possible negative is that since the time that Ba Tung defected, they might have decided to move somewhere else. We haven't picked up any activity around the place. But it's still worth a shot."

Bartlett and Clint Wilson agreed, as did Colonel Thanh when we went to see him. With our successes at An Tinh and Loc Hung, Thanh had become a firm believer in the data bank and he was delighted by this new prospect. "Maybe next we'll go after the 101st in the Ho Bo Woods," he said, laughing. When he asked what I expected from the operation, I told him that my main objective was to capture Nam Cuong alive. "What I'd like," I said, "is for you to close off the whole area, then bring troops down the main trail to the bunkers. I have a former NVA sapper who can lead them in and deactivate the mines."

"Fine," said Colonel Thanh. "First I'll soften up the area with artillery, then my RF will follow your sapper in. We can use two command choppers. Colonel Bartlett and I will be in one of them directing the artillery, and you and your interpreter will be in the other directing the sapper." This wasn't exactly what I had in mind. An artillery bombardment would give Nam Cuong plenty of advance warning. I was hoping they might just have the balls to go in with a megaphone and take the place by surprise. I also didn't like the idea of using separate choppers, but I immediately understood that the province chief did not want me and my interpreter on this hookup with the RF troops. But Colonel Thanh was insistent about the two choppers and especially about the artillery. A bombardment would shatter the bunkers' defenses and detonate a lot of the mines; to him that was worth the loss of surprise.

Technically an observer, there was nothing I could do but back off. Colonel Thanh, I knew, was a first-rate province chief. But I also knew his priorities would be to eliminate the N-10 headquarters and protect his troops. Intelligence gathering might be important to him, but it definitely did not head the list.

Despite my disagreement with Thanh about procedures, I was still excited about the prospects of the operation. Two days later when we lifted off from the Bao Trai airport at 0530 the anticipation hadn't worn off at all. I had briefed Truong, the sapper, carefully; he was to have his radio on at all times and call me instantly if any problems developed. I had real fears for his safety—South Vietnamese troops had little affection for North Vietnamese sappers, even former sappers, and he was going to be out in front of them going into a firefight.

At 0540 we were over the area and a minute later the province chief in his own chopper started directing artillery fire onto the target. He was very accurate, correcting one way, then another, then zeroing in on the bunkers, covering them in explosions of smoke and dust. After thirty rounds or so we saw the RF begin to move down the trail. At the same time Truong's voice came over the radio. He was leading them in, he reported, now he was picking up mines along the trail and at the sides, they were easy to detect, he was deactivating them, one . . . two . . . three . . . four . . . By the time he counted twelve the RF were near enough to start firing into the bunker entrance areas. Truong was shouting something over the radio, but just then we began taking ground fire ourselves and the door gunners opened up with a racket that momentarily drowned out his voice. Clasping the phones tight to his ears, Albert started cursing. Then suddenly the gunners stopped and there was silence except for the flap, flap, flap of the rotor. Over the radio Truong was yelling: "They killed everyone. There's only a girl left alive down here with a smashed-up leg." Through Albert, I ordered Truong to protect her and make sure she came out of it alive. We had to get at least one prisoner out of this.

In another minute we had put the chopper down at the edge of the bush area next to the trail entrance. By the time I got down to the bunkers Colonel Bartlett and Colonel Thanh were already there, and the wounded girl, the only survivor, was being attended to by a medic and troops were going through the complex. With Truong standing next to me, an RF lieutenant reported what had happened. Several of the N-10 people had been killed by the artillery fire, and the RF shot three more when they tried to get out of a bunker entrance. The lieutenant was very uncomfortable telling me this, but Truong was right there and the lieutenant knew we'd get the full story soon enough anyway. One of the three who had been shot turned out to be the N-10 colonel, Nam Cuong. He had been wounded first, then, when the soldiers arrived, they just blew him away. When Colonel Thanh heard this, he ripped into the lieutenant for having allowed something like this to happen, directly contrary to his orders. But however angry Thanh was, it was all over and we had lost what might easily have been our most important source to date. Nobody was going to bring Nam Cuong back.

The wounded girl identified herself as Thi Be. She was a courier, she said, sixteen years old. She ran messages between Nam Cuong and Saigon. As an RF officer talked to her, Albert began to sift through the metal ammo cases packed with documents that the soldiers were bringing out of the bunkers. "Ong Gia, this stuff is amazing," he said. "It's full of directives from COSVN sapper command, training manuals, correspondence, target lists, the whole works." Just looking at the quantity of material, I knew that at least some of it would prove valuable. But a few minutes later Albert hissed, "Ong Gia, come here. Look at this." He was leafing through what looked like an ordinary school notebook. "Ong Gia, these are names and addresses of the sappers in Saigon. Real names, contacts, everything. It's signed by Nam Cuong and Nguyen Thi Kieu. Do you know what this means?"

"Yes," I said, "it means I better get Colonel Dinh in here immediately to protect this stuff." I knew too well how valuable these names were. If the province chief kept the material, he and the special police would be fighting like cats and dogs over it. Thanh I knew was honest, but someone else was bound to get hold of it and either sell the documents off or sell the people off. "Albert," I said, "I want you to stay here with these documents, just baby-sit them while these guys take them back to the province. I'm going to get Dinh down to talk to Thanh to try to get him to release them to me."

Back in the helicopter, I called Lou and told him to try to have Dinh at the Monastery in thirty minutes. A half hour later I was in my office with Dinh describing what had happened. "Albert is sitting with the documents now," I told him. "The important thing is to get what we can now; we're better prepared to handle these documents than anybody else. After we get what we need, we can give them to Saigon." Dinh was just as alarmed as I at the thought of handing material over to the special police before we processed it. He, like many ARVN officers, held even worse opinions of the police than I did.

The first job, then, was to get the documents out of Hau Nghia province, which Dinh succeeded in doing in short order, working it out with Colonel Thanh. At the new interrogation center, we immediately began logging and prioritizing documents, translating the immediately important ones. In addition to the name and address list of all the N-10 operatives and support personnel in Saigon, there were reports on all the jobs the battalion had undertaken going back years. The agent making each report had included a diagram of the location, how much plastic or other explosive he or she had used, how it had been placed, what the timer had been set for, how many had been killed or injured, the effect of the explosion on the building. The reports were completely objective and all in the first person: "I did this, I did that, then I did the other." They were unbelievably cold-blooded. But none was more hair-raising than the report by Nguyen Thi Kieu herself—N-10's nineteen-year-old handler in Saigon—entitled "How I blew up the Tu Do Club." She wrote how she had bought a wig and makeup and had practiced to give herself the appearance of a Saigon bar girl. Then she had applied for a job as a cocktail waitress at the Tu Do. After working there for several weeks she had brought in the plastic with a timer inserted and had placed it under the bandstand. When it went off, it blew the bandstand through the ceiling, killing all the musicians as well as the people on the dance floor and maiming many of the other customers—most of them Vietnamese. This report, like the others, was a copy, with a notation that the originals had been sent to COSVN for their records. Obviously Nam Cuong had kept his own archives.

When we saw what we had, we were astounded, as were Don Gregg and Jack Martel when I told them. This was our opportunity to roll up the N-10 Sapper Battalion completely, or even better, roll up most of them but recruit one and keep him out in the field: a sapper who would be contacted again some day. Yet for all the talk and momentary excitement, we all knew this was unrealistic. Saigon was not in our jurisdiction, and the N-10 material would inevitably have to be turned over to the special police. The days of unilateral American action on something like this were long past; indeed they had never really been.

In the end Colonel Dinh and I put our heads together and decided that he himself would take the material to General Bay, current director of the Special Branch Police. And so he did. General Bay was extremely appreciative for this, even making the unusual gesture of driving out to Bien Hoa to thank me personally. He assured Dinh and me that the police investigation in Saigon would be handled in a completely professional manner and that he would keep Dinh regularly informed.

Over the next two months or so, Bay was as good as his word, and Colonel Dinh received updates, which he discussed with me. But after that Dinh ran into a stone wall. When I asked him to level with me about what was going on he said that he had been told that all the N-10 agents had been arrested, but that he had not been able to get any more specific information. "OK," I said, "if they've been arrested, let's get some of them sent out here for interrogation. Nobody could object to that." But Dinh told me that the general had personally asked him to back off and let the police handle it to the end. "What are they doing?" Dinh said. "They tell me, 'We're still investigating. The surveillances are alive.' I know that they did send a team up to Nguyen Thi Kieu's family home in Suoi Sau to try to pick her up. But they got lost. They barged around there for a while, then ended up in Trang Bang district headquarters. It's obvious they missed her in Saigon. And if she ever was at home, she's long gone now. As far as the rest of the sappers are concerned, who knows? My own guess is that they're selling them off to their families. They're picking them up, confiscating everything they have, then putting a price on their heads."

Dinh, who was an honest man, thought the police were ransoming the N-10 agents off. Personally I didn't believe they would let the sappers live, not after all the murdered police and blown-up police stations. But that too was conjecture. Dinh was sure we would never find out what happened to them. And he was right; we never did. It was a dismal end to what might have been a brilliant operation.

8

VIETCONG HOTEL

By the time we hit the N-10, Jack Martel, Gregg's new deputy, had his feet firmly on the ground. He had kept close tabs on things as we went about renovating the apartment house and transferring the operation in from its various locales. It seemed almost as if he took a personal pride in watching the new center take shape. "What shall we call it, Orrin?" he said one day, then laughed. "We've got the PICs of course, then there's the CIC [Colonel Dinh's Corps Interrogation Center], and in Saigon there's the NIC [National Interrogation Center]. Why don't we call this one the DeForest Interrogation Center? Orrin's DIC? What would you say to that?" "I don't think so, Jack," I said, "though it's a nice idea. But what about something a little less risqué, like the Joint Interrogation Center—the JIC?" So we agreed on that, among ourselves we'd call it the JIC. For radio and other Agency communications we would use the code name "Hotel," since the JIC had all the appearances of a hotel for Vietcong and North Vietnamese. We would also need a cover, "Something to do with the National Police would be good," Jack thought. And soon a sign went up on the front of the building announcing in bold blue letters above the barbed wire: "National Police Convalescence Center." Not that everyone in Bien Hoa didn't know what it was. People would walk by and the prisoners would wave to them from the balconies in their distinctive purple pajamas.

Knowing how the operation was expanding, and understanding my need for people, Jack busily looked for new personnel. Shortly after we opened the JIC, he came to me with news that he had acquired two American case officers. "One of them, Gary Maddox, is here now," he told me. "He was supposed to go to Binh Duong, but the officer in charge there thinks he's a little slow and doesn't want him. It's a ridiculous thing. Gary's from Texas and has a major-league drawl. But that's the only thing slow about him as far as I can see. He's a college graduate and looks like a decent prospect. Do you want to take him?" "You're damn right I want to take him," I said. "Send him right over."

"I've got another one coming," Jack went on, "Sam Capone. We're hiring him and his wife. His wife has a master's in English and I'm bringing her on as a reports officer. Sam was in Vietnam for a tour as an army captain before he joined the Agency. But I don't have a specific assignment for him yet. You can have him too if you'd like." "Fine," I said, "I'll take anybody I can get. If there are others you can line up I'll take them too. I've got enough work for four or five more. The more people I have here, the more reports you'll see coming out of this base every month. You get me more people and you'll see a hundred a month."

The next day Sam and Gary showed up. They both seemed enthusiastic about joining the operation and went about getting themselves oriented without any delay. It didn't take long before it was clear I had a couple more good case officers.

Once Sam and Gary were broken in, I divided the work force into four interrogation teams—Bingo, Buffalo, Gekko, and Tiger, one working under me directly and the other three under Lou, Sam, and Gary. Each team consisted of three Vietnamese interrogators and two translators, and each operated separately. They had their own separate entrances and completely compartmentalized areas in the JIC, including dining facilities, so that the sources each team was working never had contact with one another. With all the Lams and Phats and Nguyens among the interrogators and other employees, I began to give them nicknames: Lam Number One, Lam Number Two, Lam Number Three, Gekko Number One (Gekko team's lead interpreter), Tiger Number Two, and so on. Within a short time everyone on the base, Vietnamese as well as Americans, was using these names.

While the teams and sources were set up in the main building, the data bank itself along with the ten typists and clerks under Mr.

Thiet, who managed and coordinated the files, was housed in a forty-foot trailer that fit nicely inside the compound at the side of the hotel. Meanwhile the sources, fifty to sixty at a time, were living and relaxing in the unit of whatever team they had been assigned to. When the interrogators were not working with them, they were kept busy writing detailed autobiographies and accounts of experiences they had had as VC or NVA. Those with even a little education loved this activity, and though it was primarily make-work, it provided us with a vast and occasionally useful collection of material about the whole gamut of Vietnamese life, from growing up, to schooling, to work, to romance, to marriage—in addition to the more relevant subjects of politics and war. The sources also watched television; there was a set in the lounge area of each unit. They stared at "Gunsmoke" and "Bonanza" until they were blue in the face and watched the Chinese and Vietnamese movies far into the night. TV has been called the world's best baby-sitting device, and it was that for us. But with the news and reports on the Armed Services channel it also gave them a chance to see a bit of the world in a way they had never seen it before.

Besides having their needs attended to by the domestic staff, the sources enjoyed the medical attentions of a group of Australian army doctors who lived a couple of blocks away. Don Gregg played tennis with them and had made a private arrangement for them to take care of whatever emergencies we might have. So when wounded prisoners were brought in, the Aussies would be on hand to patch them up and even do a little minor surgery. They were a good-humored, good-hearted bunch, and more than one prisoner came over to us completely after having these guys save a leg or an arm or bring them through a bout of malaria.

With the interrogators, translators, sources, specialists, the Aussies, the cooks, cleaners, typists, administrators, and an occasional family or two, the JIC seemed to be constantly seething with activity. An outsider might have said it was boiling over.

As the intelligence production of the JIC spiraled upward, Lou and I realized that we had to take measures to check on our interrogators. Although we had screened and trained each of them, the operation was now too large for the informal checking procedures I had used in the past. Defectors and prisoners were often difficult subjects, and I didn't want some less-than-adequate interrogator to start dreaming up stories and passing them off as intelligence.

After discussing this concern with our base chief of support and with technical services from Saigon Station, I decided on a simple solution. People had been complaining that with all the writing and reading going on we were short on light fixtures. So one day thirty-five or forty typical old Asian-style table lamps were brought into the JIC. They went perfectly with the Salvation Army furnishings and were distributed around the JIC—even Lou and I got one for our desks. They were, of course, bugged. Technical services had put devices in each one with a pinhole on two sides of the solid wooden base that would pick up anything said in a room. The bugs fed into recording machines that were installed in a shabby (but well secured) armoire I had in my office. The system picked up everything—from bedrooms, lounges, dining rooms, workrooms, and interrogation rooms—so we got most of the JIC's casual conversation as well as the interrogation sessions.

After the lamps were distributed, I had an American linguist come out from Saigon for several days to listen in on each of the teams. We found that all the interrogators were working hard and effectively, using the methods they had been trained in and writing accurate reports of their sessions—except for two. On his second day, the linguist tuned in on Lam Number Two and Fat Phu of the Bingo team working on an interrogation report together. Their source had been uncooperative and they hadn't been able to get to first base with him. Sitting together in their workroom (with the linguist listening in) they discussed what to write and how to write it, fabricating a report that would sound decent to me.

After the linguist went back to Saigon, I let a couple of days go by (so that no one would associate this incident with the American's presence), then I called Lam Number Two and Fat Phu into my office. Base was forcing me, I told them, to make cutbacks in JIC personnel. I was sorry, but I was going to have to let them go. They could collect their checks immediately.

After this I used Albert to monitor the bugs. Each day we'd listen in on a random basis to a different interrogation team. Other times I'd check on Albert himself, taping his conversations and sending them in to our linguists in Saigon. I wanted to confirm absolutely that all the people I had working for me were honest, that they were handling interrogations properly, that there was not a hint of brutality, and that they were not fabricating reports. To my great satisfaction, in the four years we ran the JIC, Lam and Phu were the only ones we found trying to get away with something.

With the JIC up and running I suppose it was in the normal course of events that my house at 15 Cong Ly evolved into a kind of annex. I used the large bedroom at the rear of the house for prisoners to whom, for one reason or another, I wanted to give special attention, particularly women who I thought would respond to another woman's friendship (at one time I had three female Vietcong living there). My Lan was especially good at this. She took care of them, cooked for them, talked to them about their families, even took them shopping in the Bien Hoa market. On the other side of the house I had three smaller bedrooms that we later used for debriefing spies who came in for live meetings. I equipped one of these rooms with a two-way mirror and an audio-video setup so we could monitor what was being said and put it on video tape.

I also built what I called the Hoa Binh bar out on my patio. It boasted a big lacquered wood table under a thatched roof, tree stumps for seats, a small refrigerator, and all the comforts and necessities of a watering hole. The case officers and interrogators —all of them highly attuned by this time to the importance of rapport—would bring sources there to relax and talk casually. Few of the VC or NVA would ask for hard liquor, but they would savor a beer as if it were the most precious thing on earth. Even more of them wanted a Coke, or tea, and Lan saw that everybody was taken care of and that a comfortable atmosphere prevailed. A number of the middle- and higher-level North Vietnamese who came said they were amazed, that the French would never have invited them to sit down in their own homes and have a beer with them.

As the JIC staff developed into a more closely knit group, there was some kind of function at 15 Cong Ly almost every night. Lou, Sam, Gary, and the other case officers who later joined the JIC would come over for a drink after work, often bringing along some of their interrogators and perhaps a source or two. Everyone— Americans and Vietnamese from both sides—would sit around the bar and talk in such a friendly way that we could momentarily forget that we were in the middle of a war (at least we could if the Vietcong out in the Tan Uyen rocket belt were not slamming rockets into the city that night). The first night Jack Martel came over he couldn't believe his eyes. "My God, Orrin," he whispered, taking me a step aside, "you've got defectors and prisoners over here. What if there's a flap?" "Jack," I said, "there's not going to be any flap. It's not the nature of these people to run away from this situation. They've got hot meals; they have no place to go. The Nungs are around. I'm keeping the prisoners locked up in the back rooms at night anyway. Don't sweat it."

I also had Old Man Lam over there most nights to keep an eye on things. Pham Van Lam (known to everyone either as Old Man Lam or Lam Number Three) was an accomplished administrator. In his late sixties, he was a North Vietnamese of dignified bearing who years before had been a province chief for the French. With

so many Vietnamese employees, and with all the inevitable problems and disputes, I needed a personnel manager, and in Vietnam
an older man is what you want for that job. Old Man Lam was
tactful but he was also assertive, as many Northerners are. In addition to Vietnamese, he spoke fluent French and decent English.
A die-hard Dai Viet nationalist, he had come south after the Geneva agreement in 1954 and knew everybody in the Dai Viet Party,
including those who were well placed in the Saigon hierarchy.
Naturally eliciting respect from the other Vietnamese employees,
he did a first-rate job of keeping the JIC running on an even keel
and keeping the personal squabbles and difficulties away from my
door.

Old Man Lam was my personnel manager, but as I gained confidence in his abilities and as our own relationship became stronger
I also started using him as liaison between me and Colonel Dinh.
Colonel Dinh loved company and valued his connection with the
JIC (a feeling I reciprocated), and I knew that in the Vietnamese
way of doing things it was important to maintain some kind of
personal contact with Dinh almost daily. Old Man Lam had the
stature and personality to play that role perfectly, supplemented by
an occasional visit by myself or Lou. So first thing each morning
Lam was in Dinh's offices, exchanging information and greasing
the spoon with the colonel.

I also knew that Dinh was an inveterate collector of spies. He
was proud of the fact that he had his own spies in the National
Police headquarters, in Special Branch headquarters, and in the
ARVN general staff. He was that kind of guy; he wanted to be
informed, and he wanted his own people doing the informing. So
I thought, OK, Old Man Lam can be Dinh's spy in the JIC. Let
him make friends with Lam and let him think that Lam will tell
him everything that's going on, especially the things that Orrin
might not want him to know.

Consequently, on his morning visits Old Man Lam would tell
Dinh little tidbits and cultivate the relationship. It was amazing
when you thought about it. Dinh and I were good friends, totally
cooperative with each other, and yet it was still necessary to play
games like this. It could easily have gone deeper too. The CIA has
a penchant for what it calls "incompatible operations," that is,
recruiting agents in friendly governments. And once I had things
going well with Dinh, Jack Martel asked me to pitch him. "It looks
good on paper, Orrin." But I was always disgusted by incompatible
operations. "I don't need to, Jack," I told him. "Dinh's perfectly
cooperative now. He'll do whatever I want or whatever I ask that's

within reason. He tells me things all the time, good rumors, hard inside information, anything that comes down the pike." (One of Colonel Dinh's more interesting nuggets was that John Paul Vann had been killed by Two Corps South Vietnamese rangers.* "They hated his guts up there," he said. Whether this was hard information or not I did not know, but it fit. Vann was an abrasive man with a foul mouth, given to embarrassing Vietnamese commanders in public. He'd meet a commander of a unit out in the field someplace and he didn't care who was standing around. He'd tell him right there, "Hey, you dumb son of a bitch, you couldn't run an operation against the VC if you were the last one in the world." It made no difference to Vann that "face" was the most significant thing of all to an Asian. You simply cannot embarrass a Vietnamese, at least not in front of someone else. Not unless you are ready to make an enemy for life, one who will get his revenge if he possibly can. He will watch and wait and be patient, and he'll just brood on it until he finds a way to do it.)

Although I didn't discuss it with Jack, my bias against incompatible operations was fairly deep. I did not like the idea of recruiting your friends, attempting to turn someone in a friendly foreign government into a spy for the United States. The only advantage to it was, as Jack said, that it looked good on paper. I knew that a fair percentage of the CIA supergrades had made their careers with incompatible operations, but many fieldmen considered it a cheap way to go. With incompatibles you don't have to go through all the hard and tedious work of trying to penetrate an enemy organization. All you have to do is take a shot at signing up your friends. They're so much easier to develop. In a lot of cases, of course, its embarrassing to them, and if you do succeed you've made them traitors to their country.

Besides, most incompatible operations don't work anyway. It was comical to think that a significant member of the South Vietnamese government was actually going to be your spy. He was going to be the one to decide what he was going to tell you anyway. So why the hell pay him for it? One of the CIA's recruited agents in the Vietnamese government was a senior staff officer very close to President Nguyen Van Thieu. His crypt was Lingus, though I thought it could more appropriately have been Cunnilingus, especially when I read the synopses of his reports in the Agency's monthly intelligence bulletin. The man never reported a single thing that we wouldn't have found out regardless.

---

* Vann was the subject of Neil Sheehan's A Bright Shining Lie.

This general was a well-known crook anyway, but if a man is going to spy for money, he's not too reliable a person in any event. With enemies that's a given and you take whatever precautions you can. But when you've turned a friend into an agent, you've traded a relationship that is open to one degree or another into a shaky one that is not likely to get you any better results. You are also taking a serious risk of poisoning your own waters. It's a lousy trade-off. Dealing with spies is a dirty business under any circumstances. But when you're dealing with them as members of a friendly government, it's twice as dirty.

With the various operations we had pulled off by now in Trang Bang district, Albert and I had developed a special relationship with some of the people there, in particular with Major Ngo, the district chief, and with one of the Phoenix advisers, a hard-charging American army captain by the name of Tim Miller. We had accomplished the first roll-up operation in An Tinh without any help from Major Ngo; we had used Provincial Reconnaissance Unit troops and had done it completely independently. At that time we did not know anybody in the district well and we didn't want them getting too close to our operations. We didn't trust them.

After the operation, though, Colonel Thanh, the province chief, had sent me word that Major Ngo would be very honored if I would come visit him. Honored, like hell, I thought. I was sure Ngo had gotten the idea for this invitation from Miller and Miller's immediate Phoenix boss, Major Williams, both of whom had to have the ass for me after what we'd been able to accomplish in An Tinh, which was, after all, under their jurisdiction. It didn't take much imagination to figure out how their welcome might go: "Nice to see you, Mr. DeForest. Just what the fuck did you think you were doing in our district without even telling us about it?" "Here we go," I said to Felix. "We're supposed to go up there and get chewed out by those guys, a couple of snot-nosed Phoenix advisers who don't know their butts from a hole in the ground."

But what the hell, I thought, I might as well play it to the hilt. So I requisitioned a fancy blue-and-white Agency chopper for the trip, something I almost never did. "Listen," I told Albert on the way up, "when I start talking to these birds there's no point in you being there. Ask permission from Major Ngo, then get down to their Phoenix office and talk to the Vietnamese guys there. Tell them you represent the old man from Bien Hoa and see what you can find out."

Major Ngo, Major Williams, and Captain Tim Miller were all

waiting in the Trang Bang district headquarters. The reception was
very cordial. Major Ngo said how happy he was to see me and
offered his congratulations that the An Tinh operation had gone
so splendidly . . . as he had heard. "Splendidly," he said. Pretty
damned good English.

"Thank you," I answered. I had wanted to come down here, but
my advice from his superior, Colonel Thanh, had been to go ahead
with this operation unilaterally, then come to see him and his two
American officers. "I wanted to tell you that beforehand," I said.
"I'm old enough to understand these things, so you don't have to
chew me out about it." "Well," said Miller, a short, stocky guy
wearing unbreakable glasses, "It's nice that you understand. Now
that you've had your operation and gotten your goodies, just what
the hell is your understanding about helping us out here?"

The man was a pugnacious character, ready to kick me right in
the ass. But he lost a little of his fire in the discussion that ensued.
I told them that this was the first roll-up operation we had tried,
and that by rights they were the ones who should be doing this
kind of thing. "Now tell me about your Phoenix program," I said.
"Tell me what you're doing and how you think I might be able to
help you do it." I said this to Miller and the major, though the
major was a kind of retiring type who seemed to leave things pretty
much to his captain.

The major said something in a soft voice about how they didn't
have too much going on. Then I asked the usual question: "Do
you have anything, for example, on the An Tinh party committee?" "Well, we do have a little card file here in the Phoenix office,"
the major answered. "What kind of a card file?" I asked. "Well, it's
alphabetical by names of people we suspect to be members of the
Vietcong." At this Miller broke in in a disgusted tone. "That
doesn't work. Nothing out here works!" Right in front of his boss.
"This is my second tour in Vietnam. Nothing worked my first tour
and nothing still works."

"Listen," I said. "I'll make you an offer. You know I have Ba
Tung." "Yeah, you stole him away," said Miller. "He was a good
deal for you, wasn't he?" "Yes, he was, and we've been very successful with him. We've been working hard on Trang Bang for six
months and we've got quite a bit." Then I explained the data bank
and gave them an overview of exactly what we did have. "My God,"
said Miller, "if we had that here, we could go out and capture these
guys with the PRU or RF." "Of course you could," I said. "And
ultimately I'd like to help you do that. My primary aim isn't that
kind of an operation. What I'm really after is spies." "Would you

Crew of the B-29 Superfortress Forbidden Fruit, 20th Air Force, 73rd Bomb Wing. I'm the tail gunner, third from right in the front row.

On discharge from the Army Air Corps in October 1945. I had flown thirty-five missions, and earned five air medals and a Distinguished Flying Cross.

(Left) The Monastery, CIA headquarters, Military Region Three.
(Right) The Bien Hoa Province Interrogation Center (PIC) located at
the rear of the Monastery.

Our first private interrogation house in Bien
Hoa. Entrances are on either side of the
doctor's office. To the right is the barbershop.

Lan in 1970. Soon after she moved in with me,
I was feeding her extended family.

Ong Gia (as I became
known) and Albert, my
interpreter.

Our Joint Interrogation Center (JIC),
code name Hotel Alpha.

With Old Man Lam, the JIC's personnel
director, four months before the fall of
Saigon.

The roll-up operation in An Tinh village. We rounded up the Vietcong who worked undercover as "legal cadre."

Our informant, the defector Ba Tung, identifies a Vietcong cadre in An Tinh.

Families of the Vietcong we captured during the roll-up operation. I am standing.

(Top) Colonel Thanh's widow in mourning, with nine of her ten children. (Middle) The funeral procession for Colonel Thanh. (Left) I cross the plowed minefield during our attack on the Subregion One Security Section bunkers.

Artillery hits the North Vietnamese Army's N-10 Sapper Battalion headquarters.

Captain Tim Miller (in glasses and a bush hat) gives directions during a Phoenix operation in Trang Bang.

(Left) Lan and I, in the garden in front of our house at 15 Cong Ly.

(Right) Standing at the entrance to the Hoa Binh "Peace" Bar, which was where we relaxed with our Vietcong informants on the back patio of 15 Cong Ly. (Below) Lan and I at our wedding in Bellflower, California, on August 20, 1976.

With my adopted children, To Thi My and Hai.

Lan and I today.

mind if I had a look at what you've got there?" asked Miller. "Of course not, I'll take you back with me right now on the chopper. I'll also introduce you to some sources from here that you probably didn't even know we have."

I left the meeting impressed with Major Ngo's patience and directness and even more so with Miller, who had decided to drive to Bien Hoa the following day and take me up on my offer. When he arrived at the JIC I showed him around, explaining what was what and how the operation worked. Then I took him straight into the card file. That was the ideal teaching tool, because it was so visual, with everything laid out in a nice organized way that could be seen and understood.

When I showed Miller the Trang Bang subject file, he came unglued, "Holy cow, look at this," he said, so loudly that the secretaries all stopped for a moment and stared at him. I showed him Ba Tung's card file. I also told him about Tu Duc, the not too cooperative military proselyting chief, and described what we had learned from him. Miller was first astounded, then thoughtful. "What I'd like to do," he said, "is come up here, get the information, and take it back. Then I'll put together some kind of team down there that I can take out in the daytime. We can pop in on a house and snatch guys whose names and addresses we have." "Tim," I said, "I'll go one step further. I've got six or seven guys who are real fine VC soldiers. I've kept them around here in case something interesting came up. I'll be happy to give them to you for your team, on a kind of permanent loan."

So Miller interviewed each of my specialists, most of them local guys from Hau Nghia: Hai Duc, the COSVN recon company commander; Nguyen, the Cu Chi district MI sapper and hotshot explosive expert; Phan Van Chau, another sapper (I liked sappers; they were so well trained, so good); Truong, the North Vietnamese I had used in the N-10 operation; Ba Tung himself; Quang Viet, a veteran VC platoon leader; and Quang Manh Duc, a village security cadre.

Miller told them what he had in mind and asked if they wanted to work with him and get a little salary. He did not anticipate any military action; what he wanted was a patrol team that would identify and arrest people as part of the Phoenix program. When they all accepted, he was ecstatic. He was even happier when I told him that neither I nor any one person at the JIC knew everything we had on Trang Bang. The card file was so voluminous it would be a full-time job for one man to master it. As successful as we had been already, we had done little more than scratch the surface, so there

was a wide-open field of action for him. "Make copies of all the
Trang Bang cards and take them back. With your own data bank
you'll be able to get the hamlet books [the official family registers
for each hamlet] and collate the cards with the names in the hamlet
books. You'll be able to identify people, locate them, and catch
them."

On his first trip Miller stayed for three days, studying the data
bank during the day and sleeping at my house at night. Subse-
quently he came back to Bien Hoa a number of times to continue
researching the material and organizing his approach. After that,
he picked up his team and took them back. Then he got to work,
doing exactly what Phoenix was supposed to do. He collated information, marked his targets, then took his team out into the hamlets
and picked them up. He was doing in Trang Bang exactly what the
FBI might do in the U.S.—find your man, knock on his door at
five or six o'clock in the morning, and arrest him. No shoot-outs
unless it was absolutely unavoidable. Everyone involved knew that
a dead VC wasn't going to do us any good at all.

Then Miller would interrogate them. But it wasn't too difficult.
When some local VC was confronted by a Ba Tung or Hai Duc,
he'd invariably talk. What was the use when you were staring at the
former village secretary or the former area recon captain? Ba Tung
would say, "Tell them what they want to know. This war's over
anyway. We're working for Americans; we're not working for the
government, I guarantee you. I've been over in Bien Hoa with
them for the last six months. Nobody in the GVN's involved in it.
All the Americans want to know is what's going on."

When Tim had debriefed them they'd be sent in to Colonel
Dinh, who would transfer significant sources to the JIC, where
they ended up talking not only to our interrogators but to the other
Vietcong and North Vietnamese we had there who had come over
to our side. "Yeah, I've been here for three months now," one of
them would say. "They treat you great, great food, the works. Go
ahead, cooperate. If you play your cards right you can run this
thing to the hilt, maybe they'll keep you here. They're certainly
keeping me here. Hey, what's for dinner tonight, chicken or fish?"

Of course it was the rare source I kept for an extended period.
Once the interrogation was over, prisoners would be classified A,
B, or C, then sent back to the province for trial. What usually
happened after they were convicted was that their families would
buy them off, if they had the money. If they didn't, the prisoners
ended up in the Hau Nghia province jail, which by this time was
overloaded. In the year that Tim and his Phoenix team operated,

he filled the place up. Of the more than two hundred VC he captured, perhaps twenty-five were what I considered "very significant," district- or subregion-level personnel.

Tim Miller was the kind of guy who didn't much care what people thought as long as he got his job done. He was up-front and outspoken. He was the kind of person who gave credit where he thought it was due; in this case, instead of claiming that his roll-ups were Phoenix operations he gave full credit to the CIA, even though Phoenix was run by CORDS. When Miller reported his successes in Trang Bang he invariably expressed his debt to the CIA for their "guidance and help."

For this lack of discretion Tim got in trouble with Richard Funk-hauser, who had taken Charlie Whitehouse's place as head of CORDS. Whitehouse had been a prince of a man, not just a gentleman, but also intelligent and capable, always looking at the bottom line and at what would work. It was Whitehouse who had helped us set up the data-bank operation in the first place. He was a man you could be frank with and expect a straight answer from, whether it was to your liking or not.

Funkhauser was a different story. I had had a couple of briefing sessions with him, and my impression was that he had a high regard for trivia and irrelevant details. He was, I thought, a connoisseur of bullshit. Ask him a tough question and what you were likely to hear was "Er, um, ah, hem, hem." "For God's sake, don't tell Funkhauser anything," said Don Gregg, who had a good feel for the practicalities of interagency cooperation, "never tell State anything unless you're backed into a corner."

"You're not supposed to be working for the CIA in Bien Hoa," Funkhauser had fumed at Tim Miller, who was in and out of our data bank frequently. "You're supposed to be working in Trang Bang. So get your ass back to Trang Bang and keep it there." Of course Tim, being the person he was, just went ahead and did what he wanted anyway. He'd sneak in the back door, then stay in my house at night and laugh about it. "Captain Miller," he'd say, doing a vicious imitation of Funkhauser's pseudo-British manner of speech, "I want you to stay out of Bien Hoa. Go back to your district and stay there. You are a Phoenix operator and you are to remain a Phoenix operator."

But though Funkhauser might have been pissed off, Major Ngo, the district chief, was tickled pink, and over time we became good friends. He'd invite me up for lunch, asking Clint, the officer in charge, to put the call in for him over the Agency radio. "Hotel Alpha," Clint would come in, "this is Big Rancho. Old Trango

Bango wants to see you for lunch." So I'd chopper in, pick Clint up at his place, and drive with him down the back road to the district headquarters, right past the patch of woods that hid the now defunct N-10 Sapper Battalion bunkers.

One thing that I did not get in Trang Bang was the cooperation of my prisoner Tu Duc, the Trang Bang military proselyting chief. He had, of course, given us a significant amount of background information. But despite our patience, and despite the pressure on him, he had never really opened up. He had never compromised his own set of values. We did not, for example, learn the identities of his network of agents, the legal cadre proselyters who worked so effectively at penetrating ARVN.

But hope springs eternal and I still wanted to keep Tu Duc around. He was under a good deal of psychological stress, and as we milked more and more from him and as the idea took hold in his own mind that he had already given us some information, I thought that he might eventually just cave in and give us the rest. I even tried to put him on Tim Miller's team. After all, Miller was only picking up people who had already been identified. Tu Duc wouldn't be betraying anyone. If he would help with that, maybe it would bring him across the psychological barrier. But the idea was a no-go. He wouldn't do it.

My next step was to "burn" him, not something I was happy to do, but I felt it was my last chance to break him. The idea was to take Tu Duc along on some of the roll-up operations in his home area and expose him as if he were part of the effort, compromising him in front of his own people.

So on Miller's next action in Loc Hung he took the proselyting chief along and had him stand next to him while they were parading people by, as if Tu Duc were helping with the identifications—which he was not. The villagers saw him and of course knew who he was. Then Miller took him out on one of his long patrols. He walked him right through the center of the district where all eyes were on him and the information would undoubtedly be passed immediately to Ba Be, the Vietcong's Trang Bang district chief, that the prisoner had gone over.

But that too had no effect on Tu Duc's willingness to cooperate, although the emotional strain on him was obvious. Even though he had not given us any operational information, Tu Duc considered that just by talking to us he had betrayed his comrades. And now, having seen him with the roll-up team, his comrades would think so too. He even talked about it with me when I offered to switch his status from prisoner to *hoi chanh*, to make things easier on him. "No," he said, "I'm not a *hoi chanh*. I'm Tu Duc. I'm a section chief. Don't make me feel even worse about this." You had to admire him.

Without any more tricks in my bag, I had just about made up my mind that there was no point in keeping him any longer and that the time had come to send him back to Colonel Dinh. But before I got around to doing it, one night at about nine o'clock Albert ran into my house yelling, "Ong Gia, come with me, quick. Tu Duc's at the hospital. He tried to kill himself." The province hospital was just down the street, and when I got there Tu Duc was lying on a table with a Vietnamese doctor trying to get a transfusion into him, his blood pressure down to sixty over thirty and falling. He had cut a huge gash in his arm below the elbow with a razor— deep and almost around the entire arm. It was hard to believe he had been able to do that to himself; he must really have sawed away at it. Blood was still welling through the pressure bandages.

The medics finally got an IV into his ankle, then they got another one into his groin. He was so far gone and had lost so much blood that the veins, difficult to locate in Vietnamese anyway, were already shrinking. But when the transfusions started going in, his blood pressure stabilized, then slowly started to rise. Before long it was evident that they had saved him, though not by much.

I left Tu Duc in the hospital four or five days to recover, then had him taken back to the house (we were still keeping him in a separate house). When I visited him I told him that what he had done was stupid, that it wouldn't change anything. "Besides," I said, "you haven't hurt the party any with the chicken feed you've been giving us. You haven't compromised yourself. So you don't have to feel so bad about it. Besides, this is war. We're all doing things we don't like." "Well," he said, shaking his head slowly, "I feel very bad about being here. What I would like you to do, Ong Gia, is take me out of here and put me in jail." And when he recovered fully, I did that.

One of the guys I gave to Tim Miller was Nguyen, the former Cu Chi sapper, the goofy one. He was an expert recon sapper and a good-natured boy, but not too clever. To make himself useful while he lived at the JIC, he did carpentry and all sorts of handyman work. He also managed to fall in love with a little girl by the name of Mai, who was there being interrogated. We had caught Mai in one of the Trang Bang roll-ups; she had belonged to a VC village medical section. A beautiful girl with classic features, she

could have been a model for the most discriminating artist. She
was also smart and ambitious, a go-getter. Anyway, Mai and Nguyen met in the JIC, and, unbeknownst to me, a JIC romance had
flourished.

One morning Old Man Lam knocked on my office door with the
two of them in tow, asking if I could see them for a moment. I was
a little surprised, since Lam knew how tight my schedule was and
that I expected him to handle the personal problems. "Ong Gia,"
said Lam, "please see them. They want to get married." That was
a surprise. It was also, I thought, a mismatch. "Lam," I started,
"neither of these two speaks English so let's just you and me talk
about it. This is one lousy idea. What in the world is Mai doing?
Anyone can see that this joker isn't good husband material, especially not for someone as bright as she is." "Ong Gia," said Lam,
"it doesn't matter. She's already pregnant and they want to do the
right thing. What's more, they want you to perform the marriage.
They don't have any family here, of course, and they can't very
well go home. So they've decided that you are the right one to
officiate. They would be honored by it. I think you should do it."

In the end, I not only officiated, I had the wedding at 15 Cong
Ly, with Lan doing the organizing and cooking. We invited all the
key personnel from the JIC as well as a number of girls from the
data bank, so that it had the look of a reasonable family gathering.
Everyone was dressed up—all the women in ao dais—the elegant,
silken traditional dresses that always give a feeling of dignity and
beauty to any affair. A Buddhist altar had been constructed against
the living-room wall, with candles, figurines, and flowers on it. I
served as the head of Mai's side of the family, while Old Man Lam
served Nguyen, the sapper's, side. I made an honest mistake, handing Mai the incense first, which indicated that she was going to be
the boss; at least that was the way I interpreted it. Everybody
laughed about that. Then, as the senior family member, I announced that they were man and wife.

In the dining room we had two large tables set up, and Lan and
her helpers served a delicious Vietnamese wedding dinner with *cia
gio*, spring rolls, rice, and salad. Lam made his speech in Vietnamese. Nguyen and Mai went around the table to each person, ex-
pressing thanks for their gifts—everyone had given them an
envelope with a little money to help them get started. In front of
everybody, Nguyen hugged me, saying in very broken English that
here he was, an ex-Vietcong, marrying his wife, also a Vietcong, in
Ong Gia's house. "Cannot believe," he mumbled, on the verge of
tears. Then Mai hugged me too.

. . .

My reputation at the JIC was partly due to the fact that I always seemed to know what was going on, even things I had no right to know (no one but Lou and Albert knew I had the place bugged). All the Vietnamese had known that Lam Number Two and Fat Phu were phonies, and then one day I had just got rid of them. No doubt I wasn't really omniscient, but then again it was hard to tell about these things. I also developed a reputation as a good palm reader; just the sort of pseudoscience the Vietnamese are addicted to—all of them, from the most educated down to the poorest peasant. Whenever one of my typists or translators got married and pregnant, I would take a close look at her palms, manipulate them in what I imagined was the orthodox manner, then hazard a guess at the sex of the baby. By some fluke I had called six pregnancies in a row as boys and six times boys were born. At least as far as I was concerned it was a fluke. But to my staff, with their active interest in occult phenomena of all sorts, it seemed to be something more than a coincidence.

Keeping to tradition, a couple of months after the wedding Mai came to me to have her palm read. She and Nguyen were living at the JIC. Nguyen would be out with Tim Miller's team for a week or more at a time, after which he and the others would come back for a brief rest and tell enthusiastic stories about how they had picked up five VC here and seven there, as if it was the most fun they had ever had. Squeezing Mai's palm for a minute I said, "Oh, sweetheart, look at this, you're going to have twins." I was just teasing her. Twins in Vietnam are basically unheard of; in nine years I never saw or heard of any, and my impression was that the Vietnamese themselves didn't know what to make of them. One man told me that twins were the worst evil luck, while another said that twins would ensure great riches. So, though I knew twins were rare, I never knew what the Vietnamese really did think about them.

Needless to say, five months later Mai gave birth to a set of twins. I thought, Oh, my gosh, I can't believe it. But the Vietnamese employees began to look at me strangely. They were thinking, That old bastard, maybe there is something weird about him.

Not long after the wedding I received a cable from Saigon Station stating that they were holding a man named Dong Van Ly. He had defected a year earlier, then had agreed to cooperate. He was extremely knowledgeable about Military Region Three and he was available for transfer to Bien Hoa if I was interested. I cabled right back, "Absolutely!" When the dossier arrived, Ly was identified by Station as the former intelligence chief of the NVA 101st. I felt as if I had inherited a fortune. The 101st operated in Subregion One and was maybe the most famous of all the North Vietnamese regiments. If this guy was the chief of intelligence he had to know everything there was to know about the subregion. As G-2, he would have been in on the staff meetings of the region's military affairs sections, which meant he would have known all the top military and intelligence people. And that meant operational leads. Did I want him? Put the guy on the first jetliner.

So Dong Van Ly came out to Bien Hoa, with his wife, also an ex-cadre, who had defected after he had gotten word to her to come over. In my office we drank tea and chatted. Ly was large for a Vietnamese, with a tense muscularity about him. He was dynamic; he exuded energy. I got the feeling right away that this was a take-charge individual, that he must have been a hell of a fighter and officer. As I talked to him about his background, I was struck by the feeling that if I was ever going to get a spy in Subregion One it was going to be through this guy. That thought lurked even as he led me through his fascinating personal story.

Dong Van Ly had been a regroupee. As a young man he had fought with the Vietminh against the French, then had gone North after the Geneva conference in 1954. Like other regroupees he had expected a nationwide election in two years that would allow him to return home. When that didn't happen, he was angry and bitter. He didn't like living in the North, though as a devoted party man he never gave any indication of it. But he was overjoyed when infiltration of the South began in 1959. He knew that eventually he would be sent.

Starting in 1959, he served for three years as an intelligence agent operating out of Laos. Then, in 1962, he started training for his own trip down the trail, making forced marches shouldering thirty kilos of bricks in his pack. In August of that year, he received his own orders. By this time he was a company level intelligence officer. They drove in covered trucks to the Vietnam-Laos border, where the Ho Chi Minh Trail began in the foothills of the Laotian Cordillera. There they had traded in their North Vietnamese Army uniforms for black peasant pajamas and had gone over all their gear carefully to remove any telltale Northern markings. According to the doggedly maintained fiction, there were no NVA personnel in South Vietnam.

His trip down the trail had been hair-raising, taking him more than four months. Of the 150 men in his unit who began the march, only a handful reached the end of the trail together. Many died or had to linger on the trail to recover from malaria or one of the other tropical diseases that infested the jungle.

When he arrived in the South, he fought throughout the Region Three area, eventually rising to the rank of colonel and intelligence officer of the 101st. During Tet in 1968, his regiment attacked ARVN Armored Command headquarters on the northern edge of Saigon but was stopped by American and South Vietnamese defenders. Trying to hold on while waiting for what he had been told would be a massive NVA second thrust, the 101st was battered to pieces. Half the regiment died waiting, and the second wave never did come. By the time it was over, most of Ly's long-time comrades were dead.

Afterward, he hid in the tunnels, choking in the fetid air and crawling on his belly through the many bombed-out sections. After the Cambodian invasion, he surfaced outside Saigon, ostensibly to make liaison arrangements. It was then that he gave himself up.

Now that Sam and Gary were working, I had just the place for Ly. Gary was concentrating on the Cu Chi district, where Ly and the 101st regiment had spent so much time. So I added Ly to Gary's Tiger team, explaining that soon I would start him on a special project, but first he'd have to go through a thorough debriefing by Gary.

Studying Ly's file, I could see that the Saigon debriefers had concentrated on exploiting him for current intelligence. But they had not looked at him as a source to learn more about the Vietcong infrastructure; indeed, since they had no background files against which to check his story, they had no capability to do anything like that. As the 101st G-2, however, he had to know practically every upper-level cadre in Three Corps, at least in Subregion One. I wanted Gary to go through Ly's story again, step-by-step. The exercise would give Gary experience at working with a significant source, and I felt certain that a thorough debriefing would open avenues into the SR 1 organization.

I instructed Gary that in eliciting Ly's story, he should be careful to get as many names and positions as he could, then check them against the data bank. As much of the infrastructure as possible should be diagramed and individual slots filled in. He was to look for ties between the cadres and between them and sources whom we had already processed through the system. He should look for linkages and networks of families and friends and identify every pattern that emerged from the data. It was Gary's first big test. "I want you to report your progress to me once a week," I told him.

Each week after that I got a complete report from Gary and within four or five weeks I had an immense pool of information and leads into Subregion One. As I had anticipated, Dong Van Ly's knowledge was comprehensive and intimate. Not only did I have an operational lead, I had fifty operational leads. It was just a matter of choosing the right one to pursue; we needed one spy there before we could get two.

As the debriefing went on, I found that Ly was quite a sympathetic individual. The chemistry between us was excellent, and Lan and Ly's wife were also becoming good friends. The two often came over to my house at night. The women would talk about things around the kitchen table while Ly and I made an effort to understand each other out on the patio. (Ly could make himself understood in English, and his fluency improved rapidly.) Ly smoked more than I smoked, and drank more than I drank. He especially liked *ba si de*, a Vietnamese rice spirit that had the kick of a water buffalo.

With a *ba si de* or two under his belt he would get to talking about his life in the North, laughing about the line given out in Hanoi—that the poor enslaved South had to be rescued from the Americans. What a sucker he had been. The difference between the possibilities of living decently in the South and the North were too ridiculous, and he and all his friends had fallen for a bunch of bullshit. That was what made him cooperate once he had come over, seeing with his own eyes what the true conditions were.

In Saigon he had been fascinated by the Americans, by their mentality and political views. He had never had an education, other than in the party schools. He had been fighting full-time since he was twelve. But he was smart and inquisitive, and he had been living the life of a hermit in North Vietnam for almost a decade, with no exposure at all to outside information. Then he had survived in the jungle and the tunnels for eight more years before he defected. Exposed to new things and new ways of thinking—even just to simple news—he began to feel sorry for himself —he had spent so much of his life in the dark, and he had so completely believed in the world the party had created for him.

Ordinarily, Dong Van Ly was the essence of a rugged, tough-minded fighting officer. But after a few *ba si de*, a touch of self-pity would come through. He was an intelligent, thoughtful man who had been a warrior from his youth. But he felt he had missed life and missed knowledge. That was his tragedy. He was, in Todd's language, an I-double plus-RA, a serious thinker who had spent his life in ignorance and was now appalled by it.

Once I had reviewed all the reports, I called Gary into my office with Ly. (By this time I was not calling him Ly, but "Luu Bach," the name of the military intelligence chief at COSVN. "That will be your code name with us," I told him. "Who knows, the word may even get back to COSVN that Luu Bach is working for us." Ly knew the real Luu Bach and was delighted with his new name. He thought it was the best joke he'd heard in a decade.) I described the data bank to Ly, telling him what we had and explaining what kind of contribution I was looking for from him. The debriefing material was voluminous, but disorganized. Now I wanted Gary and him to go back to work on it.

"I want you to concentrate on three areas," I said, "the SR 1 military intelligence, proselyting and affairs sections. [The military affairs section coordinated battle planning between local units, main-force units, and NVA units under the direction of COSVN. As the 101st G-2 Ly would have been in on every piece of planning in the subregion.] I want you to write down the names and positions of everyone you can remember, true names and code names. Then check the hamlet books to confirm identifications. Once you've named all the people, show the connections between them. Cross-reference those who know each other or live as legals near each other or have family connections with each other. For example, suppose you've got the chief of SR 1 military affairs section; obviously he knows all the chiefs of the other sections. But who else does he know? Who is he closely connected with in the organizational chart? Who are his friends? Who are his family? Get all that down on paper. Then I want you to decide which of them have vulnerabilities. Who can we target and get for ourselves as a spy. That's what we want out of this—a spy." "Oh," said Ly, intrigued, "this should be exciting."

When I looked in on Ly and Gary the next day, they had brought the data-bank card catalog drawers on the military intelligence, proselyting and affairs sections up to Gary's office. Charts and lists were spread out on the desk and on the floor and a rapid-fire conversation was going on back and forth while they worked. They looked like two bloodhounds on a track.

Three weeks later they came into my office with a paper about two and a half feet square, taped together from smaller sheets. On the paper was a diagram that showed every member of Subregion One military intelligence, military affairs and military proselyting by name, code name, position, and job description. Most of the entries had other relevant information penned in as well. Looking at the seventy or so names listed separately in the lower-left-hand corner I felt a tingle of anticipation. Among all those human beings there must be one, I felt sure, who would be our spy. As I looked through the names, I could not have guessed that among those listed was the best intelligence agent the Vietnam War ever produced, the agent we would eventually come to know as the Goldmother.

9

THE GOLDMOTHER

The master list of the Subregion One military intelligence, military proselyting and military affairs sections that Ly and Gary had put together was a beautiful piece of work, showing all sorts of interesting connections between the members. Now it would take a detective's diligence to find the ones who might lead us to an agent. "What I'd like you to do," I told them, "is go back and on a separate sheet list everybody here who has defected. Find where they're from and where they live now. Most likely they've been through our system, but maybe there are some we missed. Check the 201 files, then get whatever you can from the Chieu Hoi administration. Once you've done that I want you to determine who the defectors know among the cadres who are still active. I want to see if we can't link some of those we already have with some we'd like to have."

A week and a half later Ly and Gary were back with another big chart listing names and connections. One of those listed was a man named Cuu Long who was identified as the longtime former lover of a Vietcong female agent in the Military Proselyting section. The connection jumped out at us. There were others, but this looked like a particularly good prospect. "I know this woman," said Ly. "She could be what we're looking for. She's a very good handler, the best they have. I used to attend weekly staff meetings with her. She's a legal who works at night running agents in Hoc Mon, Bien Hoa, and Gia Dinh. She wouldn't be hard to contact either. I even know where her house is, right in Hoc Mon market." "OK," I said, "let's go through all the possibilities here. Then we'll make some decisions." "Oh," said Ly, "one more thing. After her boyfriend defected I remember hearing that she was having an affair with the Military Affairs section chief."

All of a sudden the female proselyting agent became even more interesting. A top operator whose boyfriend was the MA section boss—the woman had superb access. We knew her identity and where she lived. We knew her cover: she traveled to Saigon every morning to sell blackmarket cigarettes, occasionally sleeping over —which meant she could come to Bien Hoa without arousing any suspicion, to be debriefed by an American, for example. Her former lover was a *hoi chanh*, which meant we had a good opening to him. Put all this together and these were elements that might yield something.

I was excited, but Ly was even more excited. He was very eager to do this himself. I knew he wanted to prove to me that he could do it. And I knew he wanted it for Gary too; he worked well with Gary and in a sense had taken the younger American case officer under his wing. So I wasn't surprised the next day when Ly made his proposal. He could visit the Hoc Mon market, he said, sit in a coffee shop and watch for the female agent. She would recognize him, as he would her, and he'd get her to sit down and have a cup of coffee. Then he could make the approach.

This was precisely the kind of thing I did not want to happen. Gary and Ly had done a beautiful job of identifying this lead—an immense amount of background work had gone into it. But now it was time to cut them out, graciously of course. From here on, I would bring in Lou and his chief interpreter, Buffalo One, to handle the case.

There were a number of reasons for this. First of all, I did not want a well-known guy like Ly sitting around the Hoc Mon market. He would have no cover and the place was crawling with Vietcong legal cadres and even illegals from the tunnels, there to buy food. Someone was sure to recognize him. And once they did, anything could happen. They could track him, find out where he was living, kidnap him, or even put an assassination team on him. It was much too dangerous, and completely unnecessary. Second, I knew Ly's profile, and I wouldn't want him handling the situation himself, even if it weren't dangerous. His English, despite his rapid improvement, wasn't very good, and he was an I double plus. I didn't like those two pluses. They meant he had an overheated imagination, which in turn meant I'd constantly have to be double-checking reports. Besides Ly's drawbacks, Gary was too young to be this agent's handler. The female proselyter would accord much more respect to an older man. Lastly, as a strict matter of tradecraft it was usually wiser to use one team to identify leads and another to develop them—if you had that luxury, and in this case I did.

As a result, I told Ly and Gary that they had done a terrific job, but that I had to think about the approach for a while. That night I studied the charts, poring over them. The female agent looked great, but she was only one of several excellent prospects, and maybe not the easiest to develop. I was so shorthanded I had to rigorously prioritize our leads. As it was, we were badly overextended, writing seventy to eighty critical intelligence reports a month—an energy-draining process. (When I'd first come on, about five were being issued from the base.)

But what I wanted most was a superspy in Subregion One. A subregion cadre with a personal connection to the military affairs section chief could be that spy. Put somebody with those qualifications together with the Mad Bomber and the Reaper and our penetration of Three Corp's VC would be a thing of beauty. Staring at the various dossiers late that night, I realized I had made up my mind. We would go for her.

The next day I brought Lou in and told him I wanted him and Buffalo One to take over the case. "What I'd like you to do," I said, "is find her former boyfriend. He's the one who should make the approach. Offer him some money on a continuing basis, and ask him to make a visit to her at her home. Give him a lump sum for her and see if he can't use it to set up a rendezvous with her at my house; we can give them one of the back rooms and they can stay the night. If we get this far, the boyfriend can explain that he is working for Americans and can outline what we have in mind. Then, next morning, he can introduce his friends to her, namely you and Buffalo One."

I felt fairly comfortable that Cuu Long, the ex-lover, would jump at the chance. First of all he was a *hoi chanh*, so if he was handled properly it would be easy for him to decide it was in his interests to go along. Then there was the money, not something he'd find easy to turn down. I was also pretty sure he'd like the idea of spending a night with his old flame. He had been separated from her because of his defection, but Ly had not heard that there was any personal animosity between them. Besides, I knew that many Vietnamese men are rascals—in the sense that they do like to play around, probably more so than Americans. It may not be a universal, but it's not far from one. The female agent might also be prone. According to Ly, it was after her lover's defection that she had taken up with the MA chief. So there would likely be some romantic nostalgia on her part too. Her cover as a Saigon black marketeer would also give her the ability to stop overnight at Bien Hoa. There would be nothing to arouse suspicion on the part of her VC supervisors. What with the sex, the excitement, all that money flowing around—it was a heady mixture. It had a shot.

It didn't take long for Lou to find Cuu Long. After being processed through the Region Three Chieu Hoi system (we had him in our 201 file) he had gone to live in Binh Duong. So Binh Duong Chieu Hoi administration had his address. Long agreed to come to Bien Hoa for a discussion, and when he did, Lou told him that what we wanted to do was recruit his former girlfriend. Cuu Long was quick to agree. He was ecstatic about the money; he thought the chances were good that he could persuade her to come to Bien Hoa.

A week later Cuu Long visited his old lover in Hoc Mon, coming, he said, just to see how she was getting along. He also told her that he would love to meet her in Bien Hoa, where he could arrange a place for them to spend the night. And he had ten thousand piasters to help with household expenses. Whatever she might have thought was behind this idea, she agreed to see him, and she took the map and instructions he gave her.

On the day of the meeting, Cuu Long arrived in Bien Hoa early. Then we all waited to see if the wife would arrive. That night, just after dark, a bus pulled up at the movie-theater stop across from the JIC and a woman passenger got out. She walked south along Highway #1, toward Cong Ly. As she did, Buffalo One watched her from a balcony of the building across the street. When he was satisfied that no one was following her, he ran downstairs to his car and drove off toward my house. Ten minutes later the woman was walking down Cong Ly street. Again she was watched, this time from a second-floor window of the house at Number 15. A few yards before the dark alley that led to the rear entrance of the house she squatted and urinated in the gutter, a natural enough activity for a Vietnamese woman at night. As she did, she looked carefully around her. The street was empty.

A moment later she disappeared into the darkness of the alley. At the gate to my backyard, Cuu Long was waiting to let her in. Once inside the house he led her to a back bedroom with a mirror on the wall. Watching from behind the mirror were Buffalo One and Lou, her soon-to-be handlers.

In a small refrigerator there were refreshments, and Cuu Long, a former security officer himself, conducted the proceedings as if he were Clark Gable. It was, to say the least, a successful conjugal reunion, so much so that Buffalo One was in stitches telling me about it later. "How did you know it would work?" he asked. "I didn't," I answered. "It was just a hunch. But that's an odd question for you to ask. You know better than I do the kind of reputation you Vietnamese men have."

At a propitious moment during the night, Cuu Long told his lover that he was being paid by the Americans to recruit her. The Americans, he emphasized, not Saigon. They were offering her thirty thousand p a month; it would be great for her and her mother, who lived with her. The agent was astonished by the amount (about $70 a month). It lit up her eyes. "This is an American operation?" she asked. According to Buffalo One she sounded relieved, and she wanted confirmation. When Cuu Long told her that he would introduce her to his friends in the morning, she quickly accepted.

In their intermittent conversations during the night, the agent told Cuu Long that she was not happy with the way things were going anyway, even though she had been carrying on with her work. Listening to a translation of the tapes, I had the sense that I was in the presence of an agent who was very close to going over the line, and that we had given her the opportunity to do something she might have eventually done anyway. It's not that uncommon an occurrence, certainly it isn't exclusively Vietnamese. In recent years a number of American agents have found they could no longer abide the things they were doing and crossed the line: Phillip Agee, from the South American operation, and John Stockwell, who ran Angola for a while (John was the officer in charge in Tay Ninh during the last months of Vietnam and I was surprised his experience then didn't alienate him completely from his job and his employer). Cuu Long's wife was part of that club, alienated, though not quite enough to quit. Now, suddenly, she was being given a chance to work for herself while at the same time staying out of the hands of the South Vietnamese. For her, what we were offering was tailor-made. For us, the timing had been a stroke of luck.

The next morning, Cuu Long's ex, already dubbed the Goldmother (from the two thin golden "luong" that dangled from a string between her breasts—Buffalo One and Lou had seen them through the mirror) met with Lou and Buffalo One. They explained to her the kind of information we needed and assured her that we would not share any of the operation, especially her identity, with the South Vietnamese.

From that day on, the Goldmother came once a week to the back room at 15 Cong Ly to meet with Lou and Buffalo One (though not with Cuu Long). Until the end of the war she provided intelligence on everything that went on in Subregion One. Military Affairs was always at the top of the COSVN distribution list, and her liaison with the section chief gave her knowledge even beyond what she would normally have. She gave us the names of her own network of eleven agents, and she gave us the gist of the spy reports that were going back to COSVN. More than a "goldmother," she was a gold mine.

We knew from the Tu Duc debriefing that the Vietcong's Military Region Three sources were usually developed through family contacts of ARVN soldiers. An uncle, for example, would bring all his influence to bear on a favorite nephew who might be a lieutenant or captain. The ARVN officer would thus find himself under a lot of pressure from a respected older relative, and he would also find himself thinking about his family back on their farm in some contested area. The VC proselyters were expert at planting the seed of fear; explicit threats were almost never needed. The soldier's family was out there, and *they* were out there, and all they wanted was a little help. It was a double-barreled approach, subtle, but effective. So we had the background on how it worked, even if we never did get the identities of Tu Duc's sources.

Consequently we were well prepared to understand the Goldmother's operation. She ran a network of agents, many of them stationed at the 5th Division camp, who would report to her at her house in the market. Her most significant source was a colonel who was in charge of all supplies going to Hoc Mon and Duc Hue. Whenever the ARVN 5th Division began any sort of supply buildup or matériel transfer in preparation for an operation, the Goldmother would know about it and report it.

After reviewing the Goldmother's operation, Jack, Lou, and I decided to leave her network undisturbed. Knowing what information she was reporting back gave us a way of offsetting any real damage, as well as the means to plant false information if ever there was a serious need. But the intelligence she was supplying to her supervisors was not nearly as important as what she was giving us, which was nothing less than a fairly detailed outline of all subregional military activity one week—sometimes two weeks—in advance.

We would make this information available on an as-needed basis to ARVN and American units. We would, for example, inform Major Ngo in Trang Bang that the 101st was going to attack the Trang Bang market, or cut Highway #1 two klicks north of the district capital, on such and such a day at such and such a time. (For some reason they always did it two klicks north of the capital. It was almost a fetish.) The information was always detailed and accurate. We knew exactly when they would come in and which units would be involved. Often we even knew why. More than once their orders declared that the purpose of the operation was to "punish" the Trang Bang district chief. (It was understandable: Major Ngo regularly gave them fits.) Acting on the Goldmother's intelligence, Major Ngo would set a Regional Forces ambush along the highway complete with heavy weapons, and when the 101st tried to cut the highway, he would massacre them. He'd end up punishing them instead of them him. With this sort of intelligence reported to us weekly, we had no interest in burning the Goldmother's spies. If we burned the spies we knew we'd also be burning her.

Because political officers at the subregion level would always brief the key sections, the Goldmother had access not just to tactical information but to all significant directives and resolutions. In addition, she picked up the loose talk in the tunnels at night, of which there was plenty. One of the things the Vietcong was not good at was compartmentalizing information, that is, limiting the distribution of information to the appropriate persons. Like all Vietnamese, they loved to talk; they were gregarious, almost compulsive talkers. And they could not resist bragging about their accomplishments.

Of course in late 1971 and early 1972 they were also talking about the beating they were taking from the Americans and the South Vietnamese. So we knew then that they were suffering, that they were losing their grip even on contested areas. In one of the Goldmother's reports, she described how at one staff meeting they discussed their agent losses. Subregion One ran about seventy-five agents altogether. But the B-52 strikes on the Saigon River were wreaking havoc. The Military Proselyting, MI, and MA sections were located on the Saigon River north of the Cu Chi base camp (an area of massive tunnels) and they were taking casualties from the bombing. Their recruiting was at a standstill. The only replacements they could get were from Hanoi. Even the security squads that protected the sections were all North Vietnamese.

Because the Goldmother was so knowledgeable about ARVN and because she was intimately familiar with the geographical area, another of her functions was to identify and target significant ARVN facilities. These were delicate situations, since she was involved herself and we wanted to protect her. But we were able to stop some attacks. On one occasion she led in a sapper team with explosives, which they cached near the new Route Nine bridge, planning to come back and blow it at a later date. We informed Colonel Thao, the G-2 about this, and shortly afterward an ARVN patrol on an apparently routine reconnaissance found the cache. Thao himself developed an active curiosity about our source, but this was not the kind of thing I would share with him. I never inquired into his sources, I told him; we just knew them by code name. The "Goldmother" would have to be good enough.

The Goldmother had been developed through her old lover. At about the same time, we were trying to develop another spy through a spouse. But the end result of this attempt was not happy, and almost landed my Lan in serious danger.

In Phu Hoa one day, near the Subregion One headquarters, a VC suspect was picked up in a sweep, an extremely attractive girl of about twenty-five. We questioned her at the JIC for almost two weeks before we were able to establish her identity and the fact that she was a relatively low-level Women's Association member. The intriguing element here was not who she turned out to be, but that she had forced us to do so much work to find out. As a result Bingo team kept on the case, tracking down lead after lead in the data bank until finally the prisoner admitted that her husband was deputy chief of the Subregion One civilian proselyting section.

When Albert came to me with the report, I decided that we would try to use the girl as an avenue to her husband. Despite Co Luong's initial stubbornness, she seemed like an essentially passive person who was frightened by her capture and interrogation. It seemed to me that if we put her in a really friendly environment we might be able to win her over. I was willing to bet that after a week of living at 15 Cong Ly with Lan taking care of her, Luong would be ready to do what we asked.

This was not the first time I had asked Lan to handle VC women prisoners; it was something she was especially good at. She was not afraid of these people and she had a natural, friendly way about her that almost always elicited a warm response. I had given her firm instructions not to talk about anything related to intelligence. I just wanted her to make friends and provide companionship as one woman to another, exactly the kind of thing she would do without any urging from me.

As I expected, before long Lan and Luong became friends. The worst thing about her predicament, the VC told Lan, was how much she missed her husband. So much so that at night she often cried for him. When this came out, Albert played on it. He knew, he told Luong, a way that things might work out so it could be helpful to both herself and her husband. But only if she thought she could go back home, see him, then come back to talk to us.

Giving her the opportunity to leave was something of a gamble, but not that much of one. Luong herself was low level; there was nothing to be gained from her directly. If we could use her to catch her husband, that could bring substantial benefits, but if it didn't work we really weren't losing anything.

To give Luong a little extra motivation Albert did a bit of intimidating too. We knew where her family lived, he told her, and we knew her younger brother and sister were getting to be guerrilla age. If she disappeared into the jungle instead of coming back, some Regional Forces might happen to find themselves in her neighborhood picking up VC suspects.

Luong got the message and after thinking about it a while decided to go ahead with Albert's suggestion. Carrying an ARVN safe-conduct pass tucked into her vagina (in case she was stopped along the way), she found her way home and told her husband what had happened. She had been captured, then was turned over to the Americans, who had treated her well and had offered her money in return for cooperation. All she had to do was go back and give them a little information. Then she could come home and see him again.

Over the following two months Luong made five trips in and out of Phu Hoa, bringing with her fairly good intelligence, especially targeting information, which we fed to Colonel Thao. But after her sixth trip she did not come back. I had not had high hopes for this penetration to begin with. But now that her husband had gone along and she had been going back and forth it seemed strange that she'd just disappear. I wanted to know what had happened to her, and if the connection could somehow be saved.

By this time Lan and Luong had grown quite close and it occurred to me that Lan was perhaps the right person to try to see her. She lived in a real backwoods area that was infested with Vietcong, but a girl or, better yet, two girls on a motorbike (I could get another one of Lan's ex-VC friends to go with her) were unlikely to cause any suspicion.

Following a map that Luong had drawn of her home area, Lan and her friend Nam, who was six months pregnant, drove deep

into the hinterlands of Phu Hoa on a little Honda Fifty, Nam sitting
on the back. Nam was a former VC who had been very cooperative
and had become quite good friends with Lan. Together they traveled down Route Four, then turned off onto a side road that soon
turned into a path that wound its way through dikes and rice paddies. When they finally got to Luong's house no one was home
except a thirteen-year-old boy wearing black pajamas who ran off
into the field in back of the house as soon as he saw them coming.

Lan was frightened, sure that the boy was going off to warn the
local VC that strangers were in the area. Running after him, she
managed to catch up before he got into the trees. They were good
friends of his sister's, she told him. They had just come out from
Bien Hoa to visit her. If he came back into the house she'd fix some
of the food she had brought along.

Back in the house Lan was putting some fruit and a few sweets
onto the table when Luong walked in with her mother. All Luong's
hair had been shaved, a sign either that she had been put to shame
or that she was in mourning. While her mother prepared lunch,
she and Lan talked quietly. "I couldn't come back," Luong said
under her breath. "Something happened to my husband." Lan
understood immediately—Luong was telling her that he was dead.

Just as they sat down at the table to eat, three men in pajamas
with checkered scarves around their necks came into the house, all
of them carrying AK-47s. The scarves alone—the typical VC
adornment—would have been enough to scare Lan and Nam to
death. When Luong saw them she stood up very respectfully. Then
she introduced Lan and her friend to the men—her two uncles
and her cousin. Lan, she said, had been her employer while she
was in Bien Hoa, in a little sewing shop, and Nam was a fellow
worker. Yes, Lan said, thinking on her feet. When Luong disappeared from work she had been worried about her, so she and her
friend had come out to see if she was all right.

As Lan struggled to keep calm the men started asking her questions: Where did she live? What did her parents do? What kind of
people did she like—poor or middle class or upper class? She realized that they had started on a peasant-style Marxist interrogation.
"I like everybody," she managed to get out, "but I'm from the poor
class myself." When she said that she was from the poor class it
apparently was convincing, shop owner or no. And of course it was
true; as beautiful as Lan was, a Vietnamese would not mistake her
origin. Satisfied for the moment, the three sat down to lunch, while
Luong asked Lan to come into her bedroom so they could talk.

In the bedroom Luong told Lan, "I hope you understand what's happening here." With tears beginning to run down her cheeks she scribbled a short note and stuck it into Lan's bra. "It's for Ong Gia," she said, standing up and giving Lan a hug. "Go home and tell him that I can't come. I'm in trouble right now."

When they walked into the main room Luong had dried the tears. Taking Lan and Nam to the door she told them loud enough to be heard by the men at the table that it was rice harvest, so she wouldn't be able to come back into the city. She had to stay and help her family. Back on the motorbike Lan drove as fast as she could, Nam in back of her with a death lock around her stomach. The note said simply that she was sorry she could not come back due to personal problems. We never knew exactly what had happened, but we surmised that her husband had been killed in an air strike, and that she had blamed herself for it. We never did find out to what extent the VC knew about her activities or what her eventual fate was.

By the end of Don Gregg's tour the JIC had really hit its stride. We were now consistently producing at the level of eighty reports a month. In any given month between 60 and 80 percent of all intelligence being reported in Vietnam was coming directly out of the JIC, according to Saigon Station's monthly intelligence synopsis. And a large number of our reports were graded A, the top evaluation. Within the closed confines of the Agency, the Bien Hoa base was making a name for itself. So much so that late in 1971 Richard Helms, the CIA director, came to visit.

It was a rare occurrence. Nobody could think of when a director had actually visited a base before. When they traveled they stopped at stations, but never local bases. There was no question but that Don Gregg had pulled a major bureaucratic coup. "It will be you and me," he said, "Jack, Rudy Enders [the PRU adviser] and Bill Wheeler [the special police adviser]. If you want to bring Lou along that will be OK." We were to meet in the lounge a little before Helms's arrival time to run through what was supposed to happen.

That afternoon in the lounge Don said, "Orrin, we're not going to brief him on everything that's going on. Mainly I want Rudy to give him a quick overview of the PRU operations. If Helms asks you anything directly I want you to glance at me before you say anything. If I nod no, give the most nondescript answer you can think of. If I nod yes, you can go ahead and answer him directly." I was amazed at this, and a little upset. For his own reasons Gregg was not eager to broadcast news of the JIC. I understood he had put himself on the line, making expenditures for the program that

were not exactly in accord with his budgetary requirements. But I
took a good deal of pride in the operation and I was not going to be
muzzled about it. If Helms asks, I thought, I'll tell him the facts.

As it turned out, Gregg needn't have worried. Helms was coming
to Bien Hoa, but that didn't mean he had plans for an extended
visit. He arrived in a roar of his blue-and-white chopper, and listened to Rudy Enders' briefing. That seemed to satisfy him. He
asked no questions at all, neither of Rudy nor of me nor of anyone
else, though before he left he did express a few words of congratulations for the job Bien Hoa was doing. And with that he was back
in the chopper and gone.

In a sense, the visit was a fitting way to usher out Don Gregg's
tour, which toward the end of 1971 was coming to a close. Helms
obviously appreciated the work we were doing—he wouldn't have
come otherwise. But he appeared to have little interest in either
the details of the operation or the people involved in it. He made
an appearance, but that was all.

My overall impression of Don Gregg was not much different. He
had been there, but there was little to remember him by. The man
had been my boss for eighteen months, but I hardly knew him. He
was, in my estimation, a bureaucrat, and a good one; he had provided the support for what I was doing, but he had never fostered
anything like a relationship; either with me or with the other base
officers. He had kept himself far removed from the base's ongoing
operations and from the people who carried them out.

Since no one was really close enough to Don Gregg to give him
a farewell party, he threw himself one, as an office function in the
Monastery's upstairs recreation room. In addition to the base staff
and some of the officers in charge, Gregg invited key ARVN personnel, including Little Minh, commander in chief of Military Region Three, Colonel Thao, Colonel Dinh, and several others.
Some of the leading officers from the American Second Field
Forces were also there, all of us having snacks and drinks overlook-
ing the Dong Nai. It was a low-keyed affair without much warmth.
Jack Martel said a few words, though very few. He had been running the base as exec, but he hadn't been close to Don either.
When he finished, somebody voiced the obligatory "Speech,
speech," then Don got up, looked around, and started to talk. And
as he did, tears came into his eyes.

Looking at Lou I saw him rolling his eyes. Don was talking about
his extremely successful tour, how touched he was that he had
been able to do all the things he did, how sorry he was that he had
to leave, though of course the time had come, so he must. And all

the while there were tears in his eyes and on his cheeks. This was a
difficult man to understand, a cold fish who was moved to tears by
the thought of his own performance. Loren Snowcroft had been
such a human guy; this one was all business, an operator who could
throw himself a farewell party and cry over his own departure. As
the speech wound down I found myself wondering what in the
world the next chief of base might be like.

Bob Somerhill, the new chief of base, was a happy man. He had
spent his entire professional life in the Agency, including more
than twenty-five years in Africa as head of various Stations there.
A GS-16 already, he was now closing out a successful career. He
had volunteered for Vietnam, but this would be his last tour before
he retired. He was a man with no ambitions, and it showed in the
relaxed manner with which he approached both people and problems. He was short and heavy, with an engaging personality and a
hearty laugh, a study in contrasts with Gregg. Somerhill had a
habit of hugging people when he met them; he passed hugs around
like a father. He'd hug the secretaries each morning when he came
in, and everybody else who walked into his office was also likely to
get a little hug or a pat on the back.

We had met briefly on the day he arrived, and the following day
I got a call from Jack Martel. Apparently Somerhill had done a
good deal of research at Station, Jack told me. "He knows a lot
about the JIC and would like to have a thorough briefing on it and
a guided tour. I want to go through it again myself," said Jack, "so
I'll come along with him."

The next morning they came over. "Orrin," Somerhill began,
"I'm not going to say much; I mainly want to listen and go for a
tour. I'd also like to meet a Vietcong or a North Vietnamese if you
can arrange it." The next two hours or so we spent in the JIC going
over everything, including a detailed examination of the data bank
with its case after case full of subject files and 201 files. I explained
how the process worked and the directions we were going in, making a point of describing the various operational leads and how the
only thing preventing us from making a comprehensive assault on
VC security was our lack of case officers. Walking through the
interrogation units, we stopped to talk with one of Gekko team's
North Vietnamese sources, a sergeant who had come down the Ho
Chi Minh Trail the year before. Through Gekko One, Sam's lead
interpreter, Somerhill asked a number of personal questions: why
he had joined the army, how long he had been in, what his trip
down the trail had been like, what some of his experiences in the

South had been. It was immediately obvious from Somerhill's manner that he was an experienced interrogator, and the sergeant for his part was open and talkative. In fifteen minutes the new chief of base acquired more personal knowledge of what we were dealing with than his predecessor had in a year and a half.

When we went back to my office for coffee, Somerhill told Jack and me that during World War Two he had interrogated German prisoners of war in North Africa. They had had nothing to support the interrogations then, he said, no idea about who any of the people were they were talking to and little possibility of cross-checking. "You hoped they were telling you the truth," he said, "though you knew that most of the time they weren't. Not that you had any options in that kind of a situation. But what it meant was that as an interrogator you were working blindfolded." The data bank, he went on, was not something he had ever seen before. It seemed the ideal tool for interrogation. "What I really want to do with this," he said, "is to let people know what capabilities we have out here."

Turning to Jack, Somerhill asked him to contact the Agency's national adviser to the Special Branch Police, to bring him out to Bien Hoa and brief him on the JIC. "I'd also like Orrin to personally brief the commanding general of Region Three," he said. "I'm sure he doesn't completely understand what our capabilities are. General Hollingsworth at Second Field Forces ought to be brought in too, so that he can hear firsthand what kind of targeting is available to him. I've always been a great one for liaison. My philosophy is that our officers ought to be known to the governments they're working with, and that relevant people ought to be completely aware of what we can make available to them, if they want to use it. By the way, Orrin, you are planning to stay through my tour aren't you?" "Yes," I answered, "I'm staying to the end, whatever it is and whenever it is." "That's good," he said. "I want this liaisoning done; Jack will set it up and manage it. I also want you to get some good furniture in your office, maybe some sofas, coffee tables, a rug on the floor. You're going to be having people coming in here and I want to give them the right impression. As far as the JIC goes, I won't be bothering you at all. Just keep the results coming in."

Well, that was a hell of a great welcome, I thought when he left. With Bob Somerhill and Jack Martel running the show the work environment would be first-rate. Maybe I'd even be able to get some extra case officers.

On the other hand, all this liaison business had to be handled carefully, especially with the Vietnamese. My relationships with Colonels Thao and Dinh were excellent, but it had taken a long time to develop a high level of trust with them, and those two were straight-arrow workaholics. The same went for Colonel Thanh, the Hau Nghia province chief, and Major Ngo in Trang Bang. As far as other Vietnamese went, I was happy enough to talk to them in general terms. But any more detailed kind of cooperation might bring all kinds of potential liabilities. It was not a timely attitude, I knew, what with Vietnamization in full swing. But if the Agency's special police adviser was going to show up, it could easily lead to expectations on the part of the police themselves. And that was a disturbing prospect.

The first liaison visitor was Little Minh, the Military Region Three commander. With him came three or four of his staff officers and Colonel Thao, the G-2. That went fine. Little Minh was a quiet, unobtrusive guy, and Thao and I had been working closely together anyway. But then Jack announced that the National Police director and the Special Branch director would be coming out. Arrangements had already been made. "If they want to send their people up here to get information, they can, right?" Jack asked. "Sure," I said. "There's no harm in giving them sanitized versions of it. That's what I've been giving Colonel Dinh right along." I had met both directors before, the National Police chief during my initial briefings in Saigon, and the special police commander when he came out after the N-10 operation. This time I briefed them in detail about how the data bank worked and suggested that each of their offices ought to institute the same kind of system.

The following day the Special Branch commander asked Jack Martel if he could send a team of officers up to work on-site in the JIC; he wanted to use our resources to work on undeveloped leads to recruit agents. What he had in mind was eight or nine case officers under a major and a captain. He was conveying his request with the endorsement of the Agency's special police adviser.

This was exactly the kind of development I was dreading. Having Special Branch officers working in my office was a horrifying idea. I had had too much experience with them. I didn't trust a single one of them and I didn't want them there. "This is an independent operation," I told Jack and Bob Somerhill, "and I want to keep it that way. These people will compromise anything at any time. Look what happened with the N-10 sappers. We still can't get any details on it. Dinh says it was a shakedown all the way and I don't doubt it for a moment. We've got to keep these guys out of here." But for all the ranting I did it was useless. The special police adviser had laid it on with Bob Somerhill and Jack had already agreed to it.

It wasn't more than a week or so before these rascals came trooping into the JIC from Saigon: Major Binh, Captain Bui, and eight officers. "Where are our desks?" they said. "We're ready to work." Feeling unhappy about the whole thing, I made room for them in an office above Sam and Gary's, then had the major assign them to observe the different interrogation teams. I also gave them access to the data bank, as ordered. But nothing came of it, nothing bad (as I had feared), and nothing positive (as I had expected). They mainly sat around and marked time.

More productive liaison sessions were with General Hamlet, chief of staff Second Field Forces, and General Hollingsworth, his commander. They wanted to express their appreciation for the targeting we were giving them and to let me know they were eager to have anything more we could provide. Vietnamization might have put many American units into a defensive posture, but Hollingsworth in particular was not buying that approach. "We've got nothing but airplanes, choppers, and gunships," said one of his colonels, wearing the distinctive horse soldier cowboy hat of the First Air Cavalry. "Just give us the targeting and we'll get anything that's out there. You want to supervise it personally from a command chopper, just tell us and we'll arrange it for you."

These guys were aggressive; they just soaked up targeting information. And there was plenty to soak up. The Mad Bomber, the Goldmother, and the Reaper were all reporting enemy intentions in Military Region Three. In Paris the secret talks between Henry Kissinger and Le Duc Tho, which had been going on for more than a year and a half, had broken down. It was mid-November when Le Duc Tho excused himself from continuing the dialogue, due, he said, to illness. Within a few weeks we were aware that a North Vietnamese buildup was under way. By December 1971, sources were reporting tanks all along the border; hundreds of them were being concentrated in the vicinity of Mimot.

But even as we were straining all our resources to determine what the NVA had in mind, the Reaper and the Mad Bomber both reported a startling new COSVN directive, Resolution 20. The fallout from this resolution would soon be providing us with the highest-level informants we had yet had, and insight into the heart of the Central Office for South Vietnam itself.

10

DISASTER IN PARIS

COSVN Resolution 20 was distributed to all levels of the Vietcong hierarchy, right down to the village secretaries. It was couched in the usual revolutionary format and language, intended to inform the initiated and confuse everyone else. To the fighting units and party committees that received it, the message was chilling. Local and main forces, it said, were at low levels. Recruiting was becoming almost impossible; strongest measures had to be taken at all levels from the hamlet up to bring in new people. Even in terms of the usually objective COSVN analyses, this was grim stuff. In effect COSVN 20 was announcing to the party cadres that the movement was back at square one, that there was nothing to do except start rebuilding. And this to people who had been fighting for their entire adult lives.

Shortly after we received COSVN 20 we began seeing a new flow of disaffected Vietcong. Many of them had concluded that they just couldn't go on. After a decade fighting the French and thirteen years fighting the South Vietnamese and Americans, it was too much to ask. We also began to see a new kind of defector. High-level cadres began to walk out of COSVN itself.

The first was Nguyen Van Bay, the assistant chief of the COSVN supply section. He and his wife, a cultural cadre, just walked out through Mimot, across the border, and into northern Tay Ninh. At the district headquarters they announced that they were from "R"—the code for COSVN—and wanted to defect.

A day later the two of them were sitting in the JIC talking to Felix. They were not going to start over, they said. They were too old. They had been in the jungles for years and now nothing they could see on the horizon looked promising. They were fed up with the war and all they wanted to do was go home.

Within a week they were joined by Mai Thi Trang, a fifty-year-old COSVN political officer who came out with her Chinese husband. Like Nguyen Van Bay and his wife, Trang was smart, well trained, and highly knowledgeable, a key operative. For her too COSVN 20 had been one straw too many.

As a high-ranking political officer, Mai Thi Trang knew the truth behind COSVN 20 firsthand, province by province. Recruitment problems had grown to disastrous proportions. Those who understood what was happening believed that the relentless pressure from the Americans and the South Vietnamese had finally crushed the Vietcong. There were only about a dozen or two main-force battalions wandering around out there, where there used to be 150. Units that hadn't received substantial reinforcement from the North were so far down they were barely functional. The Vietcong's 506th Battalion in Long An, for example, was down to sixty people, most of whom were young and inexperienced. But that was typical. Battalions whose full strength had been 180 were operating at a third that number. A company of sixty now had fewer than twenty. They couldn't function; they couldn't recruit. It was much harder to get supplies; the peasants weren't giving them the same kind of help. The NVA was taking over everything. The Vietcong —the Southern revolutionary forces that had borne the brunt of this war since the beginning—was history.

For the disaffected COSVN intellectuals there were two significant points. First was the fact (as they saw it) that they could not win. Over the years of hard fighting their organizations had been decimated and their recruitment pool had dried up. They had reached the point of no return. The second was that by early 1972 the North Vietnamese presence, which had been building for almost a decade, finally reached a critical mass. This was not something the Southerners saw in terms of statistics; it was more a feeling that seemed to take hold at this time (many of course had felt it earlier). Whatever balance between South and North that might have existed at one time existed no longer. Northern soldiers and political cadres were not just reinforcements; they permeated the system in the South. Why was an NVA colonel running the Vietcong's Subregion Five H-1 Battalion? Why was an NVA lieutenant taking over the C-1 Company of Trang Bang district? Why was it that everywhere you looked, junior as well as senior NVA officers had taken leadership positions?

For the Vietcong lower- and middle-level cadres this development was confusing and disturbing. But for the intellectuals it was ominous. Many of them, even hard-line ideologues, could not help putting two and two together. And the answer they came up with was that one way or another they were lost. If the Americans didn't get them sooner, the Northerners—those Bac Viet—would get them later. And so they decided to come out. Along with them they brought an intimate and detailed understanding of COSVN's structure and procedures. We debriefed Nguyen Van Bay and his wife in exhaustive detail, and we set up Mai Thi Trang (and her husband) in the back room at 15 Cong Ly, where she acted as a kind of permanent consultant on COSVN and regional-level affairs. Our interrogators would go to her with specific questions, and Lou and I spent hours talking to her about background, decision making, and policy. Albert was in love with her. "God, is that woman smart," he would tell me after spending time with her. "She knows everything." And his enchantment was spurred by the hope that if he just talked with her enough he would eventually uncover some bit of information or some contact that might lead to an agent inside COSVN.

Another cadre who came out at this time was a district-level military intelligence operative from Trang Bang by the name of Anh Thi Ly. She had been in the Vietcong for half her life, but COSVN 20 had pushed her over the line too. Like Nguyen Van Bay, Ly brought her family—her husband and children. But unlike Bay, she was evasive. She had wanted out badly enough to defect, but that didn't mean she was eager to give us any straight answers.

Nevertheless, we had first-rate information in the data bank on Trang Bang, and when Ly understood that we were able to check what she was saying, she began to open up. She had a world of personal information on district-level personnel, though little that was operationally useful. Meanwhile, Liem, her husband, claimed that he was not a member of the VC at all, but had come out of the district so that he and the three children could stay with his wife.

I didn't believe Liem's story for a moment; it was unlikely that a relatively high-level cadre would have a husband who was innocent of any involvement. And when I showed his file to Hai Duc, the former area recon captain, he recognized him. Liem was, he said, from Cut Trau hamlet, part of Loc Hung village. Together with Albert, Hai Duc talked to Liem at length. Then he talked to his wife, probing the discrepancies in their stories. By this time I was developing a feeling that both of these people could be something different from what they were telling us they were.

Finally, after Hai Duc had discussed all his Cut Trau neighbors with Liem and had let him know that he and Albert were going down to check the hamlet books, he thought better of his story. Any thorough interrogation of his friends in the hamlet was likely to uncover more than he wanted known. So after hemming and hawing as much as he could, he admitted his involvement. He was not a formal member of the Vietcong, but he had on occasion "helped out" in the COSVN B-22 finance economy section.

The B-22 finance economy section was not an organization we had ever heard of. There was no entry for it in the data bank and nobody at the JIC remembered anyone mentioning it. Nevertheless, at this point we hit the wife with Liem's admission. Why hadn't she told us about this before? The reply was typical. She hadn't wanted to get involved; she simply wanted to pass through the system with as little trouble as possible. For the next two days Albert talked to her, even offering her a job with the JIC—and all the benefits that would mean. But the prerequisite was her total cooperation. Then Albert suggested that perhaps she too was a member of the B-22 finance economy section. But Ly adamantly denied this. Yes, she knew her husband did work as a messenger, but she never discussed it with her husband; she knew essentially nothing about the B-22.

Clearly both Ly and Liem knew far more than they were saying. So we kept at them, playing one off against the other. Finally Liem identified several others who he said were B-22 couriers. Their mission was to run money from Saigon to the An Thanh station on the Cambodian border, near Go Dau Ha district capital. Using this information to question Ly, we got her to admit that she did know about the network, and she too named a number of couriers.

All of this was intriguing, but unfortunately we could find no corroboration in the data bank for any of the names she gave us. Even Hai Duc, who had told us that he knew all units operating in the area, was stumped. The B-22 finance economy section was a surprise to him. "It must really be top secret," he said, "otherwise I would have known about it for sure."

Meanwhile Liem was opening up a bit more. He had earlier identified the two contacts he worked with: the two he did liaison

for when he worked. Now he named six others, all of them involved in the money network. They all traveled regularly, he said,
moving up to the equivalent of $50,000 a day in cash between
Saigon and Cambodia.

I had no reason to doubt Liem's word about the amounts involved, even though they were immense. If he was right, we were
talking about somewhere on the order of $1.5 million a month
flowing from Saigon to COSVN. That was undoubtedly a good
part of the financing for Vietcong and NVA activities in Military
Region Three, and if it was coming out of Saigon it meant that a
large bank there had to be involved. Either there was a VC-
controlled bank in the capital or someone very high up in a legitimate bank was working with them. Given the amounts involved,
the frequency of movement, and the kinds of banking regulations
in effect, whoever was managing the supply had to have protection
at the highest levels of the South Vietnamese government. Most
likely, I thought, a minister or deputy minister.

But try as we might we did not succeed in identifying any of the
couriers. Liem gave us code names only, and although I was sure
he was holding back, he doggedly claimed he did not know any real
names and had told us everything he was aware of. Despite all the
research we could do through the hamlet books and through our
own data and live resources, we were not able to make identifications. And there were no other leads to the organization. The
network was, as Hai Duc had said, supersecret.

When I ran out of leads I opened up the situation to Colonel
Dinh. But he had nothing on B-22 himself, and his efforts turned
up no more than mine had. Meanwhile, with other operations
developing and no slacking off in the daily intelligence reporting,
the energy drain involved in the B-22 case was becoming excessive.
We were getting nowhere. Finally I decided there was no alternative but to move it to a back burner.

Other operations were indeed developing very positively. One of
the defectors Lou was interrogating turned out to be a relative of
the village secretary in the district of Di An. Already an expert at
identifying effective cutouts and contacts, Lou found the right person in the secretary's family to approach on a straight money basis.
As usual, Lou had done his homework well. The cutout was right
and the incentive was right. Using a dead drop, weekly reports now
started coming out of Di An.

Here was another first-rate agent, developed in a way that most
people thought would have been impossible. The Vietnam War
ignited deep emotions over profound issues: revolution and Com-

munism, American geopolitical influence, the nature of life for twenty million South Vietnamese. And yet despite the ideals and passions, the most common human desires were all too evident, not just in the South Vietnamese government, which was riddled with corruption, but on the other side too. Although with the Reaper, the Mad Bomber, and the Goldmother, there were close relationships involved in the making of a spy, money was also a part of it. People just jumped at the chance to make a buck.

Unfortunately, the Di An Doozie (as we nicknamed this agent) did not last. After he had been operating about a year, he got word to us that he was positive VC security was on his trail. They were watching his movements carefully. A last message read: "Please do not contact me again. I cannot service the dead drop." His information was excellent, Grade A reports. But in reviewing the situation Lou and I decided that attempting to renew the contact through another channel would be too dangerous for him and we reluctantly let it drop.

A second agent Lou developed about the same time, however, served well right until the end of the war. This was a district-level security cadre whom Lou managed to contact through a stepbrother who was a *hoi chanh*. The *hoi chanh* told Lou that the security cadre was disaffected, angry at the war and angry at the way the Vietcong was handling it. Here again was the typical pattern: an approach through a relative, an offer of money, and if the potential agent was half fed up anyway, he would absolutely come over. The elements were simple, but manipulating them was not. Doing that well required tenacious background work, a close feel for the nature of Vietnamese social and family ties, and first-rate character judgment. There was no doubt that Lou was becoming a master of the game. With this new agent in Duc Hue, Region Three's network of spies now numbered five—the Reaper, the Goldmother, the Mad Bomber, and now the Di An Doozie and the Duc Hue Tiger.

Meanwhile, however, I found that I couldn't keep my mind away from those B-22 money runners. In one of my continuing sessions with Nguyen Van Bay, the COSVN supply section deputy chief, it came out that he knew B-22 quite well. Yes, the money did come out from Saigon several times a week, at the rate of $1.5 million or so a month. Across the Cambodian border it was delivered to a man named Ba Minh, who brought it to COSVN in Mimot. From that point the COSVN finance economy section allocated the funds and distributed them via their own couriers to all the military units in the region. With it they bought food, medicine, clothing, blankets, and even ammunition. They especially liked canned goods, which, along with other supplies, were stolen from the American PXs.

In addition to Ba Minh, the B-22 finance agent on the border, Nguyen Van Bay knew the stations along the line going up Highway #1—Saigon, Hoc Mon, Suoi Sao, Trang Bang, Go Dau Ha, An Thanh. The couriers, he said, were mainly little old ladies who carried the money in new bills wrapped around their bodies. Their supervisor was another oldster, a man who had been chief of the network for years.

This old man—Albert and I immediately christened him "Grandpa"—was a target worth shooting for. With him in our hands we would have a chance of tracing the money to its source and nailing the bank and the Saigon government official behind it. If we could bring him into play as an agent, we would in addition have specific intelligence on the whole length of the Saigon corridor. All local activity around Highway #1 would undoubtedly be disseminated to him in advance. And if at some point Hanoi planned to march on the Southern capital down this route, Grandpa and his team would be the first to know about it. We would thus have advance notice of any significant attacks along this major strategic axis.

With this kind of prize staring at us, Jack Martel was especially eager to keep the investigation alive. Maybe we didn't have anything yet that could crack it open, but Nguyen Van Bay had just confirmed and amplified what we had been hearing from Ly and Liem. If we kept at it, something was bound to turn up. B-22 was too important to shunt aside.

I felt the same way. So despite the growing level of activity in other areas, I kept Albert on the case and I stayed on it myself. But on April 5 our attention was wrenched away by developments in Binh Long, just above the Parrot's Beak. Word flashed by radio that the VC/NVA 5th Division had just swept across the town of Loc Ninh and was now headed for the province capital of An Loc. Thousands of refugees were on the road in front of the advancing troops. The great Nguyen Hue Offensive* had at last kicked off in Three Corps.

It was not exactly a surprise. In November 1971 Le Duc Tho had broken off his talks in Paris with Henry Kissinger. Within a month of the breakdown we began getting information that the NVA was

---

* Also known as the Spring Offensive or the Easter offensive.

gearing up for something big. In January specific intelligence about the buildup was coming in from the Reaper, the Mad Bomber, and the Goldmother, and intelligence reports were being submitted to Station, which was conveying them to Kissinger. Later in the spring, the Reaper reported that the focus of the thrust (in Region Three) would be An Loc.

We had, in addition, thoroughly debriefed Mai Thi Trang, Nguyen Van Bay, and the other recent defectors on NVA intentions. They had all reported that even while Vietcong forces had exhausted their manpower pools, Northern forces were beefing up all over the region.

But while there might not have been any surprises, still the VC/NVA 5th quickly overwhelmed Loc Ninh, and by April 12, the 5th, joined by the NVA 7th and 9th, had sealed off the province capital of An Loc. Inside the town South Vietnamese local forces and elements of ARVN's 5th Division prepared to hold while General James F. Hollingsworth, commander of the U.S. Second Field Forces, surveyed the besieging forces from the air, mapping their locations and preparing his own surprise. He had (as one of his colonels had told me not too many months earlier) nothing but planes and gunships and choppers. With accurate targeting information he was ready to wreak havoc.

About a month before the offensive broke I had been given another contract officer for the JIC, a young man by the name of Chuck Waterman. Chuck was twenty-five years old. To this point his entire experience consisted of the ten-week course at Langley and a couple of months of sitting on his hands in Vietnam. He was completely innocent of anything having to do with the world of intelligence. But when Jack Martel asked if I would take him, I had given him the usual answer: "I've got nothing but work over here, Jack. Send him along."

So Chuck came in, all smiles. With his beard and bright young face, he looked more like a war protester than a CIA case officer. But he was more than eager to learn. After a brief orientation I gave him a special project. "We've got half a dozen excellent COSVN sources hanging around the JIC," I told him (this was just after the COSVN 20 influx). "I want you to work with an interpreter and I want you to concentrate on targeting COSVN and main-force units in Cambodia and Vietnam, especially in Phuoc Long, Binh Long, and Tay Ninh. We already know their AO [area of operations] pretty well. But I want you to put the information together from the live sources who have come in recently. Give me targets, photographed and mapped where possible. You give me the coordinate boxes and I'll have the air force bomb the living daylights out of them."

So Chuck started. And I noticed that almost immediately he began working twelve hours a day. Every once in a while he would take a breather, coming into my office to chat about what his sources were like and what they were telling him. He seemed almost in awe of them. This was his first experience of any kind with Vietcong. And these were senior people who were totally cooperative.

By early April Chuck had made himself an expert on targeting. As the VC and NVA poured across the border and launched themselves at An Loc, we were able to feed coordinates directly to General Hollingsworth and Colonel Thao. And the strikes went in, one after another, from both the South Vietnamese and the American air forces. They plastered the Cambodian staging areas, and they plastered Loc Ninh, where the Provisional Revolutionary "Government" had been set up after spending two years in Cambodia. As fast as we put the intelligence out, F-5 and A-1 sorties would take off from the Bien Hoa and Tan Son Nhut airfields and B-52 Arc Light missions would sweep in from Guam and Thailand. For the B-52s, the target box of coordinates would be surrounded with four other boxes, so in whatever direction the enemy might move after their warnings had come through, they'd get hit.

For weeks the siege of An Loc raged, with NVA troops flooding in through the defenses, then being driven back. As the battle progressed, defectors began arriving at the JIC telling tales of massive destruction being visited on their units by the bomb strikes. Debriefing them, we were able to confirm the terrible accuracy of Chuck's data, especially against the 7th and 9th divisions in Binh Long's northern districts.

One area, however, was not bombed heavily despite the targeting —the giant rubber plantation in Tri Tam district. Colonel Dinh had developed information that there were tanks buried deep in the plantation. When he informed us, we too began interrogating for news on this and almost immediately started picking up bits and pieces. The absence of any major source on the buried tanks led me to believe that the heart of the plantation was off-limits, a secured area. But the information gathered through Colonel Dinh's interrogations and ours, and from Colonel Thao's radio intercepts, was conclusive. The NVA kept their tanks between Tri Tam and An Loc, most of them buried to the turret and draped with camouflage netting. We were fairly sure there were up to two brigades of them there. But it was not just tanks. Tri Tam was a giant storage depot. From there to the border the place was dotted with weapons, fuel, and ammo dumps.

Although we supplied targeting information all through the spring and summer of 1972, the area was bombed only sporadically and lightly. I did not know the reason for this, nor could I find out, though I conjectured that it was because the plantation was French-owned. It remained one of the war's little mysteries.

Although the buried tanks stayed safe, the same could not be said for those that were brought into action against An Loc. The North Vietnamese tankers made glaring tactical errors, even elementary ones—sending infantry in front of the tanks, for example, instead of behind them. And when the tanks did get out in the open, Hollingsworth and his ARVN counterpart, General "Fat" Toan Hung, annihilated them. Prowling the skies above the battlefield in a command chopper, Hollingsworth and the ARVN chief of staff utilized their air power brilliantly, bringing murderous firepower to bear on NVA troop concentrations and movements.

General James Hollingsworth was a gruff, aggressive officer, not known for his refined manners. I had met him five or six months earlier during one of Bob Somerhill's liaison affairs. That had been a civilized meeting under fairly relaxed conditions, but a month or so of vicious fighting had done nothing for Hollingsworth's temperament. Nevertheless, as An Loc wore on and the NVA besiegers were broken up and pulverized, he came to Bien Hoa again, this time to thank us for the intelligence we were delivering. For a month we had been hand carrying reports from the Mad Bomber and the Reaper to Hollingsworth's G-2 the minute we'd put them together.

On this occasion Hollingsworth asked me to brief him on some of the interrogation techniques we used. He had his own interrogation team working with Colonel Dinh in the Corps Interrogation Center and I was familiar with their activities there. By and large they did an excellent job, but their mission was to identify and analyze enemy order of battle and I knew they did not look at the whole picture. Standing in front of Hollingsworth with a drawing board and pointer, I gave him an overview of our operation and described the nature of our material. As I did, the general turned around in his seat to glare at his colonels, lined up stiffly a few steps behind him. "Why don't you motherfuckers report intelligence like this?" he growled. From the look on his face no one could have guessed that these men and their ARVN counterparts were in the middle of chewing up and spitting out three enemy divisions.

. . .

A month or so before the Nguyen Hue Offensive kicked off, I had been called down to Hau Nghia by Clint Wilson. They had a prisoner there, he said, whom he wanted me to talk to. They had established that this man was a Cu Chi district security cadre, a hard core, but they hadn't been able to get anything else out of him. Maybe I could.

As it turned out, I wasn't able to elicit any more operational information than Clint had. But although the VC was surly and uncooperative, there were some things he didn't mind talking about. It was true, he admitted, they were hurting for cadres. They also knew their security had been breached, especially around Cu Chi and Trang Bang. Although he didn't mention it by name, I had the feeling he was referring as much to the N-10 Sapper Battalion as to anything else. That had hit them really hard.

Yes, we had hurt them in those areas, he said, there was no secret about that. But they weren't sitting still either. One of the things they were going to do was kill the province chief. They had had him targeted for a good while and it was just a matter of time before they got him. He said this in a kind of arrogant, bragging way, looking me straight in the eye. You've had some fun, he was telling me, but we're going to have ours too. We're going to kill your top gun out there. As he said this I felt a prickly sensation along my back. This guy knew only that I was an American intelligence officer, not that I had been responsible for so much of the damage he was talking about. He had no idea of the impact it had on me to hear that it was Colonel Thanh who was going to pay.

Colonel Thanh's handling of Hau Nghia had brought him respect from all sides. Everyone, including the American advisers in the province, had good words to say for him. He was an honest, capable administrator and an effective military officer. Even Colonel Dinh thought he was a great guy, and Dinh tended to be scathing when it came to the subject of GVN province chiefs.

When I told Dinh about the security cadre's remarks, he had the man picked up and brought over to Bien Hoa; he wanted to hear those words for himself. In the course of a general interrogation, Dinh brought it up. What was it, exactly, that he had said to the American about Colonel Thanh in Hau Nghia? "What I said," the security cadre answered, "is that we're going to kill him. You want some significant information from me? OK, here it is. We're going to knock off the province chief."

When I had first heard this boast I told Clint Wilson to warn Colonel Thanh. Now that Dinh and I were both convinced this was no idle threat, we told Thanh ourselves directly. Specifically, we thought it likely they would try for him with a command-detonated mine. Thanh was notorious for being all over the province in his jeep. He should do as little driving as possible, we cautioned, and nothing that someone tracking him might anticipate and plan for. Another jeep should always drive in front of his. "Take it seriously," we told him. "These guys are really out to get you."

Several weeks after we talked to the security cadre I got a call from Colonel Dinh asking me if I could come over to the CIC immediately. "It's very important," he said. When I got there he was sitting behind his desk with tears in his eyes. Fifteen minutes earlier he had received a telephone call with the news that Colonel Thanh was dead. Early that morning an outpost had been overrun in Duc Hoa district and Thanh had rushed out immediately to check the casualties and provide whatever personal encouragement he could. Colonel Bartlett had pleaded with him not to go, but Thanh refused to listen. Some of his men had been killed and it was his business to visit the unit. Left with no choice, Bartlett had jumped into his own jeep and had followed. Near the overrun outpost a mine had exploded directly under Thanh's vehicle, blowing it fifteen feet in the air. The blast had killed him instantly.

That afternoon Dinh and I traveled to Hau Nghia to offer our condolences to Madam Thanh, now a widow with ten children. The next day we went to the funeral in Gia Dinh together with Colonel Bartlett, Clint Wilson, and Captain Stu Herrington, the Phoenix adviser in Duc Hoa. It was a sad affair for all of us. The GVN lost a good man, and one of its most effective province chiefs.

I had first met Stu Herrington on a visit to Tim Miller, one of his colleagues in the Hau Nghia Phoenix program. Like Miller, he impressed me as an energetic, perceptive officer who was not content to sit around on his ass and do nothing. He too had come down to the JIC to look at our program and sift through the data bank, though unfortunately we did not have much on Duc Hua; it wasn't one of the districts we were concentrating on. I was sorry we had to meet again under these circumstances, though had I been able to see the future I would have seen the two of us together under far grimmer circumstances during the war's hectic final days.

Colonel Thanh was assassinated on April 20, while the battle of An Loc was still in full swing. It was a tense time. Northern forces were still on the move, while ARVN struggled desperately to hold and American air power struck viciously at massed enemy units and exposed supply lines. The future seemed unclear, both on the battlefield and on the diplomatic front. From Washington, where

Henry Kissinger was planning his strategy for renewed negotiations with the North Vietnamese, we had urgent requests for intelligence on enemy intentions. What was COSVN really trying to do?

With fighting raging near the DMZ and in the Central Highlands as well as around An Loc, we were unable to make an overall judgment about North Vietnamese objectives for this offensive. But from the Reaper and the Mad Bomber we knew in detail what they were after in Three Corps. Their intention there was to take all of Phuoc Long province and its neighbor Binh Long, where they would firmly establish the Provisional Revolutionary Government on South Vietnamese territory. According to beautifully detailed reports from the Mad Bomber, Subregion Five personnel had been instructed to make supply arrangements. That is, the objectives of the Nguyen Hue offensive, at least in Three Corps, were strictly limited. They wanted land, as quickly as possible, for psychological and political reasons.

We had what we considered substantial and reliable intelligence to that effect, and we also reported factual intelligence from the Reaper and the Mad Bomber that there would be no general offensive on Saigon. Despite subsequent theorizing, in the spring of 1972 there was nothing at all to indicate that COSVN was looking for an ARVN collapse. They did not expect it and were not prepared for it. They had no intention whatsoever of trying to move on Saigon. They were scared to death of the United States Air Force; if they had to come down a highway, they knew they would be massacred. That was why we did not expect anything profound. They could not do it. What they did want and expect were those two provinces.

Years later Richard Nixon wrote in his memoirs that by the beginning of May he and Kissinger were face-to-face with what looked like a total South Vietnamese cave-in. "It was conceivable," he wrote, "that all South Vietnam would fall." Echoing Nixon, Henry Kissinger wrote in *White House Years* that on the eve of his May 2 meeting with Le Duc Tho, the North Vietnamese special envoy may well have felt that "a complete South Vietnamese collapse was imminent." Indications were, as Kissinger put it, that "in Hanoi's judgment the rout had begun." But despite the fall of Quang Tri (the day before Kissinger's meeting) and the noose around An Loc, that was not what the intelligence was saying. On the contrary, our intelligence was that we were not facing any kind of all-out offensive. And what Nixon and Kissinger had on their desks was our intelligence.

· · ·

Since we were dealing with limited North Vietnamese objectives and not a full-scale attempt to crush the South Vietnamese army, there was only one reasonable conclusion to draw. By taking land North Vietnam was looking to strengthen its position in the field in order to support what would be its real focus—the Paris negotiations. The May 2 session between Le Duc Tho and Kissinger bore no fruit because at that point it seemed that Northern forces might be able to take more than they already had. But as Lou and I reviewed the intelligence, it seemed clear that the North Vietnamese would get serious just as soon as the dust began to clear. All their planning that spring was aimed not at a final showdown but at achieving a treaty.

On May 12 the last serious attempt to overrun An Loc ended in a crushing defeat for the attackers. Badly mauled, the Vietcong 5th Division withdrew from the action, leaving the 7th and 9th, also severely hurt, to continue a siege that was now clearly a no-win affair. The balance shifted as ARVN dug in throughout the country. Once again, as in Tet, the enemy had overextended himself and had paid the price in stunning casualties. On June 22 the North Vietnamese accepted a renewal of negotiations.

Now, as Kissinger and Le Duc Tho sat down together again, we received requests to report any ripple of information we might pick up concerning the North Vietnamese negotiating posture. Specifically, Kissinger needed to be advised of any instructions to Vietcong and North Vietnamese field forces that might give an indication of Hanoi's intentions.

By the end of July we were getting not just ripples, but waves. Reports came in from the Mad Bomber and the Reaper that the NVA now had directions to identify specific locales that might be taken. The Goldmother confirmed this information. We could expect land grabbing, she said, particularly in Subregion One. Units were even being given flags to plant in areas they captured. Whatever was about to happen would be a very public exercise.

At the same time Radio Hanoi and the Vietcong's Radio Liberation were trumpeting a new, strident theme. According to the broadcasts, revolutionary forces had won ground in every area, the great Nguyen Hue Offensive had liberated significant parts of the homeland. In fact the offensive had managed to do little, at an extremely high cost. But the radio broadcasts exaggerated what they could, using the most triumphant language they could muster. As the dust of the fighting settled, Hanoi's new direction began to emerge. The great divisional thrusts that were meant to rearrange the map of South Vietnam had been a bloody failure. The idea now was to brazen out the defeat, take whatever parcels of land might be available, and make as big a show as possible of the whole enterprise.

By August we had gathered enough intelligence to recognize that the North Vietnamese expected a successful conclusion to this round of negotiations. No longer were they playing for time or seeking to use the negotiations as an element in their long-range strategy. Before long we began to understand that they even had a schedule in mind; in early September we were picking up indications that they expected to reach agreement with the United States somewhere near the end of October. Instructions were disseminated from COSVN throughout Subregions One and Five to methodically seize land—even small units were now being given tactical objectives and mission dates. And many of these were risky operations involving significant exposure. Things were drawing to a head and Hanoi was desperate to show the flag. By October 1 we had a balls-out push on our hands.

With the cranked-up fighting, a rush of defectors and prisoners came through the JIC, straining the interrogation teams to the limit. At the same time, reports from agents in place seemed to double, two-thirds of them relating to the massive land-grabbing campaign. In October we submitted 107 intelligence reports to Saigon, the base high.

Unfortunately, Lou was on leave during this frenzy, which meant among other things that I had taken over handling the Mad Bomber myself. On October 27 Gekko One came into my office directly from servicing the Bomber's dead drop. This time the message was urgent. "I don't even think you'll have time to report this," Gekko told me. "The Mad Bomber says that the H-1 Battalion is going to wipe out Song Phu village in Binh Duong, south of Phu Cuong city. They're planning to overrun it tomorrow morning. He's drawn it out in detail. They're coming in from Tan Uyen district, walking at night. After they cross the river, they'll take the rice fields running, then hit the village at exactly 0600. They're bringing all their flags with them."

This village was located at a significant crossroads only three klicks south of Phu Cuong, twelve or thirteen klicks from Saigon. If they were successful, it would give the NVA a strategic foothold on the capital's doorstep, a hold that the peace agreement might make permanent. I immediately cabled a report to Saigon, then had a copy hand carried to Colonel Thao. Almost immediately Thao's right-hand man was back in my office briefing me on what was in the works. The information was so detailed on timing and movement that Thao thought he could get them with air strikes. He had already alerted a squadron of A-1s, propeller-driven planes that while slow and clumsy could carry a hell of a bomb load. "We're going to put a whole squadron on them," he said.

The next morning at dawn the Vietcong's Subregion Five H-1 Battalion came out of the woods and crossed the river, right on schedule. Then, just as they were in the middle of their sprint through the rice fields the A-1s roared in out of the east. With no place to hide, most of the battalion tried to scramble back across the river to the safety of the jungle. Fewer than half of them made it. When Colonel Thao helicoptered in an hour later to see what had happened he found ninety bodies in the paddies and evidence that more had been dragged away. In essence the H-1 Battalion had been wiped out as a fighting force. "You've got one hell of an agent there," he said as he described the operation to me, "one hell of an agent."

In reviewing the land-grabbing operations, both those that were being beaten back and those that were succeeding, one overwhelming fact was evident: COSVN was straining all its resources to have forces in place in the vicinity of Saigon prior to the conclusion of a peace treaty. Most of the forces were purely NVA and even the Vietcong units were half Northern fillers. Like many of the old-line Southern Vietcong who had defected since the beginning of the year, we found ourselves wondering whether these North Vietnamese and so-called VC (but substantially North Vietnamese) units were claiming land for the South or for the North. Once there was a cease-fire, to whom did these units owe allegiance? Obviously it was not to the NLF.

Moreover, there would hardly be any point to making the land-grabbing efforts and taking the kind of losses they were taking if they were not planning to remain in place. As early as the beginning of October we understood that these people would be staying right where they were, in whatever positions they were occupying when the agreement was eventually signed. At night Colonel Thao and Colonel Dinh would come over and the three of us would talk about this, wrapped in gloom. It was hard to absorb, hard to accept. These fuckers were not going home; they had no intention of going home. Judging from their actions, this was something that Kissinger must already have agreed to. It must have been incorporated in the agreement. The three divisions with which we in Three Corps had been so viciously engaged for so many years would still be with us after the treaty. Under those circumstances it could hardly be called a "peace" treaty, a shocking realization. It left us with a feeling of distant menace, as if a disaster was forming just over the horizon. With a treaty like that, how could the war not end badly?

11

GRANDPA AND THE MONEYRUNNERS

In the early-morning hours of October 12, 1972, at Gif-sur-Yvette, Secretary of State Henry Kissinger and North Vietnam's "Special Advisor" Le Duc Tho reached agreement on the substance of what would become known as the Paris Accords. Exactly a week later, Kissinger arrived in Saigon to extract Nguyen Van Thieu's approval of the terms he had negotiated, the most troubling of which was that Northern forces would remain right where they were. On October 22 talks between the American secretary of state and the Vietnamese president ended in an explosion. Thieu would have none of it. His ally had betrayed him. Leaving the North Vietnamese Army in his country meant only one thing to Thieu and South Vietnam: death. As far as Thieu was concerned there would be no agreement, not without significant modifications in the terms, especially the withdrawal of the hated North Vietnamese.

While Nixon applied pressure to force Thieu to back down, Kissinger once again began meeting with Le Duc Tho. As these ill-fated talks got under way we once again received requests to report any information about Hanoi's intentions. But we turned up nothing. At this point defectors were coming through the system in larger numbers than anytime since the summer—more than 300 a month. It was as if now that an agreement was at hand many Northern soldiers saw this as a last chance to come over. Most of those who defected did not see the treaty as a victory for the Communist side (as almost all the Southerners did). What they saw was that they would be sitting out there in the jungle for another eternity. They thought they would be a lot better off in Saigon.

But they brought no news other than that they were aware there would be an agreement. Even when the talks between Le Duc Tho and Kissinger broke off in mid-December, we learned nothing. To the extent that that week's defectors knew anything at all, they believed this was just a temporary delay. The COSVN chiefs themselves had said nothing relevant in their directives. Perhaps they too knew nothing. All indications were that despite Le Duc Tho's return home the negotiations would still go forward.

Nixon and his advisers obviously understood differently. To them, Le Duc Tho was delaying matters purposely in order to create mounting domestic pressure on the administration and to ripen the American conflict with Thieu. The North Vietnamese, those "tawdry, filthy shits," as Kissinger called them (according to Nixon), had decided there would be no agreement after all, at least not now. For their part, Nixon and Kissinger decided that they would not put up with Hanoi's attempt to scuttle the agreement. On December 18, seven days before Christmas, the bombs started to drop on Hanoi and Haiphong.

In Bien Hoa we were elated. Information came from Saigon Station that the B-52s were using smart bombs, putting them right down the chimneys. That evening Colonel Tuong and his F-5 flyboys came over to celebrate. "They really did it," said Tuong, whose information on this was better than ours, "the smart bombs really plastered their headquarters areas. If they take out the main centers in Haiphong, this war will be over right now."

The bombing lasted eleven days, enough to force the North Vietnamese back to the negotiating table. I cannot speak for other CIA bases, but in Bien Hoa there was no optimism when the bombing stopped. The attacks had scared the Politburo, but they had not in our view been enough to make Hanoi believe we were serious about really putting an end to the war. We should just bite the bullet and get it over with, I thought. Then it would be over, instead of dragging on to some horrible bloody end one year or three years or five years down the pike.

We had an opportunity to grasp here and we were not seizing it. If we bombed Hanoi and Haiphong just once, as we had bombed the Japanese cities during World War Two, the North Vietnamese would have thrown up their hands and gone home. That was my considered opinion after having studied the Vietnamese character closely for years and having dealt with thousands of Vietcong and Northern defectors and prisoners.

No doubt my thinking was influenced by the fact that I had flown the B-29s over Japan. There was nothing pleasant about those raids over Tokyo and Yokohama and Kobe. Yet terrible as they were, the truth is that they had shortened the war and saved innumerable lives. And they had made possible an acceptable future. The Vietnamese, as I knew from years of experience, were not like the Japanese; they were not fanatic fatalists. Hit them hard enough and they would come out with their hands up. They did not welcome destruction.

I read the papers; I knew we were at the bottom line, that Nixon and Kissinger were being bludgeoned by the press and by Congress. But I also knew very well the other guy's weaknesses, how strained they were, how beaten down and full of contradictions. How vulnerable.

But even now the United States was not willing to do what was necessary for victory against an enemy fighting an all-out brutal war. Instead, we were looking for a way out. And so we bombed only until Le Duc Tho said he would come back to the table; we did not go for the jugular, we did not press for the North Vietnamese to get out. Our government was not willing to bear the domestic pressure that continued bombing would bring when to avoid it, all we had to do was sacrifice the people of South Vietnam by leaving the Northern army in their country. We were not, after all, sacrificing ourselves.

When the treaty was finally signed in late January, a grim, sad mood took hold in Bien Hoa. It affected everybody, Americans and Vietnamese alike, though for us as Americans the sadness was mixed with shame. Our sadness was because, for all the rotten corruption in the Saigon government, we were still talking about leaving an entire people to its fate. Our shame was for the same reason. It seemed to us that Le Duc Tho had "slickied" Kissinger. We even felt that Kissinger and Nixon had concluded that we had to get out, period, whatever it took. Frank Snepp's book, *Decent Interval*, gives a sense of what the thinking was among the Agency's case officers—the only thing this treaty would do was buy enough time to save our faces, because we knew, perhaps better than anyone, what it meant to leave the North Vietnamese Army in the field.

· · ·

Bob Somerhill left after only a year, instead of the usual eighteen months, to become number three in Saigon. And our exec, Jack Martel, left at almost the same time. It was a double blow. The entire base had been humming—people working happily and productively—and it was mainly due to these two men. Bob, especially, was a first-rate manager, an intelligent, supportive person, a boss you could also call your friend.

Over dinner in Bob's house one night shortly before he left I suggested that since he was going to Station, and since he had nothing to lose (being on the verge of retirement), he would be in an ideal position to hit at the corruption that was undermining South Vietnam's ability to conduct war. He knew, as we all did, that the nation's top generals and politicians were eating the country alive.

We had, for example, for years been following the story of the great Hong Kong piaster exchange. I had learned of this originally from my old friend Bill Todd, who since 1970 had been doing intelligence work on the opium trade. In the process of tracking the flow of drug money out of Saigon, Bill had been monitoring the Hong Kong banks. For several years he had watched the wives of South Vietnamese political and military figures regularly depositing huge numbers of piasters in the Crown Colony. Carrying diplomatic credentials to avoid searches, they would transport the cash in suitcases and boxes, deposit it (losing about 50 percent in the exchange), then have it transferred to accounts in Switzerland and France. Though the CIA knew all about the hemorrhaging of South Vietnamese funds, there was nothing it could do. Almost everyone in a position to grab a slice of the pie was grabbing it. And if anyone wanted to complain, who was he supposed to complain to?

But the CIA wasn't completely impotent. Unable to close off the flow, the Agency's finance officers found a creative way of using it. The ocean of South Vietnamese piasters owned by the Hong Kong banks could be bought—at half price. And this the Agency did. It was a fine, cut-rate way of financing operations. In essence, we were taking money back from the South Vietnamese leaders who were stealing it. And so we bought billions, stacked up in great big boxes that came into Bien Hoa and the other bases and used the money to finance operations. None of us ever felt there was anything immoral about this. On the contrary, it was one way of getting something back from the thieves.

Corruption, of course, was not limited to the top. It was pervasive. Typically a regional commander would shake down the province chiefs, who would shake down the district chiefs, who would shake down the local officials. Almost without exception every National Police colonel would be on the take. Honest men like Colonels Thao and Dinh and Colonel Thanh and Major Ngo were jewels to be treasured. Corruption went from the highest to the lowest and no one was spared. When I went into a local hamlet office once to register a motorbike, the petty clerk whose job it was to issue registration certificates pulled out the drawer of his desk and waited. "You know what that means, don't you?" said Felix, who was along to translate. I did. It meant drop in a thousand p's and you'll get the registration. There was corruption at every level, a universal user's tax, if you wanted to think about it that way. But though it existed everywhere, it was most pronounced, and most repulsive, at the top, among those who were supposedly responsible for the welfare of their nation.

Somerhill knew as well as the rest of us did how bad the corruption was and how it had sapped South Vietnam's strength. But he was not optimistic. His best contact in the regime was a three-star general, "And he's playing games too," said Bob. "None of those South Vietnamese at the top will listen."

There wasn't a person on base who was happy to see Bob Somerhill leave. We were even gloomier when we heard who was replacing him—a man named John Brenley. Brenley brought with him his nickname, "Blackjack," and his reputation—blackjacking anyone or anything around him that he considered out of order. He was, it was said, a violent, touchy man.

During his first meeting with the base officers, Brenley was energetic and all smiles. He was familiar with all of us, he said, from our records. He understood what our functions were and what fine jobs we were all doing. He foresaw no changes. I looked at him, pacing the floor in front of us, a forced smile etching his mouth. No changes indeed, I thought. The man was famous for getting rid of anyone he could.

After the meeting, Larry Jones, our long-term finance officer, pulled me aside. "Ong Gia," he said, keeping his voice low, "it's started already. Before the meeting Brenley told me he wanted to review all the financial records for the provinces and for your operation. He also asked me some questions about the JIC, what you and your people do over there. Why you're not over here at the Monastery with everybody else where he can keep an eye on you. He wasn't asking in a friendly way. Something's going on."

I was stunned. "Do you have any idea what's bugging him?"

"No," said Larry, "but I'll bet we find out soon. You shouldn't have a thing to worry about though. The JIC produces practically all the intelligence, at a lower cost than any of the provinces. I'll try to keep on top of the situation and let you know what's developing." Larry and I had been good friends for several years and I knew he would observe things for me, and that his wife, Jane, would also. Jane was executive secretary to the chief of base. She had worked for Bob Somerhill and now she would be working for Jack Brenley. So at least we would have some advance warning of whatever storms might be brewing in the mind of our new boss. But I felt very uneasy as I left the Monastery to go back to my office. With the Paris treaty on our doorstep, the war was about to enter a new, crucial phase. The last thing we needed was a problem in our own backyard.

A week or so later I had dinner with Larry and Jane in their apartment at the State Department's Franzblau Building. Jane was talking about life in the office with John Brenley, and what a change there was from the fatherly warmth of Bob Somerhill. "I might as well warn you," she said, "John has been making comments about Sam and Gary. Sam's sandals annoy him, and he doesn't like the way Gary talks. He can't stand that Texas drawl of his." As soon as it was out of her mouth we all started laughing. But it was nervous laughter. I began to get the feeling that in John Brenley we were dealing with something more than just an irritable personality.

The next morning at 0730 I called a staff meeting. If Brenley was talking in his office about Sam and Gary, others might have heard about it too, and I wanted to take some steps to prevent any real blowups. I discussed some of the problems with Lou, Sam, Gary, and Chuck and asked them to please let me handle Brenley myself. I reassured Sam and Gary that I had just written excellent fitness reports on them and that Brenley would have to discuss them with me and endorse them. I didn't think anything untoward would happen—the JIC was producing beautifully and their work was a significant part of what we were doing. On the other hand, John Brenley seemed a strange man, hard to figure out. I wanted all of them to keep out of his way, keep their mouths shut, and keep their noses to the grindstone. I had just received approval myself for another eighteen-month tour and I would be going to bat for them and all the other officers at the JIC.

John Brenley did not come over for a briefing at the JIC. But he did make a tour of the provinces, and as he did, I began getting troubled calls from the province officers, asking me what sort of guy the new chief was. John was setting off nervous vibes every-where he went.

Bernie D'Antonio called a week or so later. Bernie had formerly been the officer in charge in Tay Ninh, but he and Brenley had served together in Laos and Brenley had now brought him in as his number two. Brenley had finally decided to come over to see the JIC, and Bernie, who had never seen it either, was coming along.

Fifteen minutes later Brenley and D'Antonio were making them-selves comfortable in my office while I poured coffee for them and Lou, whom I had asked to sit in. "Well," said John, looking around with a little smile on his face, "my goodness but this office is fur-nished nicely. Two beautiful sofas here, two coffee tables, and that certainly is a very nice desk you've got there." As his eyes fastened on the Chinese-red rug, it hit me like a ton of bricks—the man was jealous. He did not like it at all—this big building over here with this big office that were actually bigger than his own building and his own office. I was flabbergasted. This was a CIA colonel in the middle of a war. But there was no mistaking his tone or his look.

"Ong Gia [like everyone else he had picked up my nickname], I wanted to come over and see this JIC of yours. You've got a large staff here and it's awfully expensive to operate the way you've been doing." I started to interrupt him, but he held up his hand. "Just a moment, please, I'm not finished. Yes, expensive to operate, and I think we have to have a close look at your officers here. When you have time tomorrow why don't you come over so we can talk about their fitness reports."

As he got up to leave, I decided to give him something to think about, at least before he did anything drastic. "John," I started, "before you go I'd like to explain something about the JIC. When I arrived here four years ago we had ten active province offices, spending about fifty thousand a year for each office, not counting salaries. For that the base was putting out five or six reports a month and had one agent in development. You've been over the records so you know what the story is now. Because of the data bank we have been putting out sixty to eighty reports in average months. We're running five agents and a developmental plus some excellent leads. We've closed down five province offices and the JIC is costing about seventy percent less than the remaining five. Before we talk I'd appreciate it if you would check over my figures with Larry. I'm sure he'll be able to give you details."

As Brenley left he was grumbling something to Bernie D'Antonio and shaking his head. Frankly, it was hard to see how he might touch the JIC. There was no way to attack the operation either on grounds of productivity or finances. Besides, the JIC was Bien Hoa's bread and butter. On the other hand, it was pretty clear that the existence of an independent center of operations really bothered him. Somehow he took it as an affront, and seeing the furniture and rug had deepened his resentment. I could just imagine what Bob Somerhill would think of this—the new furnishings had been part of his approach to using the JIC for expanding our liaison activities. Somerhill would think he was dealing with a nut case. By this time that was certainly my diagnosis.

The next morning I was in Brenley's office early, bringing along five newly completed reports just for effect. When I walked in he was busily shuffling papers in a folder. "You know, Ong Gia," he started, "I want to talk over these fitness reports of yours on your officers. You've ranked some of them rather high, and I tend to disagree with you. I'm talking especially about Gary Maddox and Sam Capone. It's plain to me that Gary is pretty much a nonentity. And I can tell you that that drawl of his sounds just awful; the man doesn't have anywhere near the personality I'm looking for in an officer. And I'll tell you another thing. Sam wears sandals all the time and I will not tolerate one of our officers wearing sandals while he's on duty. Now, I've added my comments to your reports. You may not like what I've said, but it's my business to consider their career potential here, and I'm telling you that the potential is very low."

"John," I said, looking over his comments and knowing they were enough to settle Sam and Gary into another line of work once their tours were up, "you are badly mistaken about this. These are both good officers. They are hard workers and they've developed a feel for the job." Then I told him about the Goldmother operation and Gary's first-rate work in doing the background research and making the identification. But what I said made no impact. "Ong Gia, these are not career-type people, that's for sure. And furthermore, I'd like you to talk to Sam about wearing sandals." "John, wearing sandals where?" "Well, certainly not in my office, and I think he should dress like a gentleman wherever he's working." "John, Sam is a former army captain with a tour in Vietnam. He's a dedicated man. Why don't we leave his sandals alone?" Brenley stared at the wall behind my head and let out a deep sigh. I obviously did not understand what was needed here, and he could see I wasn't about to listen to reason. What I could see was that reason was no longer the guiding element at Bien Hoa base's highest level.

· · ·

While our little domestic melodrama was developing, the larger saga we were part of had reached a kind of climax, or an anticlimax. One immediate consequence of the Paris treaty was that life relaxed a little. Americans were now strictly off-limits to the Vietcong, which meant, among other things, that we could safely drive into Saigon very early on Saturday morning for a round of golf. But nothing about the situation was relaxing for the South Vietnamese. Colonel Dinh, Colonel Thao's twin for workaholism, had revved up his pace even higher and now seemed to be at the Corps Interrogation Center nonstop, poring over interrogation results and huddling with Thao to piece together their version of the Region Three intelligence jigsaw.

After dinner, though, he'd take a break and stop by 15 Cong Ly for a beer before returning to his office. But even during his break he couldn't relax. He couldn't tear his mind away from business, and especially from his main concern now—the Ho Chi Minh Trail.

The United States had promised to use its air power to prevent any gross violation of the accord by the North Vietnamese. But exactly what Kissinger and Nixon might decide was a gross violation was anybody's guess, and in the meantime the fighter-bombers and B-52s were dormant.

Apparently Nixon and Kissinger did not mean to include the stepped-up flow of war matériel down the Ho Chi Minh Trail as a gross violation. Had they done so they would have unleashed the bombers within a month of the signing. With the American air force grounded, work on expanding the trail into a modern highway right down into the southern section of Two Corps got under way. Already, early in the year, Colonel Dinh and Colonel Thao were thoroughly documenting an influx of supplies into Three Corps.

At the JIC we were picking it up too. In February 1973 we were still receiving defectors, and many of them described the stockpiling that was taking place. Supplies and military equipment were coming down from Phuoc Long and Binh Long into Binh Duong and even into Bien Hoa.

Once we had established that NVA stockpiles were growing, another fact became obvious. If they were increasing their supplies and prepositioning weapons and ammunition, then they quite clearly were preparing for an offensive. What's more, the amount of matériel coming in was far more than sufficient for the three divisions already in place, so whatever they were planning, it was on a large scale. The "withering away" of the NVA that Kissinger had spoken of was nothing more than a figment of his hopes, exactly as the South Vietnamese had so desperately maintained. On the contrary, we were watching the beginning of a major NVA buildup. And even with the American arms shipments of the previous fall, the North Vietnamese were already outgunning ARVN. We were reporting all this, but there was no response from the American government.

As the Northern buildup continued, the economic situation of the South Vietnamese army was deteriorating at an alarming rate. Colonels Dinh and Thao had no funds at all to provide soldiers at ARVN's Military Region Three headquarters with supplemental food for their families, and Dinh was having a hard time feeding prisoners and defectors even minimal rations. By this time I was sending him two hundred pounds of rice a month from the JIC, but even that wasn't nearly enough to cover the shortfall. Soldiers and air force people at the base were stealing anything they could get their hands on, Dinh told me. They were desperate to feed their families.

I knew firsthand how bad it was. Lan's brother Da was a private in the ARVN 25th Division operating in Binh Duong province. Whenever he could wrangle a two-day pass he would show up at 15 Cong Ly where he knew he would find food. In Binh Duong NVA units were dug in about fifty yards from ARVN's field positions, he said, and Northern and Southern soldiers would kid and talk to one another. Whenever they could, the ARVN boys would exchange cigarettes for rice. According to Da, the NVA were well fed, while he and his buddies were always famished. It wasn't hard to tell. Despite the regular meals Lan made for him, Da couldn't keep away from the refrigerator. At one point he even gulped down a Preparation H suppository I was keeping cool in there, thinking it was some kind of American candy—"The worst candy I ever ate," he announced to Lan. I had a good laugh about that, but Lan didn't think it was funny. "You don't realize," she told me, "how hungry he really is."

Put all together it was an ominous situation; the NVA supply buildup contrasted with the deflation of South Vietnam's economy and the raging corruption that was eating the heart out of the country. Though nothing major was imminent, there was little doubt that the future held in store a massive assault. And meanwhile there was no peace. During the middle months of 1973, the Goldmother reported that Hanoi intended to avoid main-force military action to demonstrate respect for the International Control Commission team that had taken up residence in Bien Hoa. But

small-unit actions were a different story (although even here
Northern forces were being required to make it appear as if engagements were initiated by ARVN, then to claim Southern violations
of the agreement). In reality the NVA was applying pressure in
each of Three Corps' significant areas. Ambushes, assassinations,
attacks on patrols, and assaults on outposts continued as if Paris
had never happened. Each night incoming mortar and rocket fire
blasted key positions throughout the region.

To keep in touch with conditions in the field I made frequent
trips to the provinces, talking at length with friends like Major Ngo.
In Trang Bang nothing had changed. The 101st was still in the Ho
Bo Woods, harassing the district and cutting the highway, keeping
the ARVN 25th Division on the go. "What would happen," I asked
him one day, "if the 101st decided to do something bigger? Would
you have enough supplies and ammunition to deal with it?" "Ong
Gia," Ngo said, "you know, don't you, that I have to buy my 105
shells. And I'm running out of money. So if the 101st tried to force
things, we'd be in a tough situation. I'd only be able to use about
twenty rounds, which would leave me fifty in reserve. That's all I
have."

I did know it. I had gotten numerous other reports about the
new ARVN commander for Military Region Three, a man whose
corruption was notorious in his previous command, Region Four.
We had included material on this subject in many intelligence
reports to Saigon Station, warning that the abuses were so wide-
spread that they were putting the region at risk. But it was like
shouting into the void.

To men like Major Ngo and Colonels Thao and Dinh the corruption had become unbearable. In the middle of the summer my
old boss Don Gregg, who was now Station chief in Korea, came to
visit. Most of our employees came to the party I threw for him in
my house, as well as some of our outside Vietnamese friends. In
the middle of it Dinh asked if Don and I could talk with him
privately for a few minutes. When we had closed ourselves in one
of the back bedrooms, Dinh began a rambling but impassioned
speech about current conditions. Out it came in a flood, all his
fears about what was happening and where the situation was leading. If something wasn't done to curb the corruption and deal with
South Vietnam's economic situation, the country was doomed.
Doomed. Gregg looked at him with sympathy. "We're expecting a
full-scale assault sometime next year," said Dinh. "By then we
won't be able to do anything about it."

"Yes, I know," Don told him. "We've had reports on it already
and I have personally reported exactly what you're saying now to

the chief of the Far East Division." "I'm sure it's been reported," Dinh mumbled, "but the point is that it has gotten so terrible, and that nothing's being done." And there was little Don could do either, as Dinh knew perfectly well. But he was so distraught he could not pass up the chance to make a personal appeal to a CIA supergrade. As we walked out of the room Don assured him that he would send a cable to headquarters quoting Dinh on the urgency of the situation. It was an assurance that could not have conveyed much comfort.

I had been having trouble with Albert during the preceding months. My brilliant interrogator was, as I had known from the beginning, an opium smoker. For four years he had kept it under control, but in the last few months discrepancies had started turning up in his accounts. The first time it happened I talked to him about it and warned him. When it happened again I said nothing, but watched. The third time I knew I was dealing with a pattern. There was no alternative but to let him go. Not to get rid of him; he was too good for that, and I knew he was trying. But the addiction had just gotten to be too much; he couldn't resist the temptations involved in handling money. I finally decided to send him up to Tay Ninh to serve as an Agency interpreter there. I knew he would do a terrific job, but as an ordinary interpreter he wouldn't have access to funds. I hoped that would be all he needed to get back on the path.

In Albert's place I brought in Bingo One, a first-rate interpreter who had formerly worked for a friend of mine at CORDS. The first thing I wanted him to do was to go over the entire file on the B-22 finance economy case. Though the Nguyen Hue offensive and the treaty had diverted our attention, the money runners were no less intriguing now than they had been earlier. A new pair of eyes might turn up some overlooked fact or some new way of trying to crack the network. Bingo was perceptive in his own right, not as flashy as Felix, but intelligent and thorough. I'd give him a try.

After a week Bingo presented his findings, which matched almost perfectly with Felix's. The good leads we possessed had been run down; only long shots were left. Going over the material I thought that maybe something more would turn up, but if it did, it would be only by chance. I did not expect in any way that the break we needed in this year-and-a-half-old case would come from an entirely new direction.

Late one morning in August I got a call from Colonel Dinh asking me to come over to the Corps Interrogation Center for something important. On my way there I wasn't exactly panting with anticipation. Dinh had a way of calling every once in a while just to have me come over and visit him in his office. He and I talked all the time, but usually at 15 Cong Ly. Dinh, however, with his Vietnamese sense of status and propriety, felt he had to keep the relationship balanced. Every so often I'd be called over on "important business," the main importance of which was to share a pot of Dinh's specially brewed tea.

This time, though, there was more than tea waiting for me. Dinh had just taken a woman into custody. She had been picked up in Go Dau Ha district, on a spot search, with a million piasters strapped to her body. Under interrogation by Dinh's officers she had admitted that she was a courier for B-22. At that point Dinh had stopped everything and called. "So here you are, Ong Gia," he said, smiling broadly, "she's all yours."

The courier was brought into the office looking bedraggled—no doubt she had been roughed up some by the South Vietnamese interrogators. In her black pajamas she seemed thin and frail, and not at all happy with her situation. When I looked at her she refused to meet my eyes. I decided immediately that I would take her to my house and put her in the back room. I was going to treat this one with real kid gloves, let Lan take care of her for a while, talk to her slowly and gently, and see what might develop. Calling the JIC on the radio, I told them to inform Bingo that he had an immediate tennis date and to let Lan know that a guest was coming. Then I drove back home, the courier sitting next to me with a frightened look on her face.

At the house Bingo was already waiting and Lan had prepared a bedroom. As lunch was cooking, we asked the courier a few questions, enough to start doing some basic checking. Her name, she said, was Thi Nam. Yes, she had told the Vietnamese interrogators she was carrying the money for B-22. Her home was in Cut Trau hamlet, Loc Hung village. That by itself was enough to get the adrenaline flowing. Cut Trau, the same hamlet our defectors Ly and Liem were from. Both Bingo and I could feel it; if this one would open up we might really have something.

Talking with Lan a little later I explained that though Thi Nam might not be too sophisticated, she was an extremely important prisoner. She should be kept locked in the room, but treated especially well. As usual, even while I was giving them I knew the instructions were superfluous. With her natural warmth and feeling for those who were in bad circumstances, Lan would know exactly how to handle the courier.

Two days later Bingo had his first general discussion with Thi Nam. He started off by talking to her about the N-10 sapper operation, something she had nothing at all to do with. But the N-10 headquarters bunkers had been located just two miles from her house, and on an operation in which the VC had lost so much the rumors must have been flying. There was little doubt she knew at least something about it. Bingo also talked to her about Ba Tung, the former village chief whom she would also have known. Had she heard anything about what had happened to him? Did she know where he was now?

All these questions had one purpose, to enable Bingo to establish an honest dialogue with the courier. Once she felt able to talk to her interrogator without fear, once she felt a rapport with him, only then would he begin the specific questioning about the B-22. It was a process that required patience above all, though patience was the hardest quality to muster. Thi Nam obviously knew the Go Dau Ha B-22 station; she probably knew the Hoc Mon station, and perhaps other stations on the line as well. If we got lucky she might even turn out to know the moneyman in Saigon. At the very least she would give us the ability to cross-check Ly and Liem's information. Having three of them to play off against one another, what might we not elicit if we handled this right?

In the days that followed, Thi Nam turned out to be as pleasant as she was naïve and shy. Whenever Bingo tried joking with her she would laugh quickly in embarrassment. From Lan, who talked with her for hours, we learned that despite her naïveté she had a lot of native intelligence. She was also afraid of Americans and couldn't understand what she was doing in this house instead of being in jail. Her big worry was her family, who did not know what had happened to her. It was possible, Lan told her, that she might be able to get Ong Gia, the American, to pass a message to her family from her. At times he allowed that, especially if people were cooperative.

Once the ground had been adequately prepared and we had gotten to know Thi Nam a bit better, we decided that a straightforward approach had the best chance. We would tell her that we were strictly American intelligence, that we had nothing to do with ARVN, that Liem was with us also and that he had confessed. From Thi Nam we wanted an identification of the other couriers, the station chiefs, and the Saigon moneyman so that we could confirm the information Liem had given us already (a lie). We were not interested in arresting any legal cadres (a truth); we only wanted to understand the network thoroughly so that we could get to the inside (also a truth). If she worked with us she would not be endangering any of her friends.

But even at this juncture Bingo took his time, giving Thi Nam the opportunity to meditate on some of the implicit and not-so-implicit elements of her situation. We had, as she was exquisitely aware, treated her in the most humane fashion, precisely the opposite of what she had dreaded would happen to her once she fell into the government's hands. As the Americans seemed trustworthy since she had been treated decently, then maybe the Americans meant what they said about not harming or arresting the other couriers. Besides, Liem had already told them everything anyway; she would not be giving anything away.

On the other hand, what if she did not cooperate? First of all, the Americans would give her to the South Vietnamese—the interrogator had already told her that. Second, if she said nothing, or if she didn't say enough to help them get "inside," they would arrest the network on the basis of what they already knew and turn them over to the South Vietnamese too. That would be the worst thing that could happen. Looked at in that way, it made sense to work with the Americans. At least she would be saving herself and her friends.

Finally, after a few more days of discussing everything under the sun, Bingo told her that it was time to talk about B-22. By then, Thi Nam had already made up her mind to cooperate. "OK," she said, "let's talk." No beating around the bush; no attempted evasions. And then she started. She had been a B-22 courier for eight years, she said. She proceeded to identify twelve other couriers by their real names, also the moneyman in Saigon, the network chief who ran the connection between Saigon and Cambodia, and Ba Minh (whose name we already had from Nguyen Van Bay), the COSVN cadre on the other side of the Cambodian border who supervised the network chief and disseminated the orders.

And then came the shocker. Not only was our guy Liem the regular commo-liaison officer for B-22, but the network chief, a seventy-five-year-old man who lived in Cut Trau, was Liem's grandfather. Grandpa (as Albert and I had named him) was Liem's grandfather! No wonder Ly and Liem had been so evasive.

When Bingo asked Thi Nam about the moneyman in Saigon, she told him that she did not know his real name, but that he lived in Cholon, Saigon's Chinatown. She knew the house. She had been there many times to strap the money around her with belts before carrying it to Go Dau Ha station. At Hoc Mon she and all the couriers had to go through the National Police checkpoint. But they would not normally search little old ladies carrying fruit or vegetables. They'd look carefully at the young men and some of the young women, but almost never at the old ladies. And they did not ordinarily do body searches anyway. They mainly looked at ID cards, and all their ID cards were proper.

For the next three days Bingo worked to create an organizational chart of the B-22 finance economy section, identifying the legal cadres along the highway and filing all the information in the data bank. When he was finished, I talked over with him the course I wanted to take from this point on. Our purpose here was to obtain intelligence. But the only one who could provide what we were looking for was the network chief. The question was, how could we recruit Grandpa?

This wouldn't be easy, but we did have a couple of options. The most likely, I thought, would be to let Liem go home and explain the situation to his grandpa, who might then be induced to cooperate in exchange for money and for care of Liem and the children. If he went along with this we would set Liem, Ly, and the three kids up in Saigon, where it would be convenient for the old man to visit.

When we confronted Liem in the JIC (where he, Ly, and the kids were living) and told him we knew about him and about his grandfather too, he hardly batted an eye. It was almost as if he was surprised it had taken us so long to find out. It was almost a relief for him.

He also quickly resigned himself to the fact that we had a plan and he would have to help us with it. His wife had defected so he couldn't go back. He didn't want to be separated from her. As well as they were living now, they had no place to turn and no way to support themselves. He had not been disloyal and betrayed his grandfather, but fate had caught up with him. He had to cooperate; there was no other choice.

At the same time, Liem adamantly rejected the idea of approaching his grandfather directly. It wouldn't work, he said. The old man was a tough, old-line cadre, very ideologically committed. If he were faced with that kind of proposal from his grandson he would most likely just tell him to go back to his Chieu Hoi Center (Grandpa believed that Liem had defected). Then he would disappear into Cambodia to talk the situation over with Ba Minh.

If that was the case, and we had no alternative but to trust Liem's judgment on it, then we were going to have to confront Grandpa ourselves and apply whatever leverage we had available to us. But to do this we would have to utilize some sort of ruse. As I thought about it, I became convinced that the only good chance we had would be to pick Grandpa up surreptitiously, then play on his need to protect the grandson and his children (according to Liem the old man despised his wife). If we wanted to subvert a hard-core ideologue, the only way to do it would be through the family.

What we might do, I thought, would be to allow Ly to go back to the village to tell him that Liem was seriously ill in a Saigon hospital. Then when Grandpa came to Saigon to see him, we would apprehend him and take him to a safe house for interrogation. We would confront him with evidence, seek his confession and cooperation, then allow him to return home. We told Liem and Ly that they and the children would be permitted to visit Grandpa once he confessed. Then we would keep them in a safe house in Bien Hoa to give Grandpa an incentive to keep helping them. I promised Liem that we would take excellent care of the old man during the interrogation.

What I didn't tell Liem was that despite my distaste for it we were going to have to cooperate with the special police on this one. This entire operation would have to be handled surreptitiously, and we would need their cover to do it. We could not have Grandpa picked up at home by our Trang Bang team or by Major Ngo's Regional Forces, because such an arrest would be impossible to hide. I felt sure we could lure him to Saigon, but in Saigon we ourselves had no legal way to apprehend him, and we couldn't just kidnap him. Unfortunately, the special police would have to do it. We also wanted to go after the moneyman and his bank, along with whatever government minister or deputy was protecting the pipeline. And that too would require the special police. So there was no alternative; we would have to share this whole thing with them.

Once I had the operation outlined, I asked Major Binh (the special police officer whose team had been working in the JIC) to set up a safe house in Saigon where we could take Grandpa after he had been arrested. Then I arranged for my own safe house a couple of blocks away, from where I could monitor and supervise the interrogation.

In the meantime, unknown to Bingo One or to anyone else involved in the case, I cabled Hong Kong with a request to track a possible flow of money from a Communist source in Hong Kong to Saigon. Somebody had to be funding the pipeline from the outside, and the British Crown Colony was the most likely connection. Let's go after the big guy from both ends, I thought. If the special police get in my hair with the Saigon moneyman, maybe I can slip by them through the back door.

12

DEATH KNELL

In a matter of days I got a cable back from Hong Kong.
Large sums of money were being transferred electronically
on a weekly basis from the Bank of China in Hong Kong to Saigon.
But they were not able at this time to identify the recipient bank.
The cable also contained another interesting piece of news. Someone from the Agency's Vietnam operation had made an identical
inquiry eight years earlier. Eight years—if funding levels had remained relatively constant, then B-22 had carried something like
$150 million into Cambodia during those years.

With this information in hand I had Ly, the wife, go back to Cut
Trau with the news that Liem was ill. Early the next morning
Grandpa, the tiny, wizened, black pajamad peasant who had run
all that money, got on the bus from Trang Bang city to Saigon. An
hour and a half later he stepped down at the Bay Hien intersection
near Tan Son Nhut airport to change buses, and as he did, three
men pulled up next to him in an old Citroën. Identifying themselves as special police officers, they quickly ushered him into the
backseat and drove him to a house in Cholon, Saigon's Chinatown.

Waiting for him in the house was Bingo One. After offering him
a cup of coffee, Bingo started right in. "Your name is Nguyen Nhu
Binh, isn't it? Where do you live? Where are you registered?" The

old man knew exactly what was going on, and he knew that this young man in front of him knew the answers to the questions he was asking. "Yes," he said, "my name is Nguyen Nhu Binh. I live in Cut Trau hamlet, Loc Hung village, Trang Bang district."

But after that the responses came slowly and reluctantly. Bingo knew we were in a hurry. We only had two days to turn this old geezer around, three days at the most. By then he would have to be home again or he would have to cope with some unexplainable disruption in his schedule. We were sure his supervisor would buy the cover story we had established. When Vietnamese visit a relative in the hospital, they don't go home. They stay all night and sleep on the floor. So one night in Saigon would be fine, two nights would be fine. But Grandpa had to see Ba Minh twice a week. And we didn't want him missing that meeting.

Because of the rush, I had told Bingo One that he had to be able to level with Grandpa soon after they started talking. So despite his evasiveness, Bingo told him that we did in fact know exactly who he was, that we knew Ba Minh as well, and that we knew his agents. Once he heard that, the oldtimer put two and two together—the only way we could have gotten our information was through his grandson Liem or through the runner Thi Nam. One or both of them must have spilled everything.

Midway through the morning Bingo took a break and brought the interrogation tapes over to the house on Phan Thanh Giang Street where I was waiting with Chieu Hoi Lan and two translators. I wanted to keep up with this interrogation as it unfolded. As the translators got to work, Bingo told me about Grandpa. To look at him he seemed an absolutely typical old peasant—pajamas, straw hat, rubber sandals, teeth stained black from chewing betel. With his wrinkled skin and ruined mouth, he seemed even older than his seventy-five years—a backcountry elder who lived in a little hut right near the old pagoda next to a small garden of corn and manioc that he tended daily.

According to Bingo, when you looked at him sitting there dipping into his can of betel nut while the juice dripped into the corners of his mouth, you could not believe he was who he was. It seemed too incredible. But when he talked it was obvious this wasn't any run-of-the-mill peasant. "He's tough," Bingo said, "he's smart and he's knowledgeable. I asked if he was aware that Northerners were running the entire Vietcong effort in South Vietnam and he deflected it. 'All I do is what the party tells me,' he said. 'I just follow my orders.'"

And it was incredible. This man had never been to school a day in his life, but he was good enough to run a system that had probably funneled $150 million or more to the Vietcong over a period of eight years; he had not had a single problem until his courier Thi Nam was picked up in a random check. And even that wouldn't have meant anything if his grandson hadn't decided to go with his wife when she defected. For eight years they had been running that money under the noses of the Vietnamese police.

The first interrogation tapes were mainly discussions about Grandpa's family and his general background. But it was obvious he wasn't eager to answer questions even on these subjects. When Bingo told him that his grandson was not ill but safe with us, he seemed skeptical. Not knowing what to believe, he had decided not to believe a word. He was evasive about everything until Bingo One told him outright that we had Thi Nam in Bien Hoa and that she had told us everything about B-22. Once he demonstrated that to Grandpa's satisfaction, he seemed to loosen up a little. If we knew everything anyway there was hardly any point in keeping up the pretenses.

Late that afternoon I had several other tape transcripts to go over. I was reading as fast as Chieu Hoi Lan and my translators in the safe house could translate. It was easy to see that now Grandpa was being more cooperative, and that he was getting along better with Bingo, even asking him about his family. No question, the interrogator had established his rapport.

That night Bingo came over to my safe house and we discussed how to move the interrogation forward. He had gotten the old man, he thought, to the point where he would listen to a pitch. It was Thi Nam's information that had done the trick. There was no question Grandpa realized he was caught in a corner. We knew all these things, and of course he had to be thinking about what we were going to do with our information. Under more leisurely circumstances we might just let him stew for a while. But we were in a hurry, and the man was a quick study anyway. Tomorrow would be the right time to let him know exactly where he stood and what we wanted from him.

The next day Grandpa was talking freely. He identified twelve couriers all along the line, confirming the information we had. He was one of B-22's chiefs. The other was the man who ran the Saigon end of the line—the moneyman who lived in Cholon. In fact he had no way of denying any of this. Reading the transcript late that morning, I saw that Bingo went right to work on him. "We know you're the station chief," he told him. "We have testimony, so don't deny it. You know what's going to happen if you don't cooperate? You know it, don't you? We're going to turn you over to the police. They know you; they know we've got your grandson and his family; they know we know your people all along the line. You're going to go to jail. And all your people are going to jail. What do you think is going to happen to you there? You think they won't let you have it just because you're old? You think that's going to matter to them?"

Grandpa knew he was trapped. You could hear it in his answers, his tone. What choice did he have? Then too, he was being treated well. Bingo took time out to give him a nice breakfast, then a good lunch. Bingo could be tough, but even when he put his options to Grandpa in black and white, he let his friendliness show through. Not that it was difficult for him. The fact was that Bingo was an amiable guy who was naturally good with people. So the old man liked him. Instead of finding himself confronted with some frightening torturer, here was this likable young man talking to him, addressing him with the polite and respectful *bac*—"uncle."

Right after lunch Bingo gave him the pitch. "Here's what we'll do for you, *bac*," he said. "We'll put you back on the bus and you can go home. But first I'll take you to Bien Hoa today so you can see your grandson and the children. [They were at my house on Cong Ly.] We'll all have dinner there. After that we'll sit down and talk about what we can do to take care of your family, and what we'd like you to do for us in return."

And he bought it; he had obviously been thinking about it all night and had already made his decision. "OK," he said. Just like that. That surprised me a bit when I heard it. I truly didn't think he'd come over so fast. But Bingo's impression was that he badly wanted to see his grandson, that he thought his grandson really was sick and that maybe we were not telling him the truth about his condition.

Early that afternoon Bingo took Grandpa to Bien Hoa by car. At 15 Cong Ly we put him in the big back room and let Liem and the children go in to see him. He was overjoyed; he hadn't seen any of them since they had defected a year and a half earlier (defectors tended to stay as far from home as they could get). He was especially happy to see the children. Liem and those kids were the only relatives he had left.

After giving them a couple of minutes, I walked in with Bingo. I gave Grandpa an affectionate little pat on the shoulder, then sat down with him. I had Bingo tell him that I really admired the way he handled this B-22 network; it was a sophisticated operation that he had run beautifully. "But you see," I said, "we don't give a hoot about any of that. All we want is information. We will not roll up any more cadres. We will not go get your ladies in Hoc Mon or Go Dau Ha or anywhere else. You just keep that B-22 going; it's fine with us. Get your money from the man in Saigon, take it across the border to Ba Minh. We don't care. All that's just a game to us. The only thing we're interested in is information from Ba Minh."

Well, that made sense to him. And it also made sense to him that he was dealing not with the police but with an intelligence officer who wanted intelligence. He didn't need anyone to point that out to him. So when he finally realized that we were not going to hurt him or his family or any of his people, he began responding. Bing, bang, bing. Yes, he would cooperate; he would do it. Just what exactly did I want from him? All of this over tea after Lan led the children off into the kitchen to be fed.

So I laid out the program. We would protect his family and his network from the police (he hadn't realized until now that, unlike Liem's wife, Liem had not formally defected, had not been through the system, and so was subject to arrest). We would also give him the means to take care of Liem and his family, to the tune of thirty thousand piasters a month. And we would be housing the grandson, wife, and children right here in Bien Hoa (they were my insurance policy, though there was no need to say it aloud).

In return we wanted information from COSVN via Ba Minh. We knew that Ba Minh was in and out of COSVN and that he would inform Grandpa of any serious activity in Tay Ninh or Hau Nghia provinces—or of any military developments down the whole length of the Saigon corridor. B-22 was a lifeline, and if anything was doing—from a mortar attack to a major thrust toward Saigon —B-22 would be informed so they could get their people off the highway. In other words, Grandpa would give us the ability to monitor COSVN's military intentions in one of the country's key strategic areas, perhaps the key strategic area. This was the kind of thing we wanted from him. We briefed Grandpa on how to elicit information from Ba Minh about future operations, but he needed no briefing. He and Ba Minh had been working together for ages and had a completely trusting relationship; the COSVN cadre shared everything with him that related to his operation, and much that didn't.

With this level of information to be gained, I knew there was no point in busting the network. If we arrested the whole B-22 finance economy section, we would have in our hands exactly one shipment of money and twelve old ladies. And if we did arrest them, the VC would find alternative routes or would simply establish a

new delivery system. In fact, Grandpa told us there was another
network operating from Saigon into Cambodia along Highway #4
through Long An, although he didn't know any of the details.

So although Grandpa did not know it, I had almost no incentive
to break up his network, but a great incentive to recruit him. He
also didn't know that one of my objectives in having him as an
agent was to recruit his colleague, the Saigon moneyman. This
joker was a prime target; there were all sorts of things I might do
with him. He lived extremely well in his nice house in Cholon,
never enduring any hardship. He certainly would not want to go to
jail, and he had never been anywhere near the jungle. The idea of
having to go into hiding in the boonies would have scared him to
death. So he was vulnerable. If I could recruit him, I would have a
good shot at the bank he worked with and perhaps at whatever
minister or deputy minister was protecting the operation.

The scenario wasn't hard to imagine. One day I would have
Grandpa tell him, "Hey, I have someone I want to introduce you
to. I've been working for him for two years and I trust him. And
you'd better meet him, because if you don't, we're both going to
jail." But that, of course, was down the road. First we had to establish Grandpa and authenticate him.

After our talk in Bien Hoa, Bingo began meeting with Grandpa
in Saigon. Then, when we were satisfied he was leveling with us,
we switched the site to 15 Cong Ly, where he would come every
two weeks. By early 1974 Grandpa had been reporting for several
months. Usually when he came in, I would meet with him and
Bingo in a back room. I'd have Lan talk with him too, make a good
meal and spend some time. Among his other characteristics,
Grandpa had an ironic bent. It amused him that Ba Minh was
talking about how dumb the government was. The idiots had Liem
and now Thi Nam, and still they hadn't managed to figure out the
network. I was amazed at Grandpa's wit, his quick answers and
detailed information. The man had an extraordinary memory. It
was no accident he had been chosen to run this operation.

In talking about the situation generally, Grandpa would laugh at
the Paris peace treaty. That was a good piece of work, he thought,
putting one over on Kissinger like that. He was proud of the fact
that Le Duc Tho had outsmarted his adversary, that the Vietnamese had outsmarted the Americans. But at the same time he was
concerned. He was well aware that the Northerners had taken over
almost everything. And from the beginning he was reporting that
the NVA units were a real drain on the finances. The buildup that
had been under way since shortly after Paris was being supported

in part from local Vietcong resources, and the finance economy section was straining to meet the new demands.

Grandpa's worries on this subject reflected Ba Minh's. Ba Minh was afraid the NVA might even try to take over the money link and pipeline the funds to their forces directly. According to Ba Minh, there were constant rumors floating around COSVN from General Tra right down to the lowest level about a formal North Vietnamese takeover of the Vietcong apparatus.

Grandpa was reporting Grade A information right from the start, but the Saigon end of the B-22 operation was not going well. We had gotten the moneyman's picture, and of course we knew the house. But the special police were handling this side of it and they were very, very slow. It was their job to identify the guy (Grandpa did not know his real name), identify the bank, and look into the connections. This was not a difficult thing to do, and I knew that the special police were putting everyone who went into or came out of the house under surveillance. But they never seemed to come up with anything tangible. I strongly suspected that they had in fact made the identification, but that they were up to their old tricks. There was just too much money involved here, millions of piasters a week, week after week, month after month. "We're working on it," Major Binh would tell me. "We're getting close to the identity of this guy." But that was as far as it ever went.

By this time we were getting a steady stream of intelligence from Grandpa, so this was not a major concern of mine. But it still frustrated the hell out of me. I would have liked to recruit the moneyman, and I certainly wanted whoever it was who was covering the operation. I finally got so angry I was ready to give it a shot myself. So I put my own surveillance on the house in Cholon. I used five of the girls from the data bank, and whenever we heard from Grandpa that a money pickup was scheduled, I'd surveil the place. The data-bank girls dressed in black pants and white blouses if they were meant to be city girls, in black pajamas and conical hats if they were country girls that day. One at a time they'd squat across the street and eat a bowl of noodles, watching the traffic in and out of the house, waiting for the man to emerge. I also had Liem identify the couriers in the pictures the special police had taken from the house across the street, after which we checked out the hamlet books to nail down the IDs. But the moneyman had a lot of company besides the B-22 couriers, and we were not equipped to trace these others. Nor, unfortunately, did we ever see the man himself go into a bank.

I was getting a bad feeling about the whole thing. The special police knew almost every aspect of the Grandpa operation. I had also been forced somewhat earlier to share the Goldmother operation with them. Under pressure from the Agency's national-level special police adviser, Station had decided to bring them into some of the ongoing operations. I had had to give the entire file to Major Binh working there in the JIC. Their participation worried me deeply; they couldn't be trusted not to try to turn a profit from what they knew. And this meant not only that their own investigations were likely to be fruitless; it meant that mine were in danger as well.

Meanwhile, Bingo One was proving himself a case officer as well as an interrogator/interpreter. He had handled Grandpa's recruitment flawlessly. Now, building on his familiarity with the data bank, and especially with the files on Hau Nghia province, he began to track his own leads. He became a dossier man, poring over the files until he knew each of the VC personnel in the province for whom we had cards. With that knowledge in mind he then went about examining the records of prisoners and defectors who had come out of that province. At the same time he kept a close watch on the new people being brought in. Eventually, he hoped to make an identification that would prove operational.

In the end Bingo's work paid off. Two years earlier a man had been captured who identified himself as the chief of the Loc Hung village Worker's Association. For Loc Hung, of course, our files were exhaustive, but Bingo was unable to confirm the identity of the man holding this position. So although the prisoner had been convicted as a VC and had been serving his sentence in jail, in fact no one had any way of knowing if he had told the truth about his position. Bingo One suspected he hadn't, that he had confessed to being the Worker's Association chief to cover his true identity and receive a shorter sentence (which was now just about up). Certain facts in the man's family background and biography suggested to Bingo that rather than being the Worker's Association chief, the prisoner might in reality be deputy secretary of the Trang Bang Military Proselyting Committee, our old friend Tu Duc's second-in-command.

When Bingo came to me with his suspicions I suggested that he obtain a photograph of the man from the Hau Nghia jail along with fifteen or so photos of other prisoners. Then he should show them all to Ba Tung, who would surely know both the real deputy secretary and the real Worker's Association section chief.

When Bingo did this his suspicions were confirmed. Ba Tung made the identification instantly. Bingo's man was indeed the deputy chief.

With that, Bingo and I worked out an approach. The Worker, as we were calling him, was scheduled for release shortly. Bingo One would visit him in his common jail cell, making overhearable comments about talking more about the Worker's Association. Then in private Bingo would tell the man that we knew his true identity. He would mention Tu Duc for the effect, indicating some of the details we knew about Tu Duc's life, which would suggest all the details we knew about his own life. Bingo would put a little fear into him about his family, who might easily be picked up, and about his own future—as deputy proselyting chief he of course owed several more years to the government, including another round of interrogation.

At the same time, Bingo would assure him that he was not working with the government, but with American intelligence (always a ray of hope in that). No government agencies were yet involved in these developments. But we did want to talk with him again, after his release, and we hoped he would cooperate. We suggested a rendezvous in Saigon thirty days after the Worker got out of jail.

We knew we were giving the VC a lot of slack, and we were pessimistic about his showing up for the meeting. But we also knew that on his return home the Worker would be put through a round of testing by the party. That was standard procedure, and often unpleasant for comrades of long and good standing. So after thirty days the Worker might not be too happy with the way he was being treated, especially after suffering for the revolution in jail for two years. In addition, if he looked around he would see that the VC was not the same organization it was when he was picked up in 1971. The Northern penetration of the whole system was likely to shock him. At the same time he would be considering his options. If he went underground his family might be harassed by ARVN. If he chose not to cooperate but stayed above ground, he would be arrested again. Maybe he should at least listen to what the Americans had to say.

Thirty days after his release, the Worker showed up in the Saigon noodle shop where Bingo had told him they would meet. There Bingo talked to him about the failure of the Vietcong and urged him to do what he could to protect his family and his farm. What Bingo wanted him to do was go back home and ask to be given a position, his former one if possible, something else if not. In the old days the VC never would have considered it, not until the man had been thoroughly tested, and maybe not even then. But times had changed. With so many legal cadres in prison and with the Vietcong infrastructure hurting so badly for personnel, we might get lucky. Whether he was reinstated or not, the Worker was to meet Bingo again after another thirty days.

When the Worker agreed, we had no way of telling whether he was being sincere or whether he was angling to play the double agent. We knew that was a possibility, but we decided to go ahead anyway on the principle of nothing ventured, nothing gained. If the man had leveled with his old bosses and was working for them, he would not be able to find out much anyway. He would have no access to anything. And if his object was to feed us misleading information, the agents we were already running would give us an effective check.

At the appointed time the Worker was back in the noodle shop. Tu Duc's successor had refused to reinstate him as deputy chief, but he had taken him back into the section. And having worked with him for so long, the chief was friendly and communicative. From that point on the Worker reported regularly to Bingo One. The information he brought was usually not headline news, but most often it was useful, and a year and a half later it was to be highly significant.

One of the areas the Worker was reporting was the continuing takeover by the NVA. Grandpa was reporting this too, so it was apparent that the subject was high on the list of things that were bothering the old VC hierarchy. Material from the other agents kept flowing in on this as well. By now I had turned the Mad Bomber over to Sam while Lou was busy working on several promising leads. Don, Lou's original cutout, was still servicing the agent, reporting now to Sam twice a week.

We had been running the Bomber for three years and now he began making signs that he was bored with the work (he had always had a craving for action). But he was still furnishing first-rate information, a lot of which had to do with the North Vietnamese, whom he personally didn't like at all.

The best single piece of information we got at this period, though, had nothing to do with the North Vietnamese. In mid-December 1973, the Goldmother reported that the VC were planning to blow up the giant POL farm in the Nha Be peninsula, just south of Saigon—a facility whose tanks contained most of South Vietnam's oil reserves. Her information was not complete. She did not know the number of the sapper unit that was assigned to the mission, nor did she know their plans. Only that their target was the entire dump. She was able to provide two dates—two consecutive nights.

As soon as the Goldmother's report came into my hands I notified Colonel Thao. He had long been familiar with this agent's reliability and needed no urging to take the report seriously. The POL dump's security command was notified to double their forces and to be on the highest alert those two nights.

It was beautiful intelligence, but unfortunately it did not prevent the sappers from carrying out their mission. In the early-morning hours of the second night we heard a vast roaring sound coming from the direction of Saigon. It sounded as if an atomic bomb had exploded. The next morning a giant cloud of black smoke had risen twenty thousand feet into the air to our south. "That was what intelligence is all about," I said to Lou as the two of us gazed at the blackening sky. The Arab oil embargo was at its height and we were watching thirty-five million liters of gas burn up. "Yeah," he grunted, shaking his head. "It was great intelligence. It's just too bad our friends didn't take it seriously enough."

At this time the JIC, the data bank, and the network of agents were running beautifully. We were handling the Mad Bomber, the Goldmother, Grandpa, the Worker, the Duc Hue Tiger, the Di An Doozie, in addition to the Reaper, who was being supervised out of Tay Ninh. Now, at the end of 1973, the data bank had grown to almost 100,000 names of legals and illegals (bunker dwellers and regular forces). The interrogation teams worked hard and effectively, all of the people thoroughly professional by now. With the recent addition of three new men from the Agency we now had eight American case officers.

But despite the program's successes I continued to have my problems with the chief of base, John Brenley. I had come to the conclusion long ago that Brenley was unbalanced. I had also found that the only way to minimize the consequences with him was to hit back as quickly as I could at any attack. Often he would back away from a frontal attack. But dealing with him was a constant drain. Whenever I was at the Monastery he would ask me to come into his office for a "chat," and inevitably the first remark from him would be something like, "Good to see you again, Ong Gia. How's your office looking now? Any new rugs or paintings?"

Consistent with my theory of give him an inch and he'd take a mile, I would thank him for inquiring and tell him I was about to put in a requisition for another sofa. "You know I've got to keep it looking first-class, John. I just had Little Minh and Colonel Thao in the other day and I can never tell who else might show up." I knew that would infuriate him. He did not know General Minh. There were not many Vietnamese he did know, which was how he wanted it, since he was not fond of Asians. But he still wouldn't like Minh's having come to visit me. And he hated the fact that Colonel Thao, the G-2, dropped in so often.

Ours was a strange relationship. I was aware that the man was volatile and capable of anything. I also knew he was in a state of constant turmoil about the JIC, which he regarded as a rogue elephant that existed on his base but not under his control, something he could not tolerate. Yet we talked to each other and on occasion even had dinner together. I was, I told him, the closest thing he had to a friend on base besides Bernie D'Antonio, his exec.

"What is it," I asked Brenley one night when a couple of martinis and one of Lan's marvelous steak dinners had induced a semblance of intimacy, "what exactly is it about the JIC that bugs you so much?" "It's the security," he answered. "I'm worried about security there. I think we're violating all sorts of regulations in running a huge operation like that away from the Monastery." "John," I answered, "the JIC's been running for almost four years and we've never had the slightest problem. You know what results we've had, so I don't have to go into that again. It's not productivity, and you and I both know it's not security, so what is it?" "No," he said, "it's security. One of these days I'm going to request Saigon Station's security section to come up here and inspect the JIC. Just to cover our asses."

That was a warning alarm if I had ever heard one. It sounded to me as if he was preparing an attack, and that he had already decided on his strategy.

The first stage of Brenley's attack opened up only a week or so after this dinner, but from an entirely unexpected direction. One day Bernie D'Antonio called Sam and asked him to bring the Mad Bomber file over to his office, not the kind of thing he was in the habit of asking for. The next day Bernie called me to announce that he had found a number of "holes" in the operation, mainly involving Don, the former VC captain who had been Lou's source when he originally developed the Bomber and who was still the cutout. "What the hell are you talking about, Bernie?" I asked. "What kind of holes?" "Oh, nothing special," he said, "just some things in the background investigation. If you don't mind I'd like to come over to 15 Cong Ly and run Don through the lie box."

   The following morning Bernie had Don in one of my back rooms
going through a lie-detector test. An hour later Sam came up and
told me that the box operator had said Don made some ripples on
his chart. Bernie was going to try him again after lunch.
   "Did Don look nervous to you?" I asked Sam. "Like a whore in
church," he said. I couldn't believe this was happening. Don was a
high-strung character under any circumstances, and Vietnamese
tended to produce abnormal results on the box anyway. They were
afraid of it; it excited their superstitious natures, especially the ones
from peasant backgrounds, like Don.
   After lunch Don jiggled the box again and Bernie came in to tell
me he had decided to close the Mad Bomber operation. "Bernie,"
I said, "you can't be serious. The Mad Bomber's been producing
beautifully for years, always corroborated material. A lie box
doesn't mean anything, especially for an Asian. Haven't you been
out here long enough to know that? So the cutout was nervous,
who cares? He's an ex-peasant and he's frightened. We're dealing
with a human asset here. A human asset can authenticate himself
and this man has authenticated himself a hundred times. What
about the H-1? What about three years' worth of A reports?"
   "No," said Bernie, with a tone of satisfaction, "we boxed him
twice and that's plenty as far as I'm concerned. Close the operation." I was speechless, but there was no one to appeal to. Brenley
had obviously put D'Antonio up to it. He had started his assault on
the JIC.
   So the Mad Bomber was terminated, after three years of faultless
intelligence. We stopped the payments to the cutout, we stopped
the payments to the Bomber's auntie, and we stopped servicing the
dead drop. What it must have seemed like to the Bomber I couldn't
imagine. All of a sudden his handlers just disappeared. A spy left
out there in the cold.
   A short time later Sam and Gary left the base with their wives,
their tours up. It was a terrible shame to lose them. Had they stayed
a little longer they both would have been running their own agents.
As it was, Gary had done masterful work on the background investigation that led us to the Goldmother and Sam had handled the
Mad Bomber with patience and growing expertise. But now they
were gone. It was a loss, a kind of sniping maneuver by Brenley.
Even worse, they left with their personal dossiers carrying letters
from the chief of base that ensured their contracts would not be
renewed, as indeed they were not, and both men left the Agency
for civilian life.
   But we were now nearing the end of 1974 and Brenley himself

was due to leave soon. Already we knew who his replacement would be. Hal Wiggins, who had served in central Asia, had a reputation for being a decent guy. I had already begun to feel that I had weathered a very uncomfortable situation.

Two weeks before Brenley's rotation date he called me over to his office. I thought I knew what was coming. I did not expect the man to leave without some last attempt at destruction. But now he was so close to the end of his tour that the only way he could get rid of me, I thought, would be to have me reassigned, maybe bump me up to Saigon Station. Of course I would fight it, and there was a good chance I could win. As I drove over to the Monastery I felt confident. I had faced him down before and now the man was practically a lame duck.

When I sat down across from his desk Brenley asked Jane to bring in some coffee. As we waited there was not even an attempt at small talk. Jane had a grim look on her face as she put the cup down in front of me and as soon as she closed the door Brenley started. "Orrin," he said, "I'll tell you what I have decided to do. I'm going to have to close that JIC of yours. It's out of control. It can't be handled. There is no way the base can be run properly with that JIC over there. We both know that I'm rotating in two weeks, so this is all going to be done before I leave. And I'm going to see to it that it is. I want this thing closed down and I want you out of there while I am still here to make sure that you do it. I want to watch it myself."

I sat there stunned. Calm, but stunned. Then, very deliberately, I began to talk. In the last eighteen months I had rehearsed a speech a hundred times for just this situation. But this was the wrong time for it, and it seemed to me that the words were coming out in the wrong order and in the wrong tone, hurt, and as I went on, angry. "John," I heard myself saying, "this is a mistake. This is the craziest thing I have ever heard. The JIC is the most productive organization, the cheapest, in this country. That's already on the boards. Nobody can say anything different. You can't do this. You've only got two more weeks here. Why don't you just go home and forget it? Chalk it up as a bad experience or something. But don't break down this operation. Why would you want to destroy the base's productivity? What will the new chief think when he gets here? He might have completely different ideas. Why would you destroy his base for him before he arrives?"

"I'm sorry," said Brenley, "but the security is terrible over there. You've got prisoners there. You've got a safe there. You've got documents in that safe. It's an unacceptable situation."

"John, in the six years I've been here, we've never had a security problem. We have never had a single person escape. We've never had even an attempted escape, not from the JIC and not from my house. I don't keep cables in the safe or anything else that's secret. All I keep there are sanitized reports. Everything else is immediately hand carried to the office here. Nothing's in my home safe either."

"Well," said Brenley, "I've asked Saigon to send a security team out here. They're arriving tomorrow. Let them make the decision." We both knew exactly what a security team would say, because the fact was that the JIC was not run according to the book. No one at headquarters ever would have approved a private hotel as a jail. Thank God Don Gregg, and Bob Somerhill after him, had had the balls to go along with it. They had been completely aware that almost nothing I was doing went according to the book. But they also knew we were getting the job done. "I'm going to move your data bank over here," Brenley was saying. "We'll put it out in the supply section. And I want you and Lou to set yourselves up over here. I'll make offices available for you. You can run your operation from the Monastery. As far as your other officers go, they can work out of your offices."

"John, what are you talking about? You know there's no room for my officers and interrogators here. And what am I going to do with the fifty sources I've got living in the JIC? Where am I going to put them?"

"I don't know, Orrin, and I don't care. Just get rid of them."

"We're talking to them, John. Right this minute we're talking to them. The reports that came across your desk yesterday and today, the ones that are coming tomorrow, that's where they're coming from, those people in the JIC. If I send them back to the CIC or the Chieu Hoi Center, where are we supposed to talk to them?"

"Well, go out to the CIC to talk to them. Go out to the Chieu Hoi Center to talk to them. Go and sit in their mess hall and talk to them there, at a table. I've seen it done before, so do it again."

By this time I was hearing myself talking, as if I were outside of this conversation and listening in on it. I was telling him about how it worked, that if the data bank was here and the sources were in different places, it meant a half a day to check out statements or a name or to do background research. I was telling him about the need to put the prisoners in the right environment, to create the rapport, to give them a picture they could believe in. Without that they wouldn't cooperate. I heard myself talking and I saw Brenley sitting there with that strangely skewed smile on his face. I knew the man had no concept of the damage he was about to do, that the only thing he knew, or cared about, was that he had finally gotten to me.

So I stopped talking. The room was silent, lit up only by that idiot smile. I sat there for a minute, waiting for him to say something else, then another minute. Then I got up and walked out.

Back at the JIC Lou and I sipped coffee in my office, trying to absorb what had just happened, wondering what we would do with ourselves. Everything that had been built so painstakingly over six years, destroyed overnight. And the whole thing was about an office and a desk and a rug. It was insanity, plain psychotic insanity.

But there was no way around it. I had no one to turn to to get this reversed, or even delayed. We knew that the next day Brenley would be standing in the office asking where the trucks were. And so we started making arrangements to move the files to the Monastery and the prisoners and *hoi chanh* back to the centers. But the case officers, interrogators, translators, clerks, and typists—the fifty or so people who made up the JIC staff—would be stranded. Somehow I'd have to jam them into the Monastery's halls and storage areas. Insanity. As workers began to pile desks into alcoves and corridors I wondered briefly if there was some way I might be able to get Brenley certified. But the sight of my employees milling around uncertainly woke me out of the mental haze that seemed to have settled on my brain. And as the haze cleared a little, I started looking for houses. Maybe, I thought, I could reconstruct the situation I had before Don Gregg authorized the JIC. Who could tell what the next chief of base might decide to do? Maybe he would want to put the whole thing back together. Or maybe not. Nineteen seventy four was ending, and how much more time might be left for any of us in Vietnam was something no one could tell.

13

THE BEAUTEOUS LAN

But the JIC wasn't my only problem that December, or even the most disturbing. More and more I found that Lan was in my thoughts. I was worried about her.

It had started as a troubling little dilemma more than a year ago when I had begun to accept in my gut that this was one war the United States was not going to win. After the Paris agreement I had shared the general depression. I had sat with my friends Thao and Dinh, working through the various grim scenarios that offered themselves. But the despair at that point was vague and unfocused. The signs were bad and we knew they weren't likely to improve. But while doom might be gathering, it was still somewhere beyond the horizon.

Over the last year or so, though, the situation had worsened. South Vietnam's army was deteriorating fast. They say that an army fights on its stomach, and ARVN soldiers not only weren't able to feed their families, they didn't even have enough for their own breakfasts. Morale was nonexistent. I didn't believe they would fight when the blow came, and that opinion was shared by ARVN officers I knew. As far as the U.S. was concerned, there was only one reality. There was not going to be any more help, despite Nixon and Kissinger's commitments. Since shortly after Paris we

had been reporting detailed intelligence on the North Vietnamese
buildup. The flow of traffic down the Ho Chi Minh Trail was
bumper-to-bumper, right out in the open, verified and reverified
by live sources and by photoreconnaissance. The North Vietnamese were violating the treaty massively, brazenly—flaunting the
violation right in our faces. But there had been no response. The
B-52s had stayed grounded. Who was there to send them? Nixon in
the death throes of Watergate? Ford? Even if ARVN had been
poised and eager, by now they were badly outmanned and outgunned, no match for their enemies, not without American air
power.

So the nature of my conviction that Vietnam was lost had slowly
changed. Since the spring of 1973 I had accepted it intellectually.
By the winter of 1974 I could feel it. And sometime during this
transition I had begun worrying about Lan. I had hired her as a
housekeeper; then she had become my mistress. But by 1974 we
had been together for five years and our relationship had long since
gone through its own changes.

Originally I had been attracted by her beauty, and by the fact
that she seemed to be someone I could trust. But it wasn't long
before I had begun to admire her too. I was struck by the way she
mothered that extended family of hers, all those orphans and semi-
orphans who had somehow found their way under her wing. In
five years I had watched them grow, some from infants into school-
children, others from children into teenagers. I had become, infor-
mally at least, an adoptive father, making sure they had enough to
eat, that they had medical care, that they had clothes to wear. At
any given time there might be one of them, or five, or all nine
eating in my kitchen or playing around the house or sleeping over.
From the very start I had fallen for the little ones, but over the
years I had grown attached to all of them, almost as if they were
my adopted children, which in a sense they had become.

As Lan grew into a permanent fixture in my life, I began to trust
her with more and more. Once I understood what kind of a person
I had found, I started bringing her into the operation. When I kept
Vietcong women in the house it was Lan who looked after them
and Lan who became friends with them. She was the kind of individual who made friends easily, an instant confidante. But although she knew perfectly well what was going on and what her
role was, she never considered that she was in the spy business.
The VC women were most often frightened and lonely; usually
their backgrounds were not much different from hers. As far as
Lan was concerned they were human beings and she responded to

them as one human being to another. With some of them she became and remained close.

The one mission I had sent Lan on had worked out well, although it had scared her half to death. When she and her friend, the ex-VC Nam, went to check on our lapsed agent in Phu Hoa, I hadn't really had any fear for her. Lan's dark skin would allow her to pass as a peasant and I was sure she wouldn't have any trouble even if she encountered some VC. Of course, she had encountered them and had been put through a grilling. Ever since then we had been teasing each other about it, Lan insisting that I had wanted to kill her, while I maintained that with her country looks the worst they would have done was recruit her.

Shortly after the Phu Hoa episode I decided that Lan, the kids, and her mother had to have a place to live other than the windowless room they were renting behind the bar. I had given her money for a small house and a little land just across the Dong Nai in the district of Di An. For the first time the family had a place they could call home. After a while they built a small store in front of the house, from which they sold rice and a few other staples. The store was made entirely of beer cans soldered together (not an uncommon type of construction). When I found out they were on the verge of bankruptcy for giving bad-risk local farmers rice on credit, I got Bingo One to persuade them to put up a sign he made for them—"Khong Ban Thieu," No Credit. Eventually they added a couple of tables and chairs and served soft drinks. Occasionally I'd drive by there and see four or five people at the tables, so I figured business was going all right. That was important. I wanted Lan to have a way of surviving if something happened to me.

One day when I stopped by the store Lan wasn't there and I understood one of the kids to say that she was out back near the jungle picking fruit. At least that was what I understood, though with my grasp of Vietnamese he might have told me that President Nguyen Van Thieu had just stopped by for a Coke. Driving down the track that led through the field in back of her house, I spotted Lan in the distance near the tree line. When she saw my white Colt she ran toward me waving her arms and yelling. It wasn't until she got to the car that I understood she was telling me to get out, that there were VC in the trees. Realizing that she could be a hundred percent correct, I slammed the car into reverse and bugged out in a hurry. Later Lan told me that there was a small Vietcong camp in the woods with eight or nine guerrillas always on hand. She knew them all; they visited her store at night to buy rice and snacks or to have a soft drink. I was a little surprised to hear this, but actually it was quite typical of the neighborly relations thousands of people throughout the country had with VC who were camped nearby.

An objective observer might have said that Lan and I were in love. I might have said so myself. We enjoyed each other's company, we attended social occasions together (Agency and State Department functions mostly), we talked about the kids. I cared for her and felt protective toward her and toward the whole brood. My own marriage had formally ended several years earlier, so in that sense I was a free man who could do what he wanted with his affections.

But though I might have said we were in love, I wouldn't have. I knew the East too well, and I knew myself too well. In 1974 I was fifty-two years old. Lan was twenty-five. I had lived in Japan a long time and had seen plenty of winter-spring relationships and plenty of American-Japanese relationships. I wasn't exactly a novice in the world of Asian romance. And by this time I most certainly knew the Vietnamese. There are two expressions in Vietnamese that spring to mind when it comes to romance: *ba muoi lam* (number thirty-five) means to play around, and *de dai lo* (along a wide boulevard) means to really play around. Vietnamese are notorious for playing around, at least the men are. And as for the women, well, I thought I had learned the primary lesson—that Asian women are mainly oriented toward security. Love might develop between a husband and wife, but a good marriage in Asia puts family and economic interests first.

Vietnamese, as far as I could see, seek in their marriages security for the family, not just the immediate family but the extended family. And the long war in Vietnam had introduced its own twist to romance. There were a lot of relationships between American men and Vietnamese women, but I knew very well that more often than not the Vietnamese woman had a Vietnamese boyfriend or husband at the same time. Her real commitment was to the boyfriend or husband, who would provide for her and her home over the long run, while the American was a source of temporary financial help. That didn't mean she might not feel warmly toward her GI boyfriend, but she certainly knew what the priorities were.

During the fall of 1974 I found myself thinking more and more about Lan and about her future. I began to feel that my sugar-daddy days were over, that I had to find a way to give her some protection in the inevitable future, when I would be gone. The best way, I thought, would be to separate her from me while there was still time. She and her mother had a little land and the store.

If she got married, she and a husband would be able to support themselves and fit right in. Nobody in Di An would know she had spent five years with the CIA interrogation chief.

Once I had made up my mind about this, I talked it over with Bingo One and enlisted his help. He was intelligent and sensitive, an ace translator who knew how to convey nuances and feelings as well as literal meanings. Lan's English had improved quite a bit since I first hired her, but it was still pretty rudimentary and I wanted her to hear what I had to say in Vietnamese so there wouldn't be any mistakes.

The next afternoon Bingo, Lan, and I sat down around the dining-room table at 15 Cong Ly. Speaking slowly, giving Bingo time to translate as I went along, I told Lan I wanted to see her settled down for the future. That couldn't include me, whatever the two of us might wish. I would not be able to stay in Vietnam much longer. (I didn't say that the fall was imminent. I couldn't predict exactly when that might happen and I didn't see any point in scaring her.) Perhaps she had a close friend who might be interested in a young woman with a home and a little business and a plot of land (I didn't say I knew she had a boyfriend). If she did know someone like that, someone who was himself employed, they would have enough income to get along. She was a young, beautiful woman who should have her own husband and her own children.

As I talked I knew I was doing the right thing—an old hand experienced in the ways of the East doing the right thing by his young Vietnamese mistress. Here I was, making these wonderful gestures. I had gotten the family the house, helped her build the store, made sure the kids had clothing and were going to school. And now I was giving up all this beauty, making the responsible decision—just the right thing. But when tears began dropping silently from the corners of Lan's eyes I did not feel good. I had to hesitate a moment before I could continue talking, so I could choke back something that had gotten into my throat.

In one way or another I got through the rest of it. She should leave by the end of the week. That would be enough time for her to give the housegirls any last instructions. There was no point in drawing it out. It would be better for both of us if we made a clean, quick break. When Bingo stopped talking Lan got up from the table and walked out in silence. I didn't see her face as she left, and I was glad I didn't.

That afternoon I reconvinced myself that this was the right way to handle it. Even though dissolving the relationship was sad, it was hardly the end of the world. Lan would realize soon enough that it was to her benefit to go home now and start up a more permanent life. There was a good chance that she had had similar thoughts herself. In fact it would be surprising if she hadn't. She might be attached to me right now, but she knew as well as I that there was no future in it.

Friday was the last day. Lan had been avoiding me since our talk; I knew she was hurting badly and didn't want to talk to or even look at me. At lunchtime Old Man Lam and his wife came over. I was grateful for the gesture. They were good friends and I knew Lam thought their presence might make it easier for us. Or maybe after five years he and his wife couldn't believe we were actually going through with this and wanted to see it for themselves. With one part of me I couldn't believe it either. Despite the Lams, as we stood in the kitchen looking at each other the tears started running from Lan's eyes. She was always quick with her feelings, and tenderhearted, maybe the most tenderhearted girl I had ever known. Looking at that lovely face I suddenly couldn't find a trace of the cool, experienced Asian hand who was so sure of himself. I stared at her, knowing I would not see her again, or see the kids again. It was over, for good. As Lan turned and walked out through the kitchen door for the last time I felt my own tears welling up.

Over the next two weeks Old Man Lam let me know that Lan had apparently taken what I said to heart. As I knew, there was a close family friend who was very interested in her, and it looked as if the two families might get together and decide on a marriage. Mrs. Lam, who had always been a good friend to Lan, had visited her and her mother a number of times. Lan was unhappy, but she was trying to resign herself to what had happened and look ahead.

Whatever Lan was doing, I somehow couldn't get my mind off the past. I kept visualizing scenes from our life together. I would find myself slipping into reveries at my desk or sitting in the Hoa Binh bar or having a martini or talking with Thao about the most recent piece of war news. I seemed to be spending half my time thinking about Lan and what had happened between us and the other half berating myself for acting like a high-school kid. Come on, old man, I'd think. What the hell's wrong with you? There are a million others out there just waiting for you, the same as there always have been. Is this something new to you? You're fifty-two years old, for Christ's sake.

Every night after work Lou, Bingo One, Gekko One, and Tiger One would come over to 15 Cong Ly, either by themselves or with sources they were entertaining. And almost always we'd sit and talk for a while. Lam was often there too, and he and Bingo were good company. J. J. Clark also came. J. J. was one of our administrative officers, a bright, cheerful black kid who was a top-notch worker and who regarded me as his on-site parent. J. J. had a Vietnamese girlfriend himself whom he had fallen in love with and had started thinking about marrying. I had advised him against it. Girlfriends are one thing, I had told him. But these cross-cultural, cross-racial things rarely work out. Wait till you get back, I said; you'll find a nice black girl at home and you'll have a much better chance at a marriage that will last. First-rate fatherly advice.

Now J. J. was trying to console me, giving me the same line. Under different circumstances I might have seen the humor in it. But it didn't seem very funny. My spirits sank even further when one night Lam told me that Lan's family and her friend's family had made an arrangement and that the traditional wedding dinner was scheduled for the coming Sunday. "You know, sport," I said to J. J., "I thought I could handle this without any problem, but it's not working out too well, is it?" Inside I was burning. It was just what I wanted for her, wasn't it? Get her married, settled down, protected. But I was having a hard time recalling why I was so sure I'd be able to just walk away and turn my back on her. No, it wasn't working out too well.

A week later Old Man Lam told me that he had visited Lan at her house to congratulate her on her marriage. Although the wedding dinner had been held, the couple had not started living together yet. Lan, he said, was in tears the entire visit. She had not been able to sit still. "Everything I see here is from Ong Gia," she had told him. "Everywhere I look, he's here."

That set me off. I hadn't expected any of this and I didn't want it. I didn't think I could stand it. That night I didn't sleep. God knows, I had had enough girls in my time. But none of them had affected me anything like this. I had been a cool enough customer through a couple of wars, so why couldn't I handle this? Orrin, you dumb son of a bitch—the refrain kept running through my head— what the hell did you do? Just what the hell did you do?

The next day I didn't go to work. Instead I called Lou and had him ask Old Man Lam to come over. When he did I broke it to him quickly. I had made a terrible mistake, I told him, a terrible, terrible mistake. "I have to have her back. I need to have her back in this house. I want you to arrange that for me. I'm relying on you to do it."

Lam had come over thinking I needed some company. But as I spoke, the look on his face changed from one of kindly sympathy to shock then to horror. His mouth started working, stuttering in Vietnamese, "*Ke, ke, ke, ke,*" then shouting at me in English—the man had never raised his voice in five years. "Ong Gia, what do you mean you want her back? Do you understand what you are saying? They had the wedding dinner already! They're married! You know our customs! What do you want me to do, break up the marriage?"

I tried to keep my voice low, to calm him down. He looked almost as if he were going to have a heart attack. "Yes," I said, "I know what I'm saying; I know what it means. But I did the stupidest thing of my life letting her go. I thought it was the right thing. But it's not working. I can't bear it. I just cannot function like this. You must talk to Lan about it and to her mother. You have to find some way to do it. Tell them that I want her back permanently. Have them tell the boy's family that Lan isn't compatible with him. Or find some other way. But you have to do it."

In a little while Lam had Bingo One, Gekko One, and Tiger One sitting in the living room with us, almost the whole of my Vietnamese mafia. They were as incredulous as he was, just stunned. "It's unheard of, Ong Gia," said Bingo. "The families have had their formal dinner together. Now Lan and this man are husband and wife and they have to register in the hamlet family book. What you're asking is impossible; you can't do it." As he spoke the others made approving noises and comments, looking at me and shaking their heads as if I had lost my mind.

"Bingo," I said, "I know the procedures. That's why I want to do it now, before they register in the hamlet book. I know how difficult it is. But there must be a way. People must have gotten marriages called off before, especially before they've registered or set up house. Please believe me, I know I made a mistake, and so does Lan. I'm sure of it. She'll agree to come back. It's mainly a matter of getting her mother to go along. So please try. Find some way and try."

The Vietnamese all sat there in a silence that seemed to last an eternity. Then they began talking in low voices among themselves. All I could pick up were some of the individual Vietnamese words, no general meaning. At that moment I felt that these four men were deciding my fate. Finally Bingo One looked up at me and said, "OK, Ong Gia. We've agreed that Lam can try to discuss this with the family."

Old Man Lam made his initial approach to Lan's mother in my living room. It went over like a ton of bricks. He suggested that an annulment should be arranged on the grounds that since the wed-

ding Lan had proved herself to be incapable of marriage. But the
mother wasn't buying it. At heart she was sympathetic to Lan's
plight, but she could not imagine going to the groom's family with
such a proposal. No one had ever heard of such a thing.

Lan came over to the house too, dressed in black peasant pajamas and a conical bamboo hat. She seemed gloriously beautiful to
me. We talked quietly, trying hard to keep our emotions subdued.
I told her how I felt, how I had felt since she left. How I needed
her to come back. Her feelings were the same, she said. But this
was mad, even talking like this. Why was I doing this to her? Why
was I hurting her like this? She couldn't understand it, and she
couldn't understand me. She could try to convince her mother;
she would try. But even if her mother went along, there would be
the boy's family to deal with. She didn't know how she could face
their embarrassment and hurt pride, or her own embarrassment.

With this delicate task in front of us, I asked Old Man Lam if he
could help. His age and stature made him the ideal person for it.
He had a way of smoothing over difficult personal problems, as he
had shown time and again in his years of dealing with the JIC's
sometimes steamy and involved employee relationships. He probably expected I would ask. After the initial shock of hearing me say
I wanted Lan back, he had quickly reverted to his usual calm,
dignified demeanor, ready to handle anything. Maybe he considered this just another JIC melodrama, a little unusual since it
involved Ong Gia, but essentially not much different.

Ten days after my meeting with Lan, Old Man Lam drove up to
15 Cong Ly with Lan in the front seat. She had brought a suitcase
with her and as she got out of the car she was smiling radiantly.
Old Man Lam also had a broad smile on his face. "Ong Gia," he
announced a bit formally, "I have just completed a task of immense
consequences, something unheard of in our customs. Now I pray
it will all work out." He looked at me, then at Lan. I thanked him
for what he had done, and told him I understood the meaning of
it. "I know," I told him, "that somehow it will work out happily for
everyone."

All this was going on during the last month of John Brenley's
tenure and had not helped me keep my equilibrium when he ordered me to close down the JIC. But by the time Hal Wiggins, the
new chief, came, my private life had settled down.

"I know all about John Brenley," Hal Wiggins said when I met
him. "Don't even bother telling me about him. I know about the
JIC too. I've done my homework on this and I want you to do

everything you can to rebuild the operation. The building's gone, and I don't see going out and redoing it at this point. But I understand you're making inquiries about houses. That's good. Try to get five or six of them. We've got some critical times coming up, and I want this base to be prepared as best it can. Spend whatever you need to spend on it. Larry tells me money's not a worry. And have Lou handle the reorganization. Give your instructions to him. You're overdue for home leave and I want you to take it."

Exactly whom Hal Wiggins had talked to I wasn't sure. But it sounded almost as if he had gotten himself a briefing from my former boss Bob Somerhill. Whatever the case, it was a huge relief just to have a rational person in charge again. As Larry Jones's wife, Jane, put it, it felt as if the weight of the world had been taken off our shoulders.

As far as my leave went, I had been putting it off for some time now, and Wiggins was right, I was overdue. It seemed like the ideal time too. The agent network was working fine (though I would always be pissed off about the Mad Bomber termination) and Lou wouldn't have any trouble covering for me. Lou was also capable of putting the houses together and reorganizing the interrogation operation. There was no reason he shouldn't have everything up and running by the time I got back.

So I was ready. But I was not going to go without Lan. After what we had just been through there was no way I was ever going to be separated from her again. That was a problem though. Getting a passport for a Vietnamese citizen to leave the country was a hugely expensive affair. It could be done, of course, but the payoffs involved were really stiff. Here again Old Man Lam came to the rescue. His old Dai Viet party contacts were still in good working order, and he could get help from one of our Vietnamese employees who was closely connected to a three-star general with a lot of political clout.

Within a week we were in possession of a letter from the general giving Lan the necessary permission. But even that wasn't enough. The document required the countersignature of Lan's hamlet chief, and this individual refused to sign without a hefty contribution. When he wouldn't budge on his demands, Old Man Lam decided to take the matter into his own hands. It was his responsibility to get this done and no corrupt, thieving hamlet chief was going to get in his way. So he simply signed it himself, forging the hamlet chief's signature. Then he took the papers to Saigon and came back with Lan's new passport in hand.

Two days later Lan and I took off from Tan Son Nhut airport

bound for the Philippines, Hawaii, then the mainland U.S. It was a joyous occasion—half my staff and all of Lan's family came down to see us off. It seemed as if most of them felt they had had a hand in bringing Lan and me together, and this trip to the United States must have looked like a real storybook ending.

In a way it was. Even now I could hardly believe what I had gone through. It wasn't normal, becoming a believer in true love at my age. But there it was. As for Lan, this trip was by far the most exciting thing that had ever happened to her. She was a real small-town Vietnamese girl for whom a visit to Saigon was an exciting event. Flying across the Pacific to see the United States was something she had never even imagined.

We stopped in the Philippines overnight, then spent two days in Hawaii where we toured the islands. Flying to the United States, we landed in San Francisco, then made the connection to Los Angeles. At LAX my mother and aunt picked us up for the drive to Long Beach, where the two of them had been living together since my father's death the previous year. Lan could not get over the crowds or the number of cars on the freeway. Not that there weren't plenty of people and cars in Saigon, but this was on a different scale altogether. It was impossible to absorb, as if she had been transported into some kind of futuristic fairyland.

My mother and my aunt took to Lan immediately. They went all over with us, to the shopping centers, the supermarket, the local sights. And everywhere, Lan had us take pictures, as if to be able to prove to herself that she had really been to these places. The supermarket especially was beyond her conception. Thinking of the Bien Hoa marketplace with its mud and flies and not too aromatic smells, I could understand why.

But she was dying for Vietnamese food. Hamburgers and hot dogs and mashed potatoes and gravy were not the kind of fare a Vietnamese could live on. Lan, whose English didn't sound that familiar to my mother or my aunt, tried to describe what the problem was, and eventually they understood and took her back to the supermarket. There she bought some fresh vegetables, rice, and shrimp, which she brought home and cooked, serving it with *nuoc mam*—fermented fish sauce. Mrs. Lam had warned Lan that she better take a bottle of *nuoc mam* with her, since the chances of finding any in the United States might not be too good. So she had, packing the bottle carefully in a shoe box, which thank God had saved it from breaking. My mother and aunt loved the food, though at first they turned their noses up a little at the fish sauce. But when Lan added vinegar and garlic and a little hot pepper to it

they began to enjoy even that. For the rest of the visit Lan did a lot
of the cooking, to everybody's delight.

The two old ladies were smitten by her in the beautiful ao dai
dress she wore when we went out. And they were also impressed
by the way Lan always called me "honey" or "sweetheart." That
impressed me too, since she had never called me anything of the
sort back in Vietnam. It turned out that the "honey, sweetheart"
business was Old Man Lam's idea. Ong Gia, he had said, didn't
indicate the proper level of affection. And Ong Gia Mat Do—"the
Old Man with the Red face" (which was what many of the Vietnamese called me)—certainly didn't. "So don't call him 'old man'
anything; his mother won't like it. Call him 'honey' and 'sweetheart.' That's what Americans do." Lam was also responsible for all
the pleases and thank yous I was hearing. Lam had given strict
instructions on this. Lan was not only going to the United States
as a future daughter-in-law, she was going as a representative of
the Vietnamese people. "When you come back to Vietnam," he
had told her, "I want them to remember how polite and consider-
ate Vietnamese are."

Even in the middle of this domestic interlude the war would not
go away. I wondered how things were going back in Bien Hoa. The
action had been picking up during the week or two before I left,
and the great question was whether the NVA was geared up for an
all-out offensive or whether they wanted more time to complete
their buildup and were still thinking on a smaller scale. I was watching the television news one day when the announcement came
that the North Vietnamese had taken Phuoc Long province. Oh,
oh, I thought, here it goes. This is the start of the offensive. Song
Be, the capital, had fallen—it was the umpteenth time they had
overrun the city—though they had always given it back before. But
this time they weren't giving it up, and with Song Be gone everything else had naturally fallen in line. So they had all of Phuoc
Long. They had half of Binh Long province too, and near the
DMZ they were moving on Quang Tri.

These were just names to my aunt and my mother, but they
were interested in what it all meant. This is only the beginning, I
told them. This looks like the big one coming. They'll probably
wipe out ARVN; I don't think the South Vietnamese have the will
to fight anymore. We could be facing disaster.

My older daughter, Cecile, was in college in New York, so we
weren't able to visit her, but Lan and I drove from Long Beach to
Houston to see my daughter Julie. The trip was lovely. However,
in my mind's eye I could see those four hundred tanks half buried

in Tri Tam and the bumper-to-bumper convoys of men and supplies hurrying south down the trail. The United States seemed so peaceful as we drove back through the beautiful landscapes of Arizona and New Mexico. Already Lan was thinking about the stories she would have to tell Mr. and Mrs. Lam and her girlfriends when we returned. But I had an eerie feeling about going back. Whatever was happening over there was not good. And I couldn't see exactly what it was going to mean for us in Bien Hoa, or how we were going to cope with it.

14

THE BIG ONE

It was January 2 by the time we got back and Lou already had things fairly well organized. The data bank was up and running at the Monastery, sources were living in the new houses he had rented, and the interrogation teams were operating at full capacity. Compared to the JIC the operation was slow and cumbersome, but at least it was working.

A week later our new chief, Hal Wiggins, announced that Thomas Polgar, the chief of Station who had replaced Ted Shackley, would be coming out to visit us. Polgar was more or less an unknown to the field agents. He had been born in Hungary and had done his own field work during World War Two in occupied Europe. He had also been to South America, as Station chief in Argentina. But he was a novice in Asia, and whatever impact he might have been having in Saigon, little of it had filtered out to the bases.

When Wiggins brought Polgar up to the Monastery's recreation room, all the headquarters personnel and the officers in charge were waiting. What we saw was a short barrel of a man with thick glasses and scraggly tufts of hair bordering a bald dome. Although I knew about Polgar's origins, I was a little surprised to hear the thick Eastern European accent. But it wasn't his pronunciation that was the shocker, it was what he said. "I want you to know," the voice growled in thick gutturals, "that everything is going OK. We don't see any major problems in 1975. Our reading is that the situation is under control."

It was an astounding statement. Just astounding. Eyes all around the room sought out other eyes to share their disbelief. We were on the edge of a disaster, and hearing the chief of Station say something like this was incredible, demoralizing. I wondered if he thought we needed some kind of reassurance from him (no matter how patently false) or did he really believe what he was saying. Either way it was awful. We had already had a minidisaster. Phuoc Long was gone. Of course we could have given Phuoc Long away years ago and nobody would have missed it—it had no military or political value. But still, an entire province had been swallowed. Half of Binh Long was gone too, as was substantial territory on the outer edges of Long Khanh and Binh Tuy, taken during the earlier flag-raising campaign. The North Vietnamese army was poised and hungry. Any minute now it would descend on the South Vietnamese like a wolf on the fold. But there it was. "Ve don't," the man said, "zee any machor prroblems in 1975."

Hal Wiggins was not sure what to think. He had been in country for less than a month and he was struggling to get oriented. Remarks like Polgar's weren't helping. Most mornings we would sit a while in his office and talk over the recent intelligence and the overall situation the country was facing. "Do you really think the whole thing is going down the tubes?" he'd ask. I did. The NVA wasn't building up for the hell of it; it was building up for a reason. And it was a tremendous effort. With all the ammunition and supplies it already had stored in the boonies, it could undertake a six-. month sustained offensive. Its tanks could overrun Tay Ninh, Ben Cat, anyplace it wanted. "ARVN does not have the forces to stop it," I told Wiggins. "Those three NVA divisions are at full strength. They've brought their SAMs down here. They're ready."

The only thing we didn't know about was the timetable, or even time frame, of the forthcoming offensive. We did not actually believe that the major push would come in early 1975. Even after Phuoc Long fell, it seemed as if we were in for a period of probing in force, and sharp but limited confrontations. We were going to face a nasty situation. But the real hammer wouldn't fall, I thought, until later in 1975; perhaps during Tet in 1976 would be even more likely. No one doubted that it would happen, though, and that when it did it would be devastating. And we reported exactly that, that when the big push came, South Vietnam was going to collapse—sourcing the analysis to Colonels Thao and Dinh.

By mid-January Thao and Dinh were coming over to 15 Cong Ly almost every night to discuss our assessments, a kind of informal pooling of the intelligence we all had coming in. There was no disagreement among us. NVA manpower and matériel were in place for a major offensive, but when or where the thrust would come still remained unclear. We were all picking up North Vietnamese scuttlebutt, rumors, conjectures—but no hard information. Studying the dispositions, I Corps—just below the DMZ—seemed a likely site; III Corps was almost a certainty. The NVA was positioning tanks and troops in the lower part of Phuoc Long and in parts of Binh Long, which indicated a move toward Bien Hoa, the gateway to Saigon. But we had no hard evidence, even from the agents. Ominous things were happening out there, but they were happening behind a cloud that only allowed us to catch glimpses of an outline.

But there was no conjecture among any of us about South Vietnam's inability to withstand the coming onslaught, wherever it might be launched. Phuoc Long province might have been worthless militarily, but its capture was, I believed, a crucial test of American willpower. Washington had not reacted to the North Vietnamese buildup; it had not reacted to the smaller actions that had been launched during the fall of 1974; now it had not reacted to a major assault. Thao and Dinh may not have been experts at reading the mood of the U.S. Congress, but they were among the most knowledgeable and sensitive people in Vietnam when it came to assessing military intentions and capability. They could see what the future held without the United States. And they knew and talked constantly about the urgent need for immediate reforms to help the Southern soldier, and for a comprehensive effort by South Vietnam's high command to more efficiently utilize existing supplies and equipment. Without those things happening we would be facing very hard days.

Other ominous news came from Colonel Tuong and his F-5 flyboys, who also came by to drink and talk a couple of nights a week. All of them complained about the SAMs, Russian-built antiaircraft missiles that we had reported were coming down the trail. Now the missiles had been deployed throughout the region. It was harder and harder to fly low for runs or for close observation. "They're up to something," said Tuong. "It's going to happen, soon."

Throughout February reports came in from the Goldmother, Grandpa, and Duc Hue Tiger, all mentioning the coming offensive. In the VC and NVA ranks it was common knowledge that COSVN had something big under wraps. But again, no one knew the specifics; there was nothing on schedules, units, objectives. Nor was Thao picking up any radio intercepts on military movements, which was unusual. Normally orders flowed across the airwaves to Vietcong and NVA elements, but now there was only an unnerving silence.

Even at this point we were receiving defectors into our system (though few prisoners), putting them in houses and debriefing them as quickly as we could. But their information only duplicated what we had from elsewhere, bits and pieces, rumors and gossip. But one thing did stand out: the talk going through the NVA divisions was not of negotiations, only of a complete military victory.

Through February our daily intelligence reports to Saigon Station indicated the increasing likelihood of military action. From what we could make out, almost all the tanks in the Tri Tam rubber plantations had shed their camouflage and had been deployed. Initially concentrated in southern Phuoc Long, they were now spreading into Binh Duong, Tay Ninh, and Long Khanh. Additional manpower was coming in too. Dinh now had firm information that the three NVA divisions in Three Corps had been joined by elements of three more. Already ARVN was outgunned in the region two to one. And more Northern troops and matériel were arriving every day; the flow down the Ho Chi Minh Trail was reaching new peaks of volume. It had begun to look like rush hour on the Pennsylvania Turnpike.

All this was conveyed in the stream of intelligence that crowded the channels between Bien Hoa and Saigon. Day by day we reported the growing likelihood of enemy action. Not that we needed any special information to figure that out. Every day now more rockets slammed into Bien Hoa from the Tan Uyen rocket belt north of the city. Each missile would destroy a house or two, kill or maim the inhabitants, and terrorize a neighborhood. People went about their business, but they were becoming wary, watchful. I noticed that we too had started acquiring something new, a siege mentality. During one rocket attack, my windows at 15 Cong Ly were shattered. A week later the plastic replacement windows were blown out. The noose was tightening. Everyone wondered how long we had before they closed within artillery range.

By late February, agent reports started becoming more specific. The Reaper reported that Tay Ninh would soon come under siege, but he did not report any plans for a general offensive. Information came from Grandpa that there was nothing planned for Highway

#1, which most likely meant nothing of importance for Region Three's western front. It began to appear that COSVN was planning to isolate Tay Ninh, primarily to tie down the ARVN 25th Division, not to initiate any drive toward Saigon. The major offensive looked as if it would come elsewhere. The Goldmother too reported that she had nothing on the region's western areas, but that large-scale deployments were going on to the east, facing the Central Highlands and the coast.

Early in the afternoon of March 10 Dinh called me over to his office. "It's started," he said. "They hit Ban Me Thuot this morning. With the forces we have there, there's no way to defend it." In an instant all the uncertainty of the past two months fell away. Ban Me Thuot was a small province capital in the Central Highlands. Taking Ban Me Thuot first meant one thing: the NVA's plan was to cut the country in two, on a straight line from the highlands to Nha Trang on the coast.

The South Vietnamese withdrawal from the Central Highlands that followed the defeat at Ban Me Thuot turned into a disaster in which columns of retreating troops and civilian refugees were cut off in the jungle and slaughtered by Northern artillery. In the following days the NVA began moving on the cities of Danang, Quang Tri, Hue, and other areas along the coast, intent now on cutting the country in half and grabbing Saigon's coastal strongholds and population centers.

Although there was a plan to hold these enclaves, anybody with eyes could see that the ARVN collapse that had been predicted for so long was now quickly shaping up. Hue, the old imperial capital, fell on March 26, its population dissolving in panic as they remembered the massacre of thousands of Hue civilians by the Vietcong during Tet of 1968. Danang fell on March 30, Tuy Hoa and Qui Nhon on April 1. A tidal wave of refugees swept down toward Saigon.

Somehow, a few still refused to accept the inevitable. Among these were Thomas Polgar and Hal Wiggins. Returning from a meeting with the chief of Station in Saigon, Wiggins seemed convinced that even if the debacles continued, ARVN would be able to defend Region Three and Region Four (comprising most of the Mekong Delta, South Vietnam's rice basket). I wondered where the hell Station was getting its information from. Certainly it was not from us. Our analyses were uniformly grim. The end was coming fast. In one of our regular meetings, Thao pointed out that the rainy season would be starting before long. Appreciating the ARVN collapse for what it was, the Politburo would most likely push to finish the Southerners off before the monsoon interrupted the process.

On April 9 the Goldmother reported that sapper teams had been ordered to infiltrate into positions near Tan Son Nhut airport. She also reported a COSVN briefing that stated there were to be no negotiations with the Saigon government. The objective was a total military takeover. Almost at the same time each of the other agents with access to COSVN directives reported the same information. No compromises, no negotiations, no coalition governments. The North Vietnamese army was going to swallow South Vietnam whole.

What this meant was that talk of negotiations or of a compromise settlement was nothing more than a deception, an attempt to further distract and paralyze the South Vietnamese and Americans by creating false hopes for them to snatch at. With their enemy's attention distracted by thoughts of how to achieve a compromise and what kind of compromise might be achieved, Hanoi knew the chances of the South asserting any coherent final strategy would be that much less.

The Goldmother's COSVN information wasn't exactly a surprise. It fit exactly with the appreciation Lou and I had arrived at based on our experience of their modus operandi over six years. These people had a thousand informants telling them that ARVN would collapse, that the Southern soldiers had no pay, no food in their bellies, no way to feed their families. By now they knew beyond any doubt that their moment had arrived. They knew they could win, so there was no motivation to negotiate, no reason to. Besides, a military takeover would make the North Vietnamese lords of all they surveyed. But a negotiated settlement, any kind of negotiated settlement, would necessarily involve the Vietcong and the NLF's Provisional Revolutionary Government. The Northerners had not been shunting their Southern revolutionary brothers out of leadership positions for the last five years only to restore them now.

Nevertheless, these new reports from the agents—starting with the Goldmother's visit on April 9—were the first hard intelligence that confirmed the rumors we had been picking up for a month. But although this was important news, it was difficult to know how best to handle it. The Goldmother had been reporting Grade A factual information for two years now, one report after another. And yet as far as I could tell she had not drawn anybody's attention at Station. No one there had even commented on her report of the

imminent attack on the Nha Be POL dump in December of 1973.
I thought they might have, since her information should have been
enough to save South Vietnam's petroleum reserves. But because
she wasn't taken seriously enough, that disaster took place. So I
wasn't optimistic that anybody would believe her now, even though
the report was right out of COSVN by a fully authenticated agent
(corroborated by reports from other authenticated agents).
Chances were that intelligence transmitted through the normal
channels would not have sufficient impact, at least not on this
issue, where there seemed to be a willful disbelief on the part of
Station.

Thinking this over, I pressed Hal Wiggins to see Polgar again
personally. He should accept the intelligence as definitive himself,
hand carry the reports to Saigon, and apply as much pressure as
he could. If Polgar could be convinced, maybe we would be allowed to get under way with the evacuation of our Vietnamese
employees and their families.

Hal seemed to agree and shortly afterward left for Saigon. When
he returned he said he had seen Polgar, but that the Station chief
hadn't seemed to put much stock in our reports. Instead Polgar
had told him that talk was continuing about negotiations for a
peaceful settlement. The only concession Polgar had made to the
idea that we might have to pull out quickly was the KIP list. Each
base was ordered to prepare a prioritized list of Knowledgeable
Important Persons who should be evacuated in the event of any
emergency. We were supposed to draw up the list, then present it
to Saigon Station, which would decide who would be taken out
and who not.

I was beginning to boil. Instead of taking steps to ensure the
safety of our people, Station was looking to get out those who were
"knowledgeable." No one had to tell me what that meant. It meant
that Station's contacts and friends would be high on the list. And
since Station had no Vietnamese operational agents or people who
worked in the field, the list would be composed of the generals and
police officials and politicians they were close to.

Just thinking about it gave me a rash. Steamboat Charlie
Timmes, who was still troubleshooting for the chief of Station,
personally knew every living South Vietnamese government official
and his wife from deputy province chiefs on up. In addition to
Timmes's list, there'd be Polgar's own list and the lists of the other
Station brass. Without a doubt the Agency would also be bom-
barded by every congressman and Washington official who had
ever visited Vietnam with requests to get his friends or contacts

out. In Bien Hoa we had only two individuals I would put on a KIP list: Colonels Thao and Dinh. I was determined to do everything I could to save them and their families, although I knew how hard that would be, at least as far as they personally were concerned. Both of them would undoubtably stay at their posts until the last minute. But meanwhile, what about the rest of our people?

It was hard to fathom Polgar's thinking. We did know that the chief of Station had become close to a Hungarian colonel from the ICCS, the four-power commission that had been established to monitor the Paris agreement. And we knew that the colonel was feeding Polgar information about the chances of a negotiated settlement that might in some way shift off the debacle that was building. Polgar had disseminated reports of his conversations with the Hungarian to that effect; they had come through on the monthly digest graded A. Lou and I always blinked when we saw them. Polgar, of Hungarian ancestry, speaking in Hungarian to a Hungarian colonel, undoubtedly an intelligence officer. Who did he think was slickying whom?

My feelings about what was happening in Saigon with Polgar and Ambassador Graham Martin, who also seemed to believe that a negotiated settlement was possible, were matched by those of John Stockwell. Stockwell was the last officer in charge in Tay Ninh, a tall, intelligent, Magnum-type career officer who had been brought in on an emergency basis in July when the previous officer in charge there had suddenly and without warning committed suicide. Now Tay Ninh was the scene of daily small-unit engagements, and each night mortars and 120-mm rockets pounded the capital. The Vietcong were trying to indicate that Tay Ninh would be a major target. But Grandpa was telling us no, as was the Reaper, that the action was only a diversion. Nevertheless, with the pressure mounting we pulled Stockwell back to Bien Hoa, making different arrangements for him to keep servicing the Reaper.

Stockwell's appreciation of the situation was the same as mine (the Reaper was also reporting COSVN's decision to achieve a total military victory). To him the intelligence unequivocally meant that the country was doomed and the clock was ticking down. And that meant we had to get our people out right now, while we still had time for a safe and orderly evacuation. The idea of leaving any of them behind seemed intolerable, immoral. And the more we procrastinated, the greater the chance for a screwed-up finale.

Stockwell was an aggressive, persistent guy, and he kept pushing Hal Wiggins on it. He just would not be put off. Meanwhile Wiggins was becoming increasingly irritated and upset. His Station

chief, Polgar, was telling him one thing while I was besieging him
with something else, and now he had this pain in the ass Stockwell
to deal with. And Stockwell was really bugging the hell out of him.
With both their tempers mounting, angry arguments flared between the two of them.

Meanwhile I simply went ahead and put together an evacuation
plan for Region Three's Vietnamese Agency personnel. First I established liaison with Lieutenant Colonel DeSilva, a marine officer
handling part of the helicopter evacuation task force that was now
assembling off the coast. Surveying our facilities, we decided that
using our pad on the river and a large soccer field across the street
we could put down four choppers at a time. Two more could land
on the rice paddy behind our support building at 1 Quoc Lo. At
fifty per chopper, that meant three hundred people at a shot. As
one set of choppers loaded, the second wave would be hovering.
Then they could set down and pick up the rest. We could do the
whole thing—six hundred people, including employees and families, up and out—in less than thirty minutes. Once we had worked
out the plan, DeSilva and I set up secret communications frequen-
cies and coordinated the smoke to guide the choppers in. And that
was it. We were ready for a completely professional evacuation
from the city of Bien Hoa that would have taken out every person
who wanted to go.

With these arrangements made, on April 13 I held a meeting of
all Vietnamese personnel at the support warehouse—interpreters,
translators, guards, cooks, everybody. Using Lam Number One as
an interpreter, I explained the plan and the priority system I had
arranged. All employees would be issued colored cards. Green
cards would go to the operational people, those who were at greatest risk. Translators and interpreters would receive blue cards, and
other employees—guards, cooks, carpenters, clerks, and so on—
would get white. That would be the order if there was any need to
observe priorities. But in fact I was planning to take all of them
who wanted to go at one swoop, providing Station approved the
plan. A man could take his wife and children, but no brothers and
sisters. Single persons could take their mothers and fathers. But no
boyfriends or girlfriends could come, no cousins, no nieces or
nephews, no peripheral relatives. This would be for critical people
only and their immediate families. If we could do more later, we'd
do more.

I also told them that if they opened their mouths about our
plans, then the evacuation would not work. We'd have the whole
city of Bien Hoa down on our backs. "In some cases," I said,

"you're going to have to leave your homes without telling your parents, without telling your brothers and sisters. If you do, they'll come tagging along and they'll end up trying to hang onto the landing gear. Then the whole thing will collapse. So if this doesn't work, it will be your fault. I am going to have those choppers there, period. I am arranging it; whether we succeed or not will be up to you."

When I finished, there was a buzz of talk, in Vietnamese and English. Yes, it sounded good. It sounded fair. No, no one would say a word. They were counting on me to do it; they didn't want to be left. I was taken by their calmness and enthusiasm, considering that I was talking about taking them away from their homes and the land they had known all their lives, forever. Maybe it just hadn't sunk in yet. Maybe they hadn't fully grasped that the war was over, that we—the United States of America—had lost, that they had lost.

Stockwell, still fuming over his encounters with Hal Wiggins, put together an alternative evacuation plan. John wanted to embark everyone on LSTs and go down the Dong Nai and Saigon rivers, covering the craft with helicopters and gunships. He had made logistical arrangements with the province chief, and he was sure it was feasible. He was intent on getting our people out; if we couldn't do it one way, we'd do it another. I agreed. The LST plan was feasible. It would make a good fallback if anything happened to DeSilva's helicopters.

With the plans laid on, all we needed now was the go-ahead from Station. This would be something our base chief would have to manage. But Hal Wiggins was running scared now. He did not want any problems with Polgar, and it seemed to me that he was exploring ways to get out of the country himself. Although he had been in Vietnam only three months, he had home leave coming, and his family was nearby, in safe haven in Thailand. He mentioned to me that if he was caught out of the country, I would be responsible for the base. Then he told me again, formally putting me in charge of operations.

On the morning of April 22, after our most recent intelligence had come in confirming that there would be a complete military takeover, I pleaded with Wiggins to see Polgar and tell him that we were ready to evacuate the base in a completely professional manner, taking all our employees with us. There was no more time for delay. Wiggins agreed to go in for an audience and he agreed to tell Polgar that we were adamant about our plans. But with his nerves already starting to show, I wasn't at all sure about how

convincing Hal might be, especially since Polgar and Martin
seemed so engaged with this crazy negotiated settlement idea. On
the other hand, the logic of the situation was overwhelming. Sev-
enteen miles to the east ARVN's 18th Division was fighting desperately at Xuan Loc to hold the Northern spearhead. And though
the 18th's defense was heroic, the division was being inexorably
crushed by massively superior enemy forces. They could not possibly hold for more than another few days. And once through Xuan
Loc, the Northern army would immediately start its assault on Bien
Hoa.

Consequently, I wasn't prepared for the answer Wiggins brought
back from his meeting in Saigon. The ambassador's strict orders,
he said, were that no evacuation was to take place at this point,
and Polgar had made it clear he was not going to disobey Graham
Martin's orders. On the contrary, they were negotiating. Mr. Polgar was negotiating. There was going to be a coalition government,
part Vietcong, part North Vietnamese, part Government of South
Vietnam. They apparently believed it, more than they believed
their own intelligence. Furthermore, any evacuation that might
become necessary in the future would take place out of Saigon,
not out of Bien Hoa. All evacuation plans from Bien Hoa were
vetoed, scrapped, null and void. And there was another message
too, Wiggins said. Polgar wanted Stockwell to report to him immediately.

Next day the troublesome John Stockwell went into Saigon Station where Polgar curtly told him to take the next available aircraft
out of Vietnam. Wiggins could get someone else to handle the
Reaper. A day later John left, taking his Vietnamese fiancée and
her daughter with him. I hated to see him go—he would have been
an invaluable help in what was coming.

The evening John left, Wiggins announced that the former
chiefs of base in Military Regions One and Two would visit that
night to give us their advice. Danang, the Region One base headquarters, was gone. So was Nha Trang, headquarters for Region
Two. Both situations had dissolved in an ARVN and civilian panic.
From what we had heard, Bob Shipley, the Danang base chief, had
done a yeoman's job under appalling conditions. He had now been
appointed by Polgar as acting overall operations man in Saigon.
The other former chief was a Chinese-American by the name of
Ken Jong. He had apparently just bugged out of Nha Trang leaving
everything behind. Now these two were coming to brief us on the
dos and don'ts of running an evacuation.

So we had this meeting—Shipley, Jong, Wiggins, Lou Bishop,

and myself. It was clear enough that both Shipley and Jong had gone through bad times. Jong, though, had little to say except that it wasn't our responsibility to save any of the Vietnamese. We should just close down and go home. Period. I stared Jong in the eye while he was saying this (Stockwell might have attacked him physically). You son of a bitch, I thought. We have trained these people, good people who have worked alongside us loyally for years, some of them risking their lives for us—and this is what you have to say? But before I had a chance to open my mouth, Shipley interrupted Jong. No, he said, I don't agree with that. You have to make an effort to save your employees.

But Shipley also thought that a helicopter evacuation from Bien Hoa would be too risky. There would be panic, thousands of fear-stricken civilians would try to storm the helicopters. That was what had happened at Danang where crowds of people had broken onto the runway making landings and takeoffs impossible.

I had nothing but disdain for Shipley's attitude. From a professional point of view, I told him, evacuation from Bien Hoa would not be a problem. We could do it at five o'clock in the morning, first light. Our people would be waiting and we could truck them to the landing sites. The whole thing could be accomplished in thirty minutes, and everyone would be off the ground before any of the local population was aware we were leaving. We could also arrange for ARVN guards from Colonel Thao, in addition to our own Nung guards, to deal with any emergencies.

No, said Shipley, I was wrong. There would be panic if we tried to airlift people out of Bien Hoa. It was an impasse, though not really, since Shipley was now in charge of all Vietnam operations, which at this point meant he was in charge of evacuation. I looked at Wiggins for help, but all I got was a cold stare. "Orrin," he said, "it's all going to go through Saigon. You should send Lou into the city tomorrow to start arranging for safe houses." Oh, my Lord, I thought, safe houses in Saigon for six hundred people? Now it's really going to hit the fan.

15

WELCOME TO AMERICA!

E ven during the last period, the Goldmother kept coming to Bien Hoa, always following the same routine. Getting off the bus at the station, she'd walk down Cong Ly street in the dark. Near the house she'd squat to urinate, watching the deserted street carefully from the shadows. From the moment she entered Cong Ly, Buffalo One would observe her from the second-floor balcony, also watching for a tail. When she was satisfied no one was there, the Goldmother would slip into the 150-foot alley that led to the back of the house, then through the gate and into the back room.

She was not particularly happy that her side was going to win. Neither did she seem thrilled by the new intelligence she was carrying, details about routes and dispositions of the Vietcong sapper teams that were infiltrating Tan Son Nhut from their bases in the Cu Chi tunnels. The mission of the sapper teams was to shut down Tan Son Nhut as soon as possible. They would wait for NVA main forces to make their move from Xuan Loc to Bien Hoa, then head down the Saigon highway. In advance of the main-force arrival, the sappers would rocket and mortar the airport, putting a halt to air traffic in and out.

Sensing her unhappiness, when the Goldmother reported for the last time (on April 21) I offered her a route out of the country for herself and her mother. But she said no. She had no reason to leave. No one knew about her. She'd be safe; she'd even be a hero.

Later that same evening Grandpa also came in to give his last report. Like the Goldmother, he came down Cong Ly cautiously, watching for watchers. He too ducked into the shadows, then stayed there motionless until he was convinced no one had followed him. While Lou and Buffalo continued the Goldmother's debriefing in one back room, Bingo and I talked with Grandpa in a bedroom on the far side of the house. As we talked I watched this extraordinary old man carefully, knowing this would be my last meeting with him. Highway #1 would not play a role in the final assault on Saigon, he said. There was no question about that. Nor was there any question that COSVN's objective was a military take-over. His state of mind about these last events in the life of South Vietnam seemed exactly the same as the Goldmother's. He was not euphoric about it, but neither was he unhappy. He simply accepted it. As he talked, Grandpa dipped into the can of betel nuts he always carried with him, the dark-purple juice staining his teeth and dribbling in tiny rivulets into the corners of his mouth. Occasionally, he'd pause to hawk into the second little can he used as a spittoon.

I had never quite gotten used to this Vietnamese habit; the look of it and the vaguely putrid smell put me off. But I was ready to put up with a lot more than that just to watch Grandpa in action. Nothing ever shocked this man or put him off balance. He loved this game he was playing, the intrigue, the danger, the need to mask every emotion and keep all the conflicts in balance. Like the Goldmother, Grandpa was an adrenaline junkie. Yet it seemed so incongruous—this daring spirit in the body of a gnarled, betel-chewing Methuselah. He was a kick in the ass, and I was sorry I would be losing him.

Also like the Goldmother, Grandpa declined my offer to take him along. He too would be a hero after the war. Neither of them paid much attention when I argued that with the North triumphant the future for South Vietnamese heroes might not be too enviable. What none of us knew as we talked was that within a week and a half the National Police would have fled their headquarters in utter panic leaving all their files behind for Northern security, and that Goldmother's and Grandpa's dossiers were in the files.

By now most of the Americans were gone from the Monastery; Polgar had given all nonessential personnel permission to leave the

sinking ship. Those of us who remained talked about the possibility
of a bloodbath following the takeover. But I didn't believe it. There
was no reason to think there would be slaughter in the streets. But
at the same time I was sure the new rulers would never forgive a
defector; they would not let a person who had betrayed the party
live. Mercy of that sort would have been contrary to all the norms
of party discipline. I had tracked the work of the party security
squads too long to think differently. I knew what they considered a
"blood debt," and I had witnessed the grisly "revolutionary justice"
that they habitually exacted. No, all the defectors (some 200,000 of
them), the Kit Carson scouts, the agents they could find—all of
them would disappear silently.

The Goldmother's last visit was on April 21. That same day we
started burning our files—the base files and of course the data
bank. It was a mammoth job and most of the American officers left
on base helped with it. I had previously suggested microfilming the
data bank, or computerizing it in some fashion. "For historical
purposes," I said, because you never knew if there might be some
point in the future when you would want to use something in it.
We had by this time four or five thousand cards on COSVN. We
knew the structure, and we knew a great deal about who was filling
what roles. We also had good information on most NVA officers in
leadership positions. All this data concerned individuals who could
be expected during the next decade to assume high-level government and military positions.

So I wanted to keep the data bank, thinking that someday the
information might come in handy, if only as part of the American
effort to understand the people we'd be dealing with in postwar
Vietnam. And it would have come in handy. In 1977 and afterward
the Agency was running security checks on Vietnamese refugees
who came through Thailand, and the data bank would have been
an invaluable help. The data bank could also have given us an
avenue into the Vietnamese army and military structure in Cambodia after the invasion and occupation of that country that began
in 1978. But when I requested microfilm and computerization,
John Brenley turned it down. Afterward it was too late.

There was an additional possible use for the data bank that I felt
was worth study. As early as February 1975 Lou and I began talking
about the possibility of arranging stay-behinds, Vietnamese agents
trained in the use of wireless and code. From Vietnam it would be
easy for agents equipped with radios and one-time pads to reach
the Philippines. Despite our defeat, Vietnam would remain a strategic area, providing an opening to the rest of Southeast Asia and

dominating the vital sea routes connecting Singapore, Malaysia, the Philippines, Hong Kong, and Japan. The United States had no choice but to maintain an active interest in that part of the world, and establishing an information network in Vietnam would be, I thought, reasonable and prudent. Here too the data bank would have been an essential tool. But any thoughts I had along those lines dissipated with the smoke from the burning hills of cards and manila file folders.

The pyres were still smoldering when word came that the ARVN 18th Division had ceased to exist. Xuan Loc had fallen and now there was nothing between the Northern army and Bien Hoa. As we worked to make sure that all sensitive material had been destroyed, a young case officer arrived from Station along with his supervisor. The officer, a paramilitary type, had been instructed to speak to Hal Wiggins and me about getting himself attached to General Nghi, the Southern commander who was still holding out in Phan Rang. He was supposed to stick with Nghi, he told us, monitor developments in that area, and report directly to Station by radio.

The officer's name was Lewis, a tall, pleasant-faced kid with dark hair. He seemed eager to go. When Wiggins asked my opinion, I said that the idea was ridiculous. "There's no reason for it," I told him. "We're getting every piece of information directly from Colonel Thao—all NVA forces, what they're doing, where they are. We're getting it on an hourly basis with written reports twice a day. The fall is imminent, why risk this man's life?"

But regardless, his supervisor decided to send Lewis to Phan Rang and soon afterward he left by chopper. From that point on he stayed with General Nghi at the Phan Rang air base, radioing his last report just as the base was being overrun. And that was the last we heard of him. Six months later Lewis reappeared in Hanoi and was repatriated. He arrived in the United States at the same time my friend Tucker Gougelmann did. Except that Tucker arrived in a box.

Tucker Gougelmann was a former marine colonel who held the rank of GS-16 (a two-star general) during his attachment to the Agency. In the spring of 1975 Tucker had been retired for two years, out of everything. But he was still a hard-driving, blunt man. With the CIA he had been national director of the Provincial Reconnaissance Units and had also filled in when the base chiefs went on leave. This latter job—making the rounds of the bases, spending two weeks here, two weeks there—had kept him busy for several years. He had been out to Bien Hoa in that capacity four or five times during my tours, and over the years we had become close friends. He was a good guy, knowledgeable and aggressive, but not the kind you could let get by with anything. You'd have to stand up to him or he'd just plunge ahead and make a mistake. But he recognized that in himself too, and if you screamed loud enough he'd always listen.

Tucker had retired in 1973, and since then had been living in Saigon with his wife. He could have gotten out easily enough, but he was a hard-nosed son of a bitch and he decided not to. His wife was Vietnamese; he had lived in Vietnam for many years; he considered himself, practically speaking, a Vietnamese citizen. And he was not the kind of guy who would back down from anybody. He was retired, he told me when I last saw him, completely separated from any government work. Why should he get out for these piss-ants? He'd be damned if he was going to let anyone drive him away. Tucker was a stubborn man, tall, strong, in excellent health. He was not the kind to die of malnutrition, not in the six months Hanoi had him before they shipped his body home. I knew in my heart that they had tortured him to death.

As the third week in April began, I knew Tucker wasn't leaving. I was also beginning to wonder whether the rest of us would be getting out. Station was still maintaining that we would evacuate only when it became imperative to evacuate. But even while they were prohibiting a lift-off from Bien Hoa, they themselves were making bizarre plans for alternatives to evacuation through Saigon.

If Saigon turned into a disaster, one option Station was devising would be to leave through the beaches at Vung Tau, a sort of Vietnamese Dunkirk. Should the NVA overrun Saigon while we were still there and threaten to capture all the Americans in the place, a marine landing team, three or four thousand strong, would be brought in to secure a beachhead through which an American convoy could escape.

To my way of thinking, even considering such a scheme was a sign of advanced mental confusion. Regardless of what kind of firepower we brought in, the NVA would shoot the hell out of an evacuation beachhead with artillery and mortars. Casualties would be substantial. Nevertheless, there it was. I received a cable from Station to set up a radio commo team in Vung Tau to establish emergency links with Saigon. The team would operate under the direction of an officer Station would send down.

My gut reaction was to reject this request on the grounds of idiocy. The idea was beyond the pale, especially when we still had time to get a reasonable evacuation started right now. All the intelligence was saying there would be a complete takeover. What could Polgar and Martin be thinking? What in the world was wrong with those people?

So I did not concur with the request. But Wiggins, who was now on his last emotional legs, did. As a result I sent Gekko One, Buffalo One, and Tinh Two down to Vung Tau to handle things on the spot under a Station officer with the appropriate name of Hank Shifty. But four days later, when things began to get rough around Vung Tau, I got a call from Buffalo One. Shifty had suddenly left, without giving them any instructions. Buffalo, Gekko, and Tinh were there alone. Telling them to stay put, I requisitioned an Air America chopper from Tan Son Nhut to bring them back to Bien Hoa.

The order to send the radio commo team to Vung Tau was Hal Wiggins's last. Now he too left, to see his family in Thailand. "Don't worry, Orrin," he said just before he stepped into the car that was taking him to the airport. "I'll be back in a few days. Until then I want you to take over as acting chief of base."

By April 25, with the battle lines nearing Bien Hoa, I had all our employees and their families gather at the Monastery. We knew that Northern artillery would begin falling on us at any moment. Lou had already arranged sanctuaries in the capital, six large safe houses belonging to the Agency, in addition to the Duc Hotel, which was receiving the last influx of CIA refugees from the provinces. Dividing the group of almost six hundred people into five "teams," I made Bingo One, Gekko One, Tiger One, and Buffalo One leaders along with Chau, our Vietnamese chief of support. Then we loaded everybody into the motley assortment of Broncos, jeeps, trucks, and little Colts that I was able to muster and began to drive slowly through a city that was swarming with refugees from Xuan Loc.

Riding in one of the Colts with Old Man Lam were Lan and two of the children, To Thi My and Hai. Lan and I had hardly had time ourselves to make a reasoned decision about what we were going to do. After our traumatic separation the previous December, then our trip to the U.S., we had never really discussed things. It just seemed a foregone conclusion that we would never be separated from each other again, no matter what happened.

But neither of us had actually thought through exactly what that might mean. And now, suddenly, there was no time left. When I told Lan that the collapse was coming and that I would take her with me, her first reaction was "But what about my mother?" I was shocked. In my wildest dreams it had never occurred to me that I might be taking Lan's mother along. She was an old woman, comfortably ensconced in the only place she had known all her life. What would she possibly want with the United States?

I didn't know what to say, so I told Lan that my thought was to take her and To Thi My, the little girl, seven years old now, who was her real daughter. I didn't see how I could take the others. I couldn't even get them out. There was no way to get them listed on the departure manifest that Station would be issuing for evacuees. And even if I could get them out, how could I possibly support them?

Now, with the clock ticking, we talked about the kids at length, who was actually who, what the relations were, who the parents were, which of them were living, which were dead, which could actually take their own children back, what other relatives were available for them. It was the first time we had had a direct discussion about this. We had to make arrangements for them, I insisted. I couldn't take them back under any circumstances. "You, Lan," I said. "You, To Thi My, and me. I can't manage more."

"No," she said, "I cannot leave without my mother." Her tone sounded pretty definite. I waited, silent, hoping that she would say something more, that she would take my silence for a denial and back down. But Lan's lips were drawn tight. She had said what she was going to say and that's all there was to it. So I blinked and figured, OK, I guess that means mama's coming along.

Then Lan said, "I cannot leave little Hai also. The others have somebody. But not Hai. Nobody here will love him and take care of him. I cannot leave him also." Hai was six. At that moment the whole world of the future passed in front of my eyes. I'd be taking care of my mother and Lan's mother and I'd have two little kids to raise. And then there were my own daughters, Cecile and Julie, who were grown but who still needed me. School, doctors, hospitals, orthodontists, adolescence—I could see it all before my eyes. How was I going to do this? I loved Lan, I knew I couldn't leave her, not under any circumstances. But did that mean I was supposed to go through this whole family routine again, voluntarily? How in the world had I gotten into this? And how was I going to get out? With one part of my mind I was still pondering this question when I heard myself say, "OK . . . My, Hai, and your mom. We'll just have to play it by ear. Now let's get the hell out of here."

So there they were—Lan and the two kids in the car with Old Man Lam, moving slowly into traffic as the first 130-mm shells began dropping on the nearby air base. Lam had instructions to get them settled at the Duc, then go back for the mother. He'd have to think up some kind of story to get the old lady into Saigon. God only knew what she might do if he told her that the next day she'd be on a plane to the United States.

The following day, April 26, Lou and I left Bien Hoa for what I was sure would be the last time. As we were in the last stages of shutting down the Monastery two calls came in. The first was from Colonel Thao, telling me that the Phan Rang air base had just been overrun and that the young agent who had been sent to General Nhgi in Phan Rang had been captured. The other call was from Hal Wiggins in Thailand. On a scratchy connection I heard him say, "It's all over, Orrin. I don't see any point in my coming back. You don't really need me there."

Lou and I left 15 Cong Ly that afternoon, saying good-bye to the three Nung guards who stood there in the driveway. They had chosen to stay. As we drove toward Saigon we were apprehensive, to say the least. The Bien Hoa–Saigon highway was clogged with refugees. Thousands of cyclos and bicycles wheeled their way around jam-packed trucks and Lambretta three-wheel carriers, all of them mixed in with masses of walkers carrying whatever they could on their backs or in suitcases or pushing belongings and children in wheelbarrows. Colonel Thao had warned us that the police had set up roadblocks to slow down the refugees and herd them into stations along the highway to prevent them from entering the capital. As a result, Lou and I cut onto the old road that went over Bien Hoa's twin bridges, then meandered through Di An (where the Di An Doozie had reigned as a village secretary and where Lan's house was), then through the heart of several rubber plantations. Here too the road was packed, though not quite as badly as the main highway. But while the police were doing whatever they could to keep the crowds out of Saigon, we immediately discovered that they were allowing Americans to pass, under orders no doubt. But it was still a little dicey, with the distinct possibility that a disgruntled soldier or cop would take it in his head to give us a hard time.

The situation on the road wasn't the only thing we were apprehensive about. Neither Lou nor I had any confidence whatsoever in Graham Martin's ability to carry out an evacuation. We knew from the Goldmother that Vietcong sappers would be doing their best to shut down Tan Son Nhut. The NVA was closing in on Saigon. They'd be at the Newport Bridge before we knew it. This was going to be a very hairy piece of action, military action. The entire thing could easily fall on its face. There was a possibility we could all be captured. Once the VC smashed up Tan Son Nhut, the only way out would be by chopper. And with any kind of enemy fire, a helicopter evacuation would be an exceptionally dangerous, fragile affair.

I spent the night of the twenty-sixth at the Duc Hotel with Lan. Early the next morning I reported to Bob Shipley at the embassy, telling him the disposition of my people and what officers I still had with me. I managed to get Lou assigned to work on the departure manifests. Wayne Craig, Ed Devons, and Clark Starzak, the three other officers who had stayed with me, I put to work out at the airport, making sure that those of our families Lou manifested would in fact find space on planes.

I also asked for volunteers among my Vietnamese employees, explaining that I would need runners and people to handle emergencies as they came up. Chieu Hoi Lan stayed and I put her up on the fifth floor of the embassy typing manifests. Bingo, Gekko, and Tiger also volunteered, even though they understood that I wouldn't be leaving until the very end and that if they were caught their chances of survival were nil.

That day we managed to get two families out immediately on the KIP list, Thao's family and the family of one of our field operatives from Hau Nghia. They went out on the Agency's own "black aircraft." Later that day Lou got fifty more of our people out on C-141 flights from Tan Son Nhut. Among them were Lan, her mother, To Thi My, and Hai. Lou saw to it that they were manifested, then he personally went with them to the airport to make sure they got on an airplane. I was unable to see them. Lan and I had said our good-byes early that morning, each of us trying to suppress our anxieties. I didn't even want to think about what would happen to her if I didn't get out—alone in the United States with two small children and an old mother.

But the frantic activity at the embassy soon blotted out thoughts of anything else. All the priorities were going to Polgar and Charlie Timmes. Timmes of course knew everyone—that was his full-time job—and he was getting the people he knew out. Lou and I were battling with the Station personnel chief over this all day. Our people were out in those safe houses, waiting. They were Agency employees. Some of them had been working for us for ten years. They had proved their loyalty; they had done magnificent things. We had a responsibility for them. What were we going to do, leave them to their fate? They should have priority over Saigon government officials, let alone Agency "friends." Our personnel should come first, then the bureaucrats and the others.

But it was like shouting into the whirlwind. Everyone who was anyone wanted out, and they all seemed to have friends and protectors. It was just the kind of fucking mess I had expected. I could have throttled Polgar on the spot.

The next morning we moved out twenty employees (all of them operational people with green cards) and their families, more than a hundred people altogether. But then the day turned into a personal disaster. I kept arranging more manifests, but I knew the chances of many more people getting out were slim. The Vietcong were rocketing Tan Son Nhut. It was extremely dangerous for planes to come in or take off, so the volume of evacuation was stalling. The system was jamming up. The only real hope now was to move people out from helicopter pads in Saigon.

I wasn't alone in my anger and helplessness; the chiefs of the Agency's Saigon and Region Four bases were having their problems too. None of us was able to move out personnel. We were all standing around with our fingers up our butts and our minds in Texas. Why the hell we weren't starting helicopter runs from the embassy and the other Saigon pads right now was something none of us could fathom.

In the late afternoon of the twenty-eighth Shipley came to me with the news that we had lost communication with the Region Three ARVN headquarters, which was controlling the last battle. Did I think I could go back to Bien Hoa to personally get Colonel Thao's assessment of the military situation? In a way it was a relief, something to do. I knew that Bien Hoa was at least encircled, that it was probably on the verge of being overrun. Artillery was already hitting the town when I had left with Lou, a day and a half before. No doubt a chopper would take fire the whole twelve-mile run. Still, it was a chance to take some action and get away from the impasse at the embassy.

At 5:45 I took off from the embassy roof in a blue-and-white. Fifteen minutes later the pilot landed amid bursts of artillery fire on the helicopter pad at Region Three headquarters. I jumped out and he took off immediately to circle the base at five thousand feet, above the ground fire. He would return in exactly ten minutes. Colonel Thao met me on the pad and we ran together to the nearest bunker, two runway landing mats propped up against some sandbags. With his communications out he had been about to send a messenger to Saigon when he saw the blue-and-white coming in. "For some reason I thought it might be you," he said. The intelligence wasn't complicated. ARVN was completely outgunned. They couldn't hold any longer. The North Vietnamese would take

Bien Hoa by noon the following day, April 29. From there they
would have twelve miles of open road to Saigon. "Now get out of
here," Thao shouted as a shell crashed onto the runway nearby,
sending splinters splattering against the heavy metal mats. "It's too
dangerous for you. Besides"—he was smiling now—"I need you in
Saigon to get me out of this country." As my chopper veered down
toward us we hugged each other good-bye. Maybe the last time we
see each other, old friend, I thought. A moment later the pilot was
screaming at me to get in fast, then we were hurtling straight upward into the darkening sky.

Fifteen minutes later we dropped onto the embassy's rooftop
pad. In another minute I was dictating Thao's assessment to Rosalie, a secretary from the Monastery who had also stayed behind
with me. She typed it up as I talked. As soon as Shipley read the
report he sent it off to Langley, then, with nothing further we
could do, Rosalie and I went back to the Duc for dinner.

At the Duc, Lou, Bingo, Tiger, Gekko, Chieu Hoi Lan, and
several American officers were waiting for me. They had been worried for my safety; now they wanted to know what Bien Hoa was
like. Downing one martini, then a second, I told them of the thousands of refugees I had seen along the highway from the chopper,
most of them apparently stopped outside Saigon by ARVN barri-
cades. Thousands more were milling around inside Bien Hoa,
mixed with ARVN soldiers—deserters, or men separated from their
units, many of them firing their rifles into the air. I had been able
to see the Monastery and the house at 15 Cong Ly, but little more,
except the muzzle blasts from the NVA positions around the town.

That night I lay in my bed listening to the rockets crashing into
the city at the rate of fifteen or twenty an hour, not a meaningful
barrage, but enough to keep people awake and jittery. That almost
seemed to be their purpose. It was as if the North Vietnamese were
announcing that they would be arriving shortly. They had given us
some extra time already, they were saying. Now they wanted us
out.

At 0800 the following morning, April 29, I received a call from
Shipley to get over to the embassy at once and to "bring my personal gear." There was no mistaking what that meant. At the embassy Shipley told me that Tan Son Nhut was now closed to
airplanes. But a large-scale helicopter evacuation would begin
shortly from the airfield and also from the various pads around
Saigon. The embassy would be the main evacuation point in the
city. State Department and Agency choppers would use the rooftop pad, while the big military choppers would lift off from the

parking lot. Lou and I should remain on the fifth floor until it was
our turn to leave.

Glancing down into the parking area I saw the ambassador's tree
in the middle of it, a huge tamarind, four feet in diameter and a
good seventy-five feet tall. No choppers were going to land in that
lot until that thing was down. When I asked Shipley about it, he
said that they were making preparations to take it down, but that
Martin had ordered that it not be cut while there was any chance
of a negotiated settlement.

With the news that Tan Son Nhut was closed to planes, I radioed
to the safe houses, telling each of the groups to come to the embassy immediately, any way they could. But even as I spoke I was
unsure how many would be able to make it, and I wondered if
there was some way to go and get them. Meanwhile, Bingo, Gekko,
Tiger, and Chieu Hoi Lan were still at the Duc. The Agency was
committed to getting all the people out of there, but already there
was panic in the streets, and the officer in charge of the Duc evacuation was Hank Shifty, whom I already knew from the Vung Tau
episode.

Finding Lou and Wayne Craig, I told them to each grab a Uzi;
we were going to get Bingo and the others. "I don't trust your man
Hank at the Duc," I said to Shipley. "He's the same son of a bitch
who left my guys in Vung Tau." "Well," he answered, "you can try
if you want. But it's pretty damned dangerous out on those streets.
There are roadblocks and everything else. You might have a hard
time getting through."

I had two million piasters of Lan's money with me—she had sold
her house a few days back to some rich Chinese guy who had come
down from Danang. I was sure that would get us through the
roadblocks if nothing else did. I called the Duc and told Bingo to
have everybody ready when we drove up to the front gate.

Going out the side entrance of the embassy we shoved our way
through the crowds to the two Dodge Colts we had parked nearby
and got in. As I drove slowly toward the first roadblock I had my
Uzi in my lap. I was fully prepared to blow away anyone who tried
to stop us. But there was no need. At the roadblock we stopped for
a moment and I told the policemen there, "I *di di* Duc Hotel," and
handed out a pile of money. "OK," they said, taking the piasters.
Then we were through.

At the hotel we pulled up to the gate where hundreds of people
were milling about trying to get in, thinking that once they were
inside, the Agency would somehow save them. ARVN soldiers and
police stood on the periphery of the crowd gripping their rifles.

They looked confused, unsure of what to do. I had the feeling that there was no discipline left, that anything could happen. If somebody fired a shot it could easily turn into a massacre.

At the gate Bingo, Gekko, Tiger, and Chieu Hoi Lan were waiting and they jumped right in. Three blocks later a little knot of police motioned us to stop. They obviously didn't like the looks of our having Vietnamese in the cars. Lou was driving in front of me now and I saw him grab a stack of piasters and shove it out the window at the nearest policeman—still rolling. That diverted the cops' attention and we accelerated, not knowing if they were going to shoot. I had eased the safety catch off my Uzi and had my right hand on the grip while I steered with my left. It was harrowing—we just didn't know what these people were ready to do. A little farther down the street were several soldiers pointing their rifles menacingly at the car. I tensed again, but they let us pass without even stopping.

At the embassy compound it was sickening to see the thousands of Vietnamese outside trying to get in, some crying, some screaming, many waving documents of one kind or another. With the marines pushing people back we nosed the cars inside the Combined Recreation Association (CRA) compound where we dropped Bingo and the others. There I saw what I thought was fourteen or fifteen more of our people and their families—at least some had managed to get through from the safe houses. Quite a few others were there too, many of them apparently newsmen and camera crews with their equipment. But nothing was happening. It was 10 A.M. and everybody was sitting around waiting for the powers on high to make their decisions. Up on the fifth floor a bit later I ran into Stu Herrington, whom I had known when he was a Phoenix adviser in Duc Hue. We had been to Colonel Thanh's funeral together after Thanh was blown up by the VC's Cu Chi security team. Stu had come back to Vietnam for a second tour, working for the team that was negotiating over MIAs and prisoners with the North Vietnamese.

I knew that Herrington had been out at Tan Son Nhut for some time getting people out—right up until the airport closed. Despite the ambassador's no evacuation order, he and some other Defense Attaché Office (DAO) officers had managed to "exfiltrate" thousands of employees, counterparts, and others. They had done it quietly and efficiently; C-141s had been flying out of there packed full. I hadn't been able to evacuate my own people, but the DAO's General John Murray and his people had done an excellent job of unobtrusively telling the ambassador to go stick it in his ear.

An hour later, with the tree still standing and the CRA compound filling up with people, I began to get jumpy. For some reason the NVA had decided not to come into the city yet; my own feeling was that they had decided to give us a little extra time. But even if they had, any hotheaded local commander might get the idea that it was time to come across the bridge and shoot things up. Who knew what might happen? Nervous, I told Lou that we better get Bingo, Gekko, Tiger, and Chieu Hoi Lan up into the embassy with us, regardless of what anybody thought.

Wayne Craig and Ed Devons came with us, and Stu Herrington offered to lend a hand. But on our way down in the elevator I had a little altercation with him. There was no reason for it, but I was so pissed off by this point that I couldn't see straight, and he was an available target. "Goddammit, Stu, you've been getting all those people out for weeks, all kinds of bastards. And I've got most of my employees stuck out in safe houses." "Don't yell at me," he said. "I was only doing what I could." I shut my mouth despite my frustration. There was no point in shouting at Herrington. He had only been doing his job, and doing it well—doing what I should have done.

Downstairs a crowd of bodies was surging against the gate that connected the embassy parking lot with the CRA compound. Taking a deep breath, I told the marine guard, "Open that mother, we're coming through." Then we were into the compound, trying to locate Bingo and the other three. We found them, and among our other Vietnamese employees there we also found Mingo, Ly, and Lam Number One. I was especially glad to see Ly, but I told him and the others that I needed Bingo, Gekko, Tiger, and Chieu Hoi Lan right now. I added that helicopters would be coming into the compound a little later in the day; there was nothing to worry about. Mingo started screaming, "Take me with you, take me with you," but we were already working our way back through the crowd. "I can't do it," I told him, looking back. "But you'll be all right. Don't worry."

On the fifth floor again I raced through every possibility I could think of, but there was no way of getting to the safe houses. The roads were blocked—no one knew exactly why, but roadblocks were up all over the place. Somebody's orders. I wasn't sure exactly how many of my people had made it that morning into the CRA compound, some, but not that many, and now there was no way of getting any of the others. We monitored the radio on the fifth floor. Saigon base was on constantly—the CIA base in Saigon, separate from the Station headquarters for the country. "We can't get through, come save us, please save us." It was torture listening to it, thinking of my own people in those houses, waiting for Ong Gia to come and get them, knowing I had never let them down. Saigon base personnel were also scattered all over the city. But there was nobody to do anything about it. Those voices kept coming over the radio—"Save me, save me, save me." "Come and get us at the police station," said one Saigon base interpreter. "There're thirty of us down here." "OK," said the radioman, "we'll try to get you with a bus." But they couldn't. They tried to get a couple of buses out. But with the crowds and the roadblocks, the drivers just turned around and came back.

At one point Shipley called me in to ask if I thought I could get through to the Phan Thanh Giang street State Department compound where a large group was waiting to be picked up. "Can we take these people and put them on boats down at the river?" "No, we can't," I told him. "The NVA are at the Newport Bridge. They won't allow it. They'll blast them just for the hell of it. They're keeping the pressure on to make sure we get out of here fast."

Around noon Colonel Thao called. I had given both him and Dinh the number at the embassy and told them to call me. Thao did not know where Dinh was. He himself had gotten out of Bien Hoa that morning by chopper. What should he do? I told him there was no way to get to the embassy at this point, to go instead to the CIA building at 22 Cong Ly where there was a chopper pad on the roof. Shipley knew the CIA pilot who was taking people off the roof. The pilot would be instructed to ask for Thao by name.

I kept waiting for Dinh's call, but it didn't come. I knew there was no way he would leave without his family, and he must be trying like hell to make his own arrangements. Dinh and Thao were the only GVN people from Bien Hoa that I had even considered taking with us. I would have been happy to take out Major Ngo from Trang Bang too, but he had decided to stick tight and go down fighting. But they were the only ones. Many others had asked. "I'm Major So-and-so," they would say, "I've known OSA for so many years, worked with them." But my vehicles had been jammed pack and we were facing a shaky scene in Saigon, so I had decided it would be best for others to rely on themselves. Dinh and Thao, though, I would have done anything for. And now it looked as if I was losing Dinh.

By early afternoon CIA choppers were landing and departing from the embassy's rooftop pad. Some bigger helicopters were sitting down there too, but the Army Chinooks and Jolly Greens were too heavy for the roof and had to use the compound. But that fucking tree was in the way, and for some God-knows-why reason there were still orders not to cut it down. Herrington, who's DAO group had now taken over the mechanics of the operation, was screaming bloody murder. "Cut that fuckin' tree down now," I heard him yelling. "Cut it down now!"

By three o'clock the tree was down and the heavy choppers had begun landing. I spent some time watching out the window, trying to identify our people. The CRA compound was a madhouse now that the big Hueys and Jolly Greens and Chinooks were coming in, one after another. There must have been two thousand people down there, and they all seemed to be pressing in on the gate. Meanwhile hundreds from outside the embassy complex were trying to climb over the fences, and I could see marines bashing heads to keep them out. There was not an additional inch of space inside.

Watching, I was amazed by the skill of the pilots, putting those choppers down into the enclosed space of the parking lot with no room for error, where one accident would have stopped the whole operation. Then, with sixty people or more on board, they would lift off, straight up and over the walls—an extraordinary sight. From the window I saw Ly, the former NVA colonel, and his wife get into a Jolly Green. I breathed a sigh of relief at that, but in the same instant thought guiltily of Mai Thi Trang, Nguyen Van Bay, and the other ex-Vietcong back in the safe houses, all of them high on the blood-debt list.

When I went up to the Agency's sixth-floor office a short time later, I was surprised to see Vietnamese government big shots standing around with their large families and heavy suitcases, maybe fifty or sixty people altogether. Pham Van Lam, the foreign minister, was there, and, amazingly, General Dang Van Quang was too, Thieu's fat security adviser, reputedly the most corrupt man in the country. The hallways were crowded with Polgar's and the ambassador's friends. These were not employees of the United States government, for chrissake, these were friends and their families, some of the very people who had eaten the country's heart out. And now they were standing there with their big suitcases, while my people along with so many of the Agency's other employees were being handed over to the executioners.

At about five o'clock one of the men from the finance office ran down the hall screaming that VC were in the stairwell. It seemed impossible. How could they have gotten through the gate? But somebody with a B-40 or a hand grenade could cause no end of trouble, so I yelled at everyone to get into the walk-in vault we had in the room—the former finance office. In a moment everyone there had grabbed Uzis and pistols, crowded into the vault, and pulled the door to, leaving it open a crack. After a tense couple of minutes we heard someone shout, "False alarm, false alarm," and we carefully moved back into the office. It turned out that an American Nisei State Department security man with an M-16 had been climbing the stairs from the fourth to the fifth floor. The finance officer had opened the door to the stairwell and had found himself face-to-face with what he took to be a gun-toting Vietcong. "Jesus," he said, "I could have sworn I saw a VC."

We boarded the Huey at 6 P.M. As the big chopper veered up from the embassy roof the CRA compound fell away under us. Looking down, I could see several thousand people milling around the gate, still trying to get into the parking lot. I hoped to God they would make it. But my mind told me differently. Dusk was on its way, and without lighting, any more takeoffs would be precarious. Inside the Huey we huddled together, Lou, Wayne, and myself together with Chieu Hoi Lan, Bingo, Gekko, and Tiger—the remnants of the Bien Hoa base. So many of the others were still out there in the swelter of Saigon, waiting hopelessly in the safe houses and the Duc: operatives, former VC and NVA, staffers, wives, children. We stared blindly as the chaos below grew distant and then disappeared, the Vietnamese among us grateful no doubt, my own mind numb and bitter. All right, you fuckers, I said to myself, still staring, though by now there was nothing to stare at, you've got it all. Now let's see what in hell you're going to do with it.

Forty minutes later, over the South China Sea, we raised the *Hancock*. Around the carrier, ARVN helicopters were hovering and being waved off. Others were splashing into the water or already disappearing below the waves. But the marine choppers were setting down on deck. Short on fuel and heavily loaded with the last wave of refugees, they had the priorities here. At least this once, I thought, we got the priorities right.

As we jumped down onto the *Hancock*'s steel deck, I saw Thao get out of an Air America chopper that had landed at just the same time. I almost laughed to see him. With the mess in Saigon I had no idea what might have happened at the pad where the pilot was supposed to pick him up. Dinh was not there though. After hearing nothing from him all day I hadn't expected he would be. But in the back of my mind I was hoping that somehow the two of them might have hooked up.

Already navy medics were herding us over to the ship's side rail. As they did, Thao found his way through the crowd and was now next to me as the medics told us to drop our pants and drawers and lean over the railing. Thao looked at me in surprise as a young medic none too gently administered the notorious finger wave. "Welcome to America?" asked Thao. "No," I said, trying to smother a burst of laughter, "they're just looking for drugs." I wondered what the scene must be like belowdecks where the women had been led off. What could they be thinking, those old Vietnamese ladies who had never so much as had a doctor look them over in their entire lives. Even their husbands had never had a good close-up view. Welcome to America!

Beyond the rail another 'copter crashed into the sea. Men were swimming and being pulled up into navy rescue boats circling in the choppy water. Others were being hauled up on deck dripping water and shaking with cold, their faces grim, or vacant with shock. Here and there Vietnamese soldiers were crying openly. From all around came the flap, flap, flap of the Hueys, some settling in to land, others about to ditch. So this is how it happens, I thought, this is how the United States bugs out.

GLOSSARY

ARVN Army of the Republic of Vietnam; South Vietnam's army.

BOQ Bachelor Officers Quarters.

CG Census Grievance program.

Chieu Hoi South Vietnam's "Open Arms" amnesty program.

CIC Corps Interrogation Center.

CID Criminal Investigations Division (U. S. Army).

CIO Cabinet Intelligence Office; Japan's CIA.

claymore An anti-personnel landmine.

commo liaison Communications and liaison.

CORDS Civilian Operations Revolutionary Development Staff.

COSVN Hanoi's Central Office for South Vietnam.

cutout The go-between or contact person.

DMZ Demilitarized Zone.

G-2 Military Intelligence.

GVN Government of South Vietnam.

hoi chanh Vietcong or North Vietnamese defector.

Iron Triangle The Vietcong base area located northwest of Saigon in Military Region Three.

jarhead   Marine.

JIC   Joint Interrogation Center.

klick   Kilometer.

Lao Dong   Communist Party (North Vietnam).

MACV   Military Assistance Command, Vietnam.

MI   Military Intelligence.

NIC   National Interrogation Center.

NLF   National Liberation Front.

nuoc mam   A fermented fish sauce.

Nung   An ethnic Chinese subgroup from which the CIA recruited many of its guards.

OSA   Office of Special Assistance.

OSI   Office of Special Investigations (U. S. Air Force).

pho   A type of noodle and meat soup.

PIC   Provincial Interrogation Center.

POIC   CIA's Province Officer in Charge.

POL   Petroleum, oil, lubricants.

PRG   Provisional Revolutionary Government.

PRP   People's Revolutionary Party; South Vietnam's Communist Party.

PRU   Provincial Reconnaissance Unit.

PSIA   Public Safety Investigative Agency.

PSIB   Public Safety Investigative Board; Japan's FBI.

RD   Rural Development program.

RF   Regional Forces.

SAM   Surface-to-air missile.

sapper   Specialists in laying and clearing mines and explosives.

STOL   Short takeoff and landing.

tiger suit   Camouflage battle fatigues.

VC   Vietcong.

Vietminh   The anti-French resistance front founded by Ho Chi Minh in 1941.

wiring diagram   An organizational structure chart.

INDEX